The Philosophical Investigator

Paris

Ken Ewell

THE PHILOSOPHICAL INVESTIGATOR
PARIS

iUniverse books may be ordered through booksellers or by contacting:

iUniverse
1663 Liberty Drive
Bloomington, IN 47403
www.iuniverse.com
1-800-Authors (1-800-288-4677)

ISBN: 978-1-4917-4763-6 (sc)
ISBN: 978-1-4917-4762-9 (e)

Library of Congress Control Number: 2014916848

Printed in the United States of America.

iUniverse rev. date: 09/18/2014

Dedicated to those who prefer
being lost in a book
to being found in a crowd.

Contents

The Private Investigator 1

The Modern Investigator 7
    Paris 9
    The Marais 26
    Beaubourg 41
    Les Halles...52
    Opéra Quarter 68
    Tuilleries Quarter 84
    Champs-Elysées 95
    Chaillot Quarter 110

The Postmodern Investigator 121
    Parisian Culture 123
    Parisian Pleasures.. 147
    Parisian Excursions 157
    Parisian Solitude 172

The Existential Investigator 217
    Eiffel Tower and Invalides Quarter... 219
    St-Germain-des-Prés and Luxembourg Quarter.....................235
    Montparnesse and Jardin des Plantes Quarter 244
    Latin Quarter and Montmartre 259

The Philosophical Investigator...267

The Philosophical Investigation...277

The Proustian Investigation..281

The Philosophical Invesigator Purpose.......................................283

The Private Investigator

The Private Investigator

On Sunday Sam remained in his apartment with the phone, which remained silent throughout the day, just as he'd predicted the night before. On Monday morning he was back at his usual schedule and daily rituals, when he heard a knock on the office door. He got up to let in his newest client, a distinguished-looking older gentleman, impeccably dressed in a suit and tie from an age when men were far more meticulous about their appearance. He sat down in the client's chair and Sam asked, "May I call you Will."

"Will is alright by me," he responded, "and should I call you Sam?"

"That's fine," Sam replied. "Would you care for a cup of coffee?"

Will did, so Sam poured them both a cup and then questioned his client about the case, "I understand from our short telephone conversation of last week that you have what you consider a rather unique case for me. But before I agree to take on the investigation, could you please explain a little about yourself?"

"Before retiring," Will began, "I was a writer of books on philosophy and history. In a sense, you might say I was in the same line of work as you. Though rather than being a private investigator, I was what's called a philosophical investigator, or as the French say, *le flâneur philosophique.*"

"Excuse me, Will," Sam interrupted. "Before going on you should know that I'm not familiar with much about philosophy or history. And I have no idea what *le flâneur philosophique* might be."

"I don't believe that will be a problem, Sam," Will continued, "for I have an agency in mind that will help you as regards the necessary particulars of those two trains of thought, at least as they pertain to the case. However, what I do need to know is do you have a problem with traveling overseas, for that agency is in Paris?"

Sam thought for a moment and then said, "No, I suppose I don't mind as long as the money's good."

"Now as to the money," Will replied, "I'm afraid I can only cover your expenses. Is that going to be a problem?"

Sam thought for a moment and then realized that he'd become somewhat curious about where this case was heading. So as he'd no other cases going on, nor any new ones in the foreseeable future, he answered, "No, covering my expenses is fine. But before giving you a final answer about taking on your case, can you tell me some of the particulars?"

Will reflected on Sam's question for a moment, apparently lost in thought, and then slowly said, "This may sound slightly odd to you, but something has gone missing."

"That's fine, Will," Sam interjected, "I've been on cases involving missing persons or stolen monies or valuable objects plenty of times."

"Yes, Sam," Will continued, "you no doubt have been on such cases, but I doubt ever on an investigation such as this. What has gone missing is not a person or money or a valuable object, though it is indeed valuable, and perhaps the most valuable thing in the world. What has gone missing is 'Modernity'."

Needless to say, Sam looked at him with questioning eyes and said, "What are you talking about? I've never even heard of Modernity? I can't see how I would be of any value to you on this case."

Will first smiled and then responded, "Please don't rush to any hasty decisions involving this investigation, for you're not the only person that has never heard about Modernity. In fact, most people living today haven't heard about it, which is probably why it has gone missing. The period we historians call Modernity began roughly 500 years ago, though sometime during the last century it reportedly began to disappear, first in Europe and then in America. If you decide to take on this case, your task will be to search for this most valuable object. However, if you are unable to find it, then you will attempt to discover what has replaced it, which I will tentatively call 'Postmodernity', leaving that term undefined for the time being."

"Go on, Will," Sam said, with his curiosity in this new case now quite overwhelming.

"I can see that this case does indeed interest you," Will said. "Fortunately, you don't have to work on it alone in Paris. I've contacted the Paris branch of the 'Pascal, Descartes, Voltaire and Rousseau Philosophical Investigation Services' to help you in your search, and they sent me a packet of instructions to give to you."

Will handed him the packet and then continued, "I have also arranged tickets for your flight and modest accommodations in an area of Paris known as Montmartre. Do you have any questions, Sam?"

"Yes," Sam answered, "plenty of them, though I have the feeling they won't begin to be addressed until I get to Paris."

"Very good," Will responded, "and here's an ATM card to handle your daily expenses while in the City of Light. By the way, while working on this case please take time to enjoy the sights and the sounds, and the foods and the wines, of the most culturally-preoccupied city in the world. And as well, don't forget to fall in love while in Paris, not only with the city, but also with the uniquely beautiful women that call her home. For Paris is there to be loved through the mind, the body and the heart." With that, Will stood up, shook Sam's hand, and left the office, saying as he went, "I'll talk to you when you get back."

The first thing Sam did after Will left was to check the departure date on the ticket printout, which indicated that he was leaving San Francisco in the late afternoon for a stay in Paris of two weeks. So he closed up the office, had some lunch, and went to his apartment to pack a few things for the flight. Once done, and after looking forever for his passport, Sam walked down to BART and caught the train out to SFO.

Sam's flight to Paris took off on time, and after a few hours and a few Beefeaters he fell into a deep sleep. However, somewhere in time and place he experienced the beginning of a profound change, when the private investigator Sam Marlowe disappeared from the world and was replaced by the philosophical investigator Sam Marlowe. Needless to say, only Jacques Barzun in his 2000 masterpiece, *From Dawn to Decadence*, could explain the reason for this unique transformation: "Is this a mystery or not? No answer seems conclusive if we ponder any important changes in ourselves... occasionally [caused] by an emotional shock. Again, when our minds undergo sudden, profound alterations - in opinion or belief, in love, or in what is called artistic inspiration - what is the ultimate cause? We see the results, but grasp the chain of reasoning at a link well below the hook from which it hangs."

So began my newest investigation, one I named "The Case of the Missing Modernity."

The Modern Investigator

Paris

The flight from SFO to Paris was uneventful, except for that Barzunian change that began to take place, which of course I knew nothing about at the time. Fortunately, this gave me plenty of much-needed sleep from the hurried life I'd endured on my last investigation, "The Case of the Girl in the Fishbowl." After landing at Charles de Gaulle airport, I caught a RATP coach to Gare du Nord train station, and then a local bus to my modest accommodations in Montmartre. And after a good night's rest, my search for Modernity began, first at a couple of Parisian islands, Ile de la Cité and Ile St-Louis, then at a famed final resting place, the Panthéon, and finally at an illustrious restaurant, Le Procope.

Ile de la Cité

As per my instructions, I took the Metro from Montmartre to Cité station the next morning, arriving there with enough time to have a good look around before meeting the appointed member of the agency staff. Fortunately, I began my investigation of Paris on a Sunday, which meant that both Marché aux Fleurs, the flower market, and Marché aux Oiseaux, the bird market, were in full bloom and full plume, respectively. And after being asked to move on by one of the ill-mannered bird traders - simply for making a few high-pitched cat sounds near one of the cages - I continued elsewhere with my investigations.

My next stop was at the Gothic cathedral Sainte-Chapelle, built in 1248 by Louis IX and now one of the most architecturally celebrated churches in the world. Its fifteen beautiful stain-glassed windows display over one thousand religious scenes, ones that impress even the most devout of non-believers. And if the investigator explores the church as the sun ends its daily journey across the sky, that's when the windows display themselves at their best.

Although Ile de la Cité is home to a multitude of museums and galleries, squares and gardens, and monuments and palaces, in particular, the Palais de Justice, my time was now running short. So I made my way to the most popular attraction on the little Parisian island, Notre-Dame, with the first stone of this most famous of all Gothic cathedrals laid in 1163. It took another 170 years to complete the church, which seems a long time until one considers how long it took to rebuild the San Francisco-Oakland Bay Bridge.

While sitting in one of the pews and enjoying the overwhelming immenseness of religious architecture, a priest approached me and asked, "My Son, would you like to join me in the confessional booth and confess of your sins?"

"Sorry, Father, but I'm not a member of your club," I responded politely. "Anyway, it would take too long for me to confess all my sins, even the ones of just the past week or two. However, I do have one question. When does the Hunchback show begin?"

"I will pray for you, my Son," the Father said as he walked away shaking his head.

In truth, I thought his well-intended gesture of praying for me was rather decent of him, though of course also rather pointless. Needless to say, if the Christians are right about the hereafter, a private investigator stands very little chance of ever living in the penthouse. And as I pondered over my metaphysical predicament, I heard a laugh coming from another sinner, one sitting directly behind me as if he was my conscience.

"Very well handled," the sinner said in my ear, "but would you care to join me outside?"

Without waiting for an answer, this older gentleman got up and grabbed me by the arm. We then made our way out to the benches overlooking the cathedral, where he continued with his thoughts, "I always attend this particular service, one originally established by the famed Dr Desplein and one I refer to as *The Atheist's Mass* (1836): '... this man was in all the secrets of the human frame. He knew it in the past and in the future, emphasizing the present. Desplein had no doubts. He was positive. His bold and unqualified atheism was like that of many scientific men, the best men in the world, but invincible atheists - atheists such as religious people declare to be impossible. This opinion could scarcely exist otherwise in a man who was accustomed from his youth to dissect the creature above all others - before, during, and after life. To hunt through all his organs without ever finding the individual soul, which is indispensable to religious theory.'"

After telling me about Dr. Desplein and his devout non-belief, I then questioned, "Why would a physician, one that was so clearly devoted to science and guided by atheism, establish a Mass to be held in Notre-Dame. It seems to me that his actions were at odds with his beliefs."

The gentleman looked at me and smiled, and he then offered an answer to my question, "There are good reasons for the apparent inconsistencies between the thoughts and actions of those we come across on our journey through life. The simple truth is that the discrepancies that we conceive of in the behavior of others are merely inventions of our own minds, and they are the products of forever remaining a stranger to the internal workings of those outside of ourselves."

"I don't completely understand, sir," I responded, "but you have given me something to think about. By the way, my name's Sam and I'm a private investigator from San Francisco."

"Yes, Sam, I know who you are," the gentleman replied. "I was sent here to meet with you by the 'Pascal, Descartes, Voltaire and Rousseau Philosophical Investigation Services'. My name is Honoré de Balzac, but please call me Honoré. Now come along with me, for we have a few others to meet before dinner."

Ile St-Louis

Honoré and I walked down the Rue de Cloitre Notre-Dame, passing Musée de Notre-Dame de Paris along the way. After reaching Quai Aux Fleurs, we crossed Pont St. Louis to Ile St-Louis, the smaller of the two Parisian isles. Though swampy pastureland until the seventeenth century, the island was eventually transformed into a stylish residential area, home then and now to those of a better standing in society.

Once across the bridge, the two of us meandered along Quai d'Orleans and Quai de Bethune until arriving at a small city park, Square Barye, at the eastern end of the island. My companion then introduced me to two gentlemen sitting on one of the park benches, "Good afternoon, gentlemen," Honoré began, "this is Sam, the private investigator from San Francisco that the agency told you about. And Sam, these are two of the retired founders of the agency, the philosophers Blaise Pascal and René Descartes."

"Glad to meet you, gentlemen," I cordially offered.

"Please sit beside me," said Blaise. "I have an important problem to pose to you from my *Pensées* (1669), one that many today call 'Pascal's Wager': 'God is, or He is not.... A game is being played... where heads or tails will turn up. What will you wager? According to reason... you can defend neither of the propositions.... Yes, but you must wager. It is not optional.... Let us weigh the gain and the loss in wagering that God is. Let us estimate these two chances. If you gain, you gain all; if you lose, you lose nothing. Wager, then, without hesitation that He is.'"

"Let me see if I understand you correctly, sir," I interjected. "Throughout our lives we bet that either God does exist or that He does not exist? So the question arises, which is the rational choice for a man to make? If God does not exist, then by believing in Him one suffers only a few losses, perhaps a pleasure here or a luxury there. However, if God does exist, then by believing in Him one stands to gain everything, and by not believing in Him one stands to lose everything. Therefore, a rational person should live as though God does exist.

"However, sir, I believe that there's a problem posed by your little wager. Given the world as I've seen it as a private investigator, and so speaking now as one who has grave doubts concerning the existence of a God, it would only be possible for me to feign such a metaphysical decision. And if God did exist and was all-knowing, would He not see through my little game? Therefore, I'll choose not to play the coin game with you and instead merely refrain from playing it until more evidence is at hand. In other words, I'll take my chances in life... and in death as well."

"Very well said, Sam," added René, "and in life let our minds always be directed by rational thought. Indeed, let us not engage our attention on questions that our minds are not capable of answering, for instance, the existence of God, but on inquiries of a more practical nature. Perhaps an example will suffice to illumine what I mean by this statement.

"Paris is divided into several *quarters*, which of course should indicate that the city enjoys four such neighborhoods. Unfortunately, we Parisians, not being terribly fluent in fractions, nor in English for that matter, have identified upwards of a half dozen quarters in our beloved city. But Paris is also divided into twenty *arrondissements*, otherwise known as neighborhoods for those not fluent in the French tongue. Now, if I might apply to this conundrum the first four of my *Rules for the Direction of the Mind* (1628)":

The end of study should be to direct the mind towards the enunciation of sound and correct judgment on all matters that come before it.

Only those objects should engage our attention, to the sure and indubitable knowledge of which our mental powers seem to be adequate.

In the subjects we propose to investigate, our inquiries should be directed, not to what others have thought, nor to what we ourselves conjecture, but to what we can clearly and perspicuously behold and with certainty deduce; for knowledge is not won in any other way.

There is need of a method for finding out the truth.

"With these four rules, as well as a few others, I am able to now pose the following proposition: When we direct our mental faculties to consider the object known as Paris, it is correct to conjecture that each quarter in the city is an arrondissement, and it is equally correct to deduce, with certainty, that each arrondissement is not necessarily a quarter.

"Might I also add that, in getting around Paris, an investigator can rationally comprehend the city because it is ordered rationally. Fortunately, the science of mapmaking has created many rational representations of arrondissements, some of which are quarters. Of course, as sensible as this proposition appears at first glance, in Paris there is always another philosopher at the end of every park bench with an opposing point of view."

"Naturally, that philosopher would be me, René," interjected Blaise. "Given that the universe is infinitely large, consciousness and reason cannot fully comprehend it. And since Paris is a part of the universe, any attempt to develop a rational representation of arrondissements and quarters for the city is inevitably lacking in success. Then again, you might contend that since numerous maps of Paris are readily available in any travel shop, then I must surely be incorrect on the matter. However, and as is well-known, every investigator who has ever attempted to comprehend a map of Paris lamentably admits that a reasonable understanding of the city, one that is based on a rational representation such as a map, is unfortunately fated to failure. And to conclude our little discussion, let me add that 'all the unhappiness of the men of Paris derives from one thing, that they cannot sit quietly in their own arrondissement and ponder on their quarters.'"

With that, Honoré motioned for us to move on, and we left the two philosophers to ponder over and bicker about other matters of a theoretical nature. However, I did come away from this conversation with a better appreciation for the plight of the average investigator of Paris, who while on a case must ceaselessly face the task of navigating the labyrinth of philosophies that forever befuddle the metropolitan minds of this most philosophical of cities. And perhaps this is why

Blaise noted in his *Pensées*: "Men are so necessarily mad, that not to be mad would amount to another form of madness."

The Panthéon

Returning to Pont de Sully, Honoré and I crossed over that old and venerable river, the Seine. We stopped only once for him to tell me about the march of history that that waterway had seen as it forever travels through Paris to the sea, "This timeless river has known the noble waters of Louis XIV, the clear waters of the Enlightenment, the bloody waters of the Revolution, and the tumultuous waters of Napoleon. It has also known the rebellious waters of the Second and Third Republics, the deathly waters of the First World War, and the undignified waters of the Occupation and the Second World War. And though the Seine will flow on eternally, she always knows that every few years, or maybe decades, or maybe centuries, a new current will flow along her, forever altering the people and the history of a great nation."

Once on the Left Bank, we walked up Boulevard St-Germain until reaching Place Maubert. We then continued along Rue des Carmes and Rue Valette until arriving at an enormous old church, the Panthéon. And while admiring the Temple of the Nation, Honoré told me the history of this monument, "The temple before us is only the latest in a series of memorials that have stood upon this low mount, with the original one being an oratory erected in 502 over the grave of Geneviève, who was the shepherdess that rallied the French in their fight against Attila the Hun. Six years later Clovis replaced that modest structure by a much larger church in which to celebrate his victory over the invading Visigoths, with the new basilica dedicated to Saint Peter and Saint Paul.

"During the War of Austrian Succession, Louis XV fell ill and invoked the protection of Sainte Geneviève. After his recovery the king ordered the construction of an abbatial church, though the necessary monies were not made available until ten years later. The architect designated to plan the Church of Saint Geneviève was Jacques-Germain Soufflot, who worked on his designs from 1755 to 1764, the year that Louis finally laid the cornerstone for the church. But due to unstable ground, technical challenges and concerns over the stability of the dome, the church was not completed until 1790, ten years after the death of Soufflot.

"After the Revolution of 1789, the Marquis de Villette proposed a new purpose for the church: 'In the tradition of the Greeks and Romans, from whom we have received the maxims of liberty, and as an example to the rest of Europe, let us have the courage not to dedicate this temple to a saint. Let it become the Panthéon of France! Let us install statues of our great men and lay their ashes to rest in its underground recesses.'"

Stopping there with his talk, Honoré suggested that we enter the Panthéon to view the ornate interior. And as we walked about, he continued with his history, "Villette's proposal was debated over the next two years, with his side eventually winning the argument, which allowed for Voltaire's ashes to be laid in the crypt on the twenty-first of July in 1791. Three years later on the eleventh of October, the remains of Jean-Jacques Rousseau were interned across from those of Voltaire. And during that period, the original decor of the church was altered from being a dedication to the history of Christianity to a celebration of philosophy, science, and the arts.

"Of course that would not be the end of the story, for Napoleon returned the Panthéon to its status as a church in 1806, though he designated that the crypt still house the great men of France, which in his opinion meant generals and politicians, not scientists and philosophers. But after the fall of the Empire and the restoration of the Bourbon dynasty under Louis XVIII in 1815, the Panthéon was consecrated as the Church of Saint Geneviève, with its purpose now being wholly religious.

"Needless to say, all was not over yet, for during the July Days of Revolution in 1830, Louis-Philippe d'Orleans replaced Charles X, with the church quickly renamed the Panthéon, though it remained unused over the next two decades. But after the restoration of the

Second Empire by Louis-Napoléon Bonaparte in 1851, the Panthéon was once again renamed the Church of Saint Geneviève, with its status now that of a national basilica. The church remained a religious memorial after the collapse of the Empire in 1870, though all that changed with the establishment of the Third Republic nine years later, when the church was once again renamed the Panthéon, which is the title that it has proudly worn to this day."

By now Honoré and I were standing in front of the temple's huge pendulum, an apparatus designed by Léon Foucault to evidence the rotation of the Earth on its daily journey. But the swinging mechanism must have mesmerized me for some time, for when I looked around my companion was nowhere to be seen, though I did hear a loud noise at the back of the Panthéon. And after making my way to the doorway of the crypt, I heard a phrase repeated over and over again: "Ecrasez l'infame! Ecrasez l'infame! Ecrasez l'infame!"

Wondering what the yelling was all about, I made my way through the entrance of the crypt to discover some stairs leading down to a lower level. While walking down, the loud voice suddenly went silent, and not too surprisingly, I found that there was no one else in the vault except Honoré. Rather than leave the crypt straight away, which would have been my choice as the place gave me the creeps, he suggested that we explore the final resting-place of the great men and women of France. After reluctantly agreeing to his suggestion, we began our exploration in the East Gallery, where there lies the philosopher Jean-Jacques Rousseau and the architect Soufflot. And also in this section of the gallery is the tomb of the philosopher Voltaire, which sits in back of a fine statue of that famed philosophe holding a pen in his right hand and some papers in his left.

After admiring that statue for a few moments, Honoré and I moved on to the North Gallery of the crypt, which is the final resting place for Jean Moulin, René Cassin, Jean Monnet, André Malraux, Gaspard Monge, Abbe Gregoire, Marquis de Condorcet, and Pierre and Marie Curie. But as we walked about the gallery, I began hearing that phrase once again: "Ecrasez l'infame! Ecrasez l'infame! Ecrasez l'infame!"

Trying to keep myself somewhat composed, I followed Honoré into the West Gallery of the vault, which is the final home of Eugène Lefèvre-Pontalis, François Denis Tronchet, Nicolas-Marie Songis des Courbons, Louis Antoine de Bougainville, Claude Juste Alexandre Legrand, Jean-Marie Dorsenne, Michel Ordener, and Joseph-Marie Vien. Unfortunately, my mind would allow me no peace as it continued hearing that incessant phrase: "Ecrasez l'infame! Ecrasez l'infame! Ecrasez l'infame!"

Although I desperately wanted to flee the crypt, I was too frightened to leave my companion's side. So without the necessary courage, I continued with Honoré as he explored the final remains of Maréchal Jean Lannes, Corret del la Tour d'Auvergne, François Séverin Marceau-Desgraviers, Lazare Carnot, Sadi Carnot, Victor Hugo, Émile Zola, Victor Schoelcher, Félix Éboué, and Jean Jaurès. But at some point the voice became unbearably loud, with it forever repeating its mysterious phrase over and over again: "Ecrasez l'infame! Ecrasez l'infame! Ecrasez l'infame!"

Unable to endure it any longer, I ran from the West Gallery towards the East Gallery and the exit from the crypt. But as I was passing by the statue of Voltaire, the right hand of the sculpture reached out and grabbed me by the shoulder. And at the same time I heard in back of me, "Where do you think you are going in such a hurry, my boy? Please stop for a moment and talk with me, for I am the philosophe that you know of as Voltaire."

Frozen in my tracks, I reluctantly turned around to find myself standing face to face with the famed philosophe. Truly my mind was losing control of itself, for I was not only hearing voices, but also experiencing hallucinations. Honoré was soon by my side, though instead of asking me what the matter was he addressed himself to Voltaire, "It is an honor to see you once again, dear philosopher. And I'm happy to report that your philosophical investigation service is doing well these days."

Needless to say, I was completely dumbfounded by this astonishing course of events, and I immediately began to suspect that Honoré was losing control of his mind as well. So I asked my companion,

"Good friend, am I to believe that we share the same figment of the imagination? Do you also see an old man, one that according to that tomb over there is well over three hundred years old? Is it possible that we both suffer from the same psychosis of the mind?"

But instead of Honoré answering me, it was Voltaire, who said while laughing, "No, my boy, you are not suffering from a psychosis of the mind, though your mind does suffer from a certain malady that afflicts most of the human race. And that widespread affliction is your inability to think properly, and by that I mean to think philosophically." Voltaire pointed in the direction of the other tomb in the East Gallery of the crypt before he continued, "That man over there is the philosopher Jean-Jacques Rousseau, who was awarded a literary prize by the Academy of Dijon in 1750. And he was given that honor for his essay, *A Discourse on the Moral Effects of the Arts and Sciences*, a paper that offered a philosophical view of the world that I fervently disagreed with then, and one that I fervently disagree with today."

"If I might ask a question, Voltaire," I interrupted, "a moment ago you mentioned that I needed to learn to think philosophically. But since it appears that Jean-Jacques thought philosophically, why is it that you two gentlemen didn't see eye to eye on matters? Is there more than one road to philosophy, and if so, how does a traveler know which path to journey down?"

"An excellent question, my boy," acclaimed Voltaire, "but the answer to your inquiry requires me tell you a little something about the controversial philosophy presented in Jean-Jacques' paper. The question proposed by the Academy of Dijon was whether or not the restoration of the arts and sciences had had a purifying or a corrupting effect upon the morals of society. Needless to say, throughout my life I believed that any increase in scientific knowledge would eventually promote an extension in moral philosophy, though of course any necessary and progressive changes might not occur until many years in the future.

"However, Jean-Jacques approached the question from the opposite point of view from the Encyclopédists. During my lifetime

I always encouraged the expression of controversial ideas, and I even told Jean-Jacques on a number of occasions: 'I disapprove of what you say, but I will defend to the death your right to say it.' But what is quite disturbing to me is that in his essay he cast dispersions upon the art of science itself, with those accusations causing the main river of modern liberal philosophy to branch off into two opposing streams of thought. And sadly, that disbelief in the importance of pragmatic scientific thinking, in other words, in reason, haunts liberalism to this very day, and it is a split that forever aids the efforts of those conservatives who would return us to the dogmatic ways of the past.

"Now, please listen to some of the thoughts contained in Jean-Jacques controversial paper: '[Scientific ideas often] stifle in men's breasts that sense of original liberty, for which they seem to have been born, cause them to love their own slavery, and so make of them what is called a civilized people. What a train of vices must attend this uncertainty! We shall no longer take in vain by our oaths the name of our Creator, but we shall insult Him with our blasphemies, and our scrupulous ears will take no offence. Our hatred of other nations diminishes, but patriotism dies with it. Ignorance is held in contempt, but a dangerous skepticism has succeeded it.'

"Allow me to review his points one at a time, the first one being the notion that there was an earlier age when Man enjoyed a 'sense of original liberty'. Clearly this was not the case in nomadic or agrarian societies, for the demands of existence within those highly-regulated social structures were and still are completely dependent upon forces outside the control of the individual. But astonishingly, just as Jean-Jacques thought then, so too today, many persons who champion the liberal cause still romanticize the hunters, the gatherers and the tillers of the land. No, if freedom and liberty exist anywhere, it is within the more progressive societies, where civilized people have advanced through the application of scientific ideas.

"As to the notion that scientific knowledge causes people to question their god or their country, I say all the better. Every religion originated in an earlier time, and even if this or that metaphysical system gave life meaning then, the circumstances of modern life demand a reappraisal of all religious oaths, if not an abandonment of those tenets altogether. If that is blasphemy, then call me a blasphemer.

"Now, as regards patriotism, is it not the love of one's country above all others that causes many of the problems in the world today, as it did in my day? If that is treason, then call me a traitor. But astonishingly, just as Jean-Jacques thought then, so too today, many persons who champion the liberal cause wrap themselves up in their flag and then demand that all their fellow citizens do the same. No, if scientific knowledge causes us to question the dogmas of the past and the present, whether they be religious or nationalistic, let all men forever increase their efforts in the cause of science and reason.

"And lastly, I must object to Jean-Jacques' view that skepticism in thought is a dangerous thing. If science teaches us anything, it is that the certain Truth of yesterday inevitably becomes the uncertain truth of today, and more often than not it eventually becomes the Falsehood of tomorrow. So if a man, in replacing his once accepted ignorance with newly found knowledge, finds himself in a world less certain, but more predictable, then let the skeptical minds lead the way. For truly, the dangers posed in life do not originate in those minds that remain skeptical of every answer, but in those minds that never ask any questions in the first place."

"But a man must retain some fixed beliefs that lie beyond skepticism, mustn't he?" I asked the philosopher.

Voltaire thought momentarily about what I asked, and then said, "Let me tell you the *Story of a Good Brahman* (1761): 'I met on my travels an old Brahman.... The Brahman said to me one day: I wish I had never been born.... I asked him why. He replied: I have been studying for forty years, which is forty years wasted; I teach others, and I know nothing. I am sometimes ready to fall into despair, when I think that after all my seeking I know neither where I come from, nor what I am, not where I shall go, nor what shall become of me.'

"Later on in my travels I met an old woman who never asked the questions that the good Brahmin always asked, and because of that omission she appeared to be forever happy in life. Hoping to understand this contradiction, I traveled further until the day that I ran into a group of philosophers who were told about the wise old Brahmin and the simple old woman: 'I concluded that if we set store by happiness, we set greater store by reason. But, upon reflection, it appears that to prefer reason to felicity is to be very mad.... How can this contradiction be explained?... Like all the others. There is much to be said about it.'

"However, perhaps another story is in order, one concerning the man *Memnon* (1749) and his desire for *Human Wisdom*: 'Memnon one day conceived the insane plan of being perfectly wise. There are few men through whose heads this mad idea has not at some time passed. Memnon said to himself: "In order to be very wise, and consequently very happy, one has only to be without passions; and nothing is easier, as everyone knows.'

"While still meditating in his private room, Memnon decided to never desire women, to never consume wine, to never pursue riches, and to never seek out old friends. Unfortunately, Memnon next looked out his window and was immediately distracted by a desirable woman, one whose uncle soon took him for a good deal of money. Lamenting his loss, he joined his friends for dinner, where he drank too much wine and lost even more money while playing dice. And after a heated dispute arose over the game, he lost an eye when one of his old friends tossed the dice box at his head.

"The next night a celestial spirit came to Memnon in a dream, whereupon he asked the apparition to return to him his eye, his health, his wealth and his wisdom. Rather than granting his wishes, the specter instead told him that he should simply be happy for what life had already given him. Things could be worse, as they were for his brother, who had recently lost both of his eyes. The spirit then told Memnon to give up his plan for becoming perfectly wise, for it is an impossible goal to achieve, even in this best of all possible worlds."

"Come along with me now, Sam," Honoré requested while grabbing my arm and dragging me to the exit from the crypt. "If you remain here any longer, you will never leave the side of that beloved and wise philosopher. Of course that is not necessarily a bad thing, but there are other philosophers that you must also meet in Paris.

Anyway, I will tell you the story of Voltaire while we investigate the Right Bank, for his life is one of the great tales of Modernity."

Le Procope

After leaving the Panthéon, Honoré and I walked back to Boulevard Saint Germain, which we turned left on and followed until hitting Rue de l'Ancienne-Comédie. We turned down that street to arrive at the front of Le Procope, originally opened as Europe's first coffeehouse in 1686. The place was founded by Francesco Procopio dei Coltelli, who was a coffeemaker that hailed from Palermo in Italy. After opening the establishment, the success of the coffeehouse was immediate, owing not only to the fine taste of the coffees, but also to its location near the Comédie-Francaise. And over the next three centuries, Le Procope was the meeting place for anyone who was anyone in the arts, the letters or the politics of Paris.

Before entering Le Procope, Honoré and I enjoyed the exterior of the restaurant, which for all intents and purposes is a memorial dedicated to the famous personages that ever enjoyed a cuppa java there. The most illustrious name was that of the philosophe Voltaire, who was known to consume many cups of his favorite blend of chocolate-flavored coffee every day. There were also the names of the Encyclopédists, Jean le Rond d'Alembert and Denis Diderot, as well as such writers as Jean de La Fontaine, Victor Hugo, Paul Verlaine, Anatole France, and my Parisian guide Honoré de Balzac. And from the political scene, Benjamin Franklin, Georges Jacques Danton, Jean-Paul Marat, Maximilien de Robespierre, Napoleon Bonaparte and Léon Gambetta all enjoyed a cuppa joe or two in Le Procope.

Upon entering Le Procope, we first looked about the two beautifully ornate floors of the restaurant to find just the right table for our much-anticipated dinner. The lower level of the restaurant is decorated in red and gold, and it has tile floors and glass chandeliers. The upper level is even more ornate, with mirrors and paintings adorning the walls, and a balcony for spying on unsuspecting

Parisians wandering by on the sidewalk below. After making our decision, and after returning to the first floor, we were seated in the location that Honoré knew would be just right for us, and it was the very table at which Voltaire enjoyed his many cups of coffee each day.

Having no idea what to order, Honoré handled all the particulars concerning the selection of the courses and the wine. While enjoying one of the greatest meals of my life, he told me the story of his life, "I was born in 1799 as the second child of two very strict parents. Unfortunately, I suffered health problems throughout most of my life. And though an avid reader, my independent ways caused me many troubles in adapting to the regimental teaching style in school.

"After finishing my education, I was apprenticed to a law office, but quickly lost interest in the tedious routine of studying the law. And though I eventually became a successful writer, my early attempts at publishing, printing, business, criticism, and politics all ended in failure. In addition, my relationships with family and friends were constantly under strain due to financial difficulties. In 1850 I finally married Ewelina Hańska, a longtime love, though the marriage ended five months later with my death."

At this point I considered asking Honoré how he could be dead, but decided against it seeing as how we'd just met that day. So I merely listened as he continued, "As a writer, my *magnum opus* was a collection of studies, stories and novels titled *La Comédie humaine*, which I will describe in more detail to you tomorrow. I suppose then, my literary accomplishments in life define me as a *raconteur*, a person skilled in relating stories and anecdotes interestingly.

"Now as the time is getting late and we have a very busy schedule tomorrow, let me explain what the agency has discerned about you today. Needless to say, before the service I work for attempts to arrange a philosophical investigation of Paris, especially one involving the search for something as difficult to find as Modernity, it must first decide which individuals are best suited to handle your case.

"That is why I arranged for you to first be approached by the Father in Notre-Dame, which told me that your mind tends to think along secular, not religious lines. Then I had you meet the two philosophers on the park bench, which told me that your mind tends to think along rationalist, not theological lines. And finally, I arranged a situation in the Panthéon where you could hear the voice of either of two philosophers, though not both. You heard Voltaire's message: 'Ecrasez l'infame! Ecrasez l'infame! Ecrasez l'infame!'. This told me that your mind tends to think along the lines of Modernity, not in opposition to it. If you had heard 'bon sauvage', or 'noble savage', then tomorrow I would be telling you the story of Jean-Jacques Rousseau.

"So we initiate our investigation of the Right Bank tomorrow morning, when we will begin our search for Modernity. After completing your formal studies, I will send you out to explore Paris on your own for a few days. In doing so, you will become acquainted with various aspects of postmodern investigation. And finally, your exploration of the Left Bank will be left to a longtime writer friend of mine, and he will instruct you in how to become an existential investigator. Until tomorrow, my friend, until tomorrow."

The Marais

Lying at the eastern end of the Right Bank, The Marais was called home by the Royals for most of the seventeenth and eighteenth centuries. But during the first French Revolution the area was reduced to an architectural wasteland, and it remained so until the 1960s. Today the district is home to famous museums and fashionable galleries, stylish boutiques and cultural centers, and popular cafés and trendy bistros. It's also the place where my investigation for Modernity began with the help of my personal philosophical investigator, Honoré de Balzac.

Place de la Bastille

After disembarking the Metro at Bastille station and before meeting up with Honoré, I spent some time searching around Place de la Bastille for the remains of Bastille prison, only to discover that, except for a few stone markers, the place all but disappeared during the storming of it on July 14, 1789. But as a recommendation to the city council of Paris, a new and improved Bastille prison theme park would make an excellent historical, educational and tourist destination, one perhaps built and administered by Disney and populated with the characters from the animated movie *Ratatouille*. Ah, if the French were only as far-thinking as the Americans.

My next stop was Colonne de Julliet, a memorial to those who died during the second French Revolution of July 1830. And waiting underneath that column topped with the "genius of liberty" was my friend Honoré, who took me by the arm, in the French style, as we began our search for Modernity.

As we meandered up Rue St Antoine, he began the story of France, "Starting at the beginning, which is where all reasonable tales should begin, the universe was created in a huge explosion called the Big Bang around twelve to fifteen billion years ago. Fortunately, things eventually cooled down enough to allow for the formation of galaxies, stars, planets, Earth and France, with bits and pieces of the nation showing up around six billion years ago. Of course, it should be noted that this is only the biased modern account of the world's leading scientists.

"Since truth is forever relative in the postmodern world, with everyone's opinion, no matter their level of education, now equally valid, Christian fundamentalists claim their own timeline for the beginning of the universe, and by way of it, France. And that moment was on the night of October 23, 4004 BC, when the Supreme Being, who makes himself quite scarce these days, created the universe, and by way of it, France. Needless to say, it would be judgmental to say which timeline is correct or not, though for the purposes of this history, I'll side with all those modern scientists.

"However she came to be, France enjoys a great deal of history, and it's not of an ordinary or vulgar type, but of a highly sophisticated and uncommonly cultured class. The geographical region known today as France has been inhabited at least since the *Middle Paleolithic Period* (90,000 to 40,000 years ago), at first by Neanderthal Man, who disappeared around 35,000 years ago due to changes in climate. Cro-Magnon Man replaced that early group of proto-humans, and he lasted into the *Mesolithic Period* (13,000 to 8,000 years ago), or Middle Stone Age, after which he also disappeared from the French scene. The reasons for the disappearance of Neanderthal Man and Cro-Magnon Man have long been a source of debate amongst physical anthropologists, but many experts now favor the theory that due to warming weather, those two primitive groups migrated north to Britain, where they continue to live contentedly today.

"The *Neolithic Period* (7,000 to 4,000 years ago), or New Stone Age, saw great changes in lifestyle due to a more advanced technology for making polished stone tools, which allowed early man to more effectively cultivate the land. Those changes in technology eventually brought copper tools into use about 5,000 years ago, a shift that was followed by the introduction of bronze tools later on. And with the arrival of the Celtic Gauls (3,500 to 1,500 years ago) and their iron tools, trade routes were established throughout the Mediterranean region and as far north as Britain, which of course resulted in many territorial conflicts.

"All of those disputes came to a head in 52 BC, when Julius Caesar finally subdued the last of the remaining Celtic tribes in Gaul, as well as in other parts of modern-day Europe and Britain. After that, Roman peace and stability reigned supreme until around the middle of the third century. Then over the next century the Roman Empire commenced its decline and fall, with internal conflicts and external invasions, mainly from modern-day Germany, bringing an end to *Pax Gaula*.

"Beginning in the middle of the fifth century and continuing into the sixth, various groups of Franks and other Germans settled in Gaul, with the Visigoths ruling in the south and the Burgundians ruling in the north. Unification of much of Gaul occurred under Clovis, who established the Merovingian Dynasty. Unfortunately, with the partition of Gaul between Clovis' sons and then their sons, as well as with never-ending invaders arriving from outside the region, the dynasty became more and more unstable by the eighth century. Eventually, Frankish control over Gaul was consolidated once again, this time within the Carolingian Dynasty, first under the rule of Charles Martel and later by his son.

"There now emerges in French history one of its most prominent military and political figures, Charlemagne, who reigned supreme from 771. After consolidating his power over all of Gaul, he conquered modern-day northern Italy, western Germany, northeastern Spain and the southern Mediterranean coast. In 800 Charlemagne was crowned the Emperor of Rome, a title that he held until his death in 814. And though his son managed to sustain much of the empire, in 843 the Treaty of Verdun partitioned Gaul between Charlemagne's three grandchildren, the result being a weakening of the empire.

"Over the next century and a half, Vikings from the north, Magyars from the east, and Muslims from the south invaded and settled within the borders of Gaul. Regional lords now governed what remained of the empire, with the most notable king being Hugh Capet, who founded the Capetian Dynasty in 987. In the middle of the eleventh century there arose in the north William the Conqueror, who ruled Normandy from 1047 and England from 1066. With his death in 1087, there still remained little centralized power in the lands lying south of Paris. And by the middle of the twelfth century, even Normandy and Aquitaine had been lost to Henry II of England.

"With the death of Louis VII in 1180, Philip Augustus reigned as the first *rex Franciae*, or King of France, rather than the traditional *rex Francorum*, or King of the Franks. Over many years Philip took back control of the disputed English territories, as well as regions in the northeast of France, and he also organized fiscal policies to protect and extend his growing feudal empire. Upon his death in 1223, Capetian control reached further into the south of France and continued its centralization of power throughout the lands. Also of importance, during this time the groundwork was laid for the establishment of judicial *parlements* and a royal monetary system.

"Through a succession of kings, the long line of Capetians protected and extended their control over most of western and central France, with Brittany in the north, and Burgundy and Aquitaine in the south, being the notable exceptions. And with the accession of the House of Valois in 1328, there began the lead up to the Hundred Year's War with England, which continued into the middle of the fifteenth century. At the end of this long conflict, which actually lasted for 116 years, the map of France began to appear pretty much as it does today, except in the eastern regions, which still remained under the control of the Holy Roman Empire.

"During this long and brutal war there arose one of the more interesting figures in French history, Joan of Arc, or The Maid of Orleans. She was born in eastern France around 1412, and after claiming to hear the voice of God, she led the French army to several important victories, notably at Orleans, the battle that opened the way for the coronation of Charles VII. In 1430 Joan was captured by the Burgundians and sold to the English, who tried her in an ecclesiastical court and then burned her at the stake the following year. She was beatified in 1909 and canonized in 1920, and is today one of the three patron saints of France.

"The French monarchy became both all-powerful and all-tyrannical during the reign of Louis XI, which lasted from 1461 to 1483. And during the Wars of Religion of the sixteenth century, the French Calvinist Huguenots fought a series of civil wars with the dominant Catholic Church, with the most horrific event being the massacre of three thousand Huguenots on St. Bartholomew's Day in 1572. But by the end of the century, first Henry III and then Henry IV, who founded the Bourbon Dynasty, reestablished the need for a centralized royal authority, with its theological premise being the 'divine right of kings', which is the concept that the sovereign is responsible to God alone.

"The beginning of the seventeenth century saw the accession of Louis XIII, who reigned from 1610 to 1643 with the help of the able political administrator Cardinal de Richelieu. Richelieu was responsible for putting down uprisings of the Huguenots, for securing and extending French borders, and for promoting economic change at home and in the overseas colonies. However, great changes lay ahead for the French people, who would now be governed by the most illustrious king to ever reign during their long history, and perhaps any other country's long history.

"Louis XIV, the arrogant and yet fascinating 'Sun King', reigned supreme from 1643 to 1715. Louis centralized authority in France with the help of the High Council of three or four members, and he built the awe-inspiring Versailles, with its motto *Nec pluribus impar*, or 'None his equal'. His most important counselors, firstly Jules Mazarin and later Jean-Baptiste Colbert, defused the rebellious Fronds, oversaw major economic reforms, and built a powerful army and navy.

"In 1685 Louis revoked the Edict of Nantes, which had guaranteed the Huguenots some religious freedom for almost a hundred years. As well, he demanded conformity from the zealous Catholic Jansenists. And in foreign affairs, Louis fought continental wars in the War of the Grand Alliance (1689-1697) and the War of the Spanish Succession (1701-1714), which resulted in the Treaty of Utrecht that established French borders almost exactly where they lie today.

"With the death of Louis XIV in 1715, the forces for the great political buildup to one of the most important events in French, as well as in world history, began to take shape, and it was an episode that marked a turning-point for Modernity. The *ancien régime*, first conceived of by Cardinal Richelieu and then furthered by the kings, was not only traditional, in that it supported the absolute rule of the monarchy and the Church, but also modern, in that it supported change in economic, military and scientific policies.

"Unfortunately for the traditional forces in French society, the modern freeing of the intellect resulted in the Enlightenment, which had as its influences the rationalism of Descartes, the empiricism of the English scientists, the naturalism of Rousseau, and the promotion of tolerant attitudes by Voltaire. Needless to say, once the human mind is unshackled from the myths of its ancestors, there's no stopping progressive change in the interest of a better society.

"Throughout the eighteenth century many political, social and philosophical factors furthered unrest during the reigns of Louis XV and Louis XVI. Firstly, there was the tremendous fiscal expense incurred from overseas engagements with the British during the Seven Years War and the American War of Independence. Secondly, though there were ongoing domestic reforms, they were instituted not quite fast enough for the needs and demands of French society. Thirdly, there was a power struggle between the king and the Parisian and regional *parlements*, as well as one between the aristocracy and the bourgeoisie. And lastly, there was the spreading Enlightenment philosophies concerning individual rights within a liberal society.

"All of those factors, as well as many others, were heading towards a confrontation throughout 1788 and the first half of the next year, when it became clear that the monarchy was nearing its end. The French Revolution, which was the event that ushered in the modern world for intellectuals and citizens alike in France, began in earnest on July 14, 1789, with the storming of the Bastille by an irate mob of Parisians."

Musée Carnavalet

Having now turned onto Rue de Sevigne, Honoré led us up the street to Musée Carnavalet, an oft-neglected museum devoted to the history of Paris. There are many rooms to explore in this gallery, and chronologically speaking, they devote themselves first to Roman and Medieval times, then to the Renaissance, the seventeenth century, and the reigns of Louis XV and Louis XVI. That history continues with rooms devoted to the Revolution, the First and Second Empires, and finally to the story of Paris up to the present. However, Honoré brought me there this day to investigate one room in particular, and it's the one known as "Salle de Philosophes."

The room offers a comprehensive collection of *objet d'art* inspired by Voltaire and Rousseau: the Fauteuil de Voltaire, a lovely chair with two swinging tables at which he composed his writings; a bust of Voltaire and his goblet; and Rousseau's journal and penholder. In addition, there were pieces commemorating the heated dispute between the two philosophers: the Buste de Voltaire et Rousseau and a clock-thermometer showing gold figures of the two in heated dispute.

Also in that room there are portraits of Jean le Rond d'Alembert and Denis Diderot, about which Honoré spoke, "Modernity in France triumphed in the middle of the eighteenth century with a project conceived by these two men, the great French *Encyclopedia*. Of course the modern world had been very slowly taking aim at pre-modern ways of thinking since around 1500, when science and philosophy began to replace tradition and religion as the standard-bearers of truth.

"As to these gentlemen, Jean Le Rond d'Alembert was born in 1717. Though an abandoned and illegitimate child, he was fortunate to receive an outstanding education at the Jansenist Collège des Quartre-Nations here in Paris. Although his early interests included law and medicine, he finally settled on the study of mathematics and physics. D'Alembert eventually joined the Paris Academy of

Sciences, and later on was elected to the French Academy as its permanent secretary.

"Denis Diderot was born into a bourgeois family in 1713, and in his youth he was educated by the Jesuits at Langres. After receiving his degree from the University of Paris, he remained unsettled in life, at first studying law and then turning to his interests in languages, literature, philosophy and mathematics. In the early 1740's Diderot began socializing with the intellectuals in Le Procope, as well as in other Parisian coffeehouses, and they were associations that eventually turned him away from theism to atheism.

"The event that bound d'Alembert and Diderot together occurred in 1745, when the publisher André le Breton approached the two of them about a translation of Ephraim Chambers' *Cyclopaedia, or an Universal Dictionary of Arts and Sciences*. Finding that project too limiting, they turned their editorial skills to a far more challenging one, which was the publication of the *Encyclopedia, or, a Descriptive Dictionary of the Sciences, Arts and Trades*. And from 1751 to 1772 that monumental work was published in seventeen volumes containing almost eighteen thousand articles by nearly three hundred contributors, as well as eleven volumes of close to three thousand plates.

"The two proposed quite a grand aim for their project, about which d'Alembert wrote in the *Preliminary Discourse to the Encyclopedia of Diderot* (1751): 'The work whose first volume we are presenting today has two aims. As an *Encyclopedia*, it is to set forth as well as possible the order and connection of the parts of human knowledge. As a *Reasoned Dictionary of the Sciences, Arts, and Trades*, it is to contain the general principles that form the basis of each science and each art, liberal or mechanical, and the most essential facts that make up the body and substance of each. These two points of view, the one of an *Encyclopedia* and the other of a *Reasoned Dictionary*, will thus constitute the basis for the outline and division of our Preliminary Discourse.'

"D'Alembert and Diderot viewed knowledge as not just of the liberal or intellectual kind, but also of the often over-looked mechanical, or what today is referred to as technological, aspects of life. Of course due to the vastness of their project they included contributions to the *Encyclopedia* from the greatest and most important writers, poets, theologians, explorers, scientists, physicians, engineers and economists of eighteenth-century France. In addition, they included articles from a group of intellectuals known as Philosophes, which was comprised of such philosophers as Jean-Jacques Rousseau and Baron de Montesquieu, as well as the most renowned philosophe of them all, Voltaire.

"The Encyclopédists constructed a new conception of knowledge, one based not in the dogmatic beliefs of tradition and religion, but in the pragmatic truths of science and philosophy. All of our modern ideas about the world, which are thoughts that seem so commonplace today, were bequeathed to us through their efforts and their sacrifices. However, they also championed for liberty and tolerance within a civilized society. And while doing so they advanced the view that the rule of government should not be relegated to one man or a group of ignorant men, but to an association of learned men. But since that project incorporated the rationalist and secularist attitudes of the French Enlightenment, their ideas threatened the very power structure of the French Monarchy and the Church. For needless to say, the Encyclopédists were revolutionaries whose ideas were instrumental in creating Modernity, one guided not by monarchs and priests, but by democrats and philosophers.

"Perhaps this new conception of the world is best captured in Diderot's philosophical tale, *Rameau's Nephew* (1763): 'Rain or shine, it is my regular habit every day about five to go and take a walk around the Palais-Royal. I can be seen, all by myself, dreaming on D'Argenson's bench. I discuss with myself questions of politics, love, taste, or philosophy. I let my mind rove wantonly, give it free rein to follow any idea, wise or mad, that may come uppermost.... One day I was there after dinner, when I was accosted by one of the oddest characters in this country, where God has not stinted us.'"

After telling me the tale of Rameau's nephew, Honoré said, "I'll end here the story of the philosopher's conversation with Rameau, though of course you may wish to discover the remainder of it on your own, for he can usually be found in the Regency Café or in some other establishment in this city devoted to unceasing talk. But perhaps if there is anything to be gained from acquainting oneself with this man or others of his ilk, it is to pose to oneself a most important question: Is it better to journey in life as did the wise Socrates, or is it better to travel as a happy fool, like most men in this world?"

Honoré and I spent the next hour or so meandering about the museum, and all the while he continued the story of modern French philosophy, "The sixteenth century saw Michel Eyquem de Montaigne offer his anti-dogmatic thoughts and skeptical views of the world in his *Essays*, the first philosopher to put forward his teachings in the form of autobiographical essays. The next century produced *The Provincial Letters* (1657) and the *Pensées* (1669) of Blaise Pascal, as well as the *Rules for the Direction of the Mind* (1628) and the *Meditations on First Philosophy* (1641) of René Descartes. All of these works emphasized the concepts of scientific uncertainty and philosophical skepticism, the very cornerstones of Modernity.

"Although the eighteenth century generated the minds of Voltaire and Jean-Jacques Rousseau, as well as Jean le Rond d'Alembert and Denis Diderot, it also produced another philosopher of utmost importance, Charles de Secondat, Baron de Montesquieu. *The Spirit of the Laws* (1748) is one of the philosophical cornerstones of the United States Constitution, in particular, the concept that the powers of the government are best separated into legislative, executive and judicial branches. This exceptional exercise in modern philosophy covered almost every area of political concern, including that most contentious of American issues, the difference between natural and positive law.

"Montesquieu also wrote on the integrity of political leaders, but let me quote him using your own nation as an example: 'It was long ago said that a [President] cannot be great unless he is sincere. A private person may avail himself of the obscurity in which he is placed; he discredits himself only in the opinion of a few, and the mask he wears deceives others; but a [President] who steps aside from the straight path has a witness, a judge, in every subject of the state he governs. Is it too daring to say that the greatest evil done by an unscrupulous [President] is not the damage to the interests of his government, not the ruin wrought among his people, but quite another thing, and in my opinion a thousand times more dangerous, namely the bad example which he sets?'"

Musée Picasso

With my first lesson in Modernity delivered, Honoré and I left the museum and continued up Rue de Sevigne to Rue du Parc Royal, which we followed to Place de Thorigny, the location of Musée Picasso. Unfortunately, the museum was shut down for renovations until the summer of 2013, with most of its pieces touring the great cities of the world. The temporary closing of museums isn't an unusual occurrence in Paris, and the prospective investigator is well-advised to keep one's aesthetic expectations at a minimum until actually admitted to an "open" gallery.

However, while standing outside the museum and wondering what to do next, Honoré told me of an incident of a decade back, "On the second floor of the United Nations building, just outside the Security Council entrance, hangs a tapestry donated to the U.N. by Nelson Rockefeller in 1985. It's a copy of Picasso's 'Guernica', which the most acclaimed artist of the twentieth century painted to draw attention to Hitler's bombing of the Basque village of Guernica, during which 1,600 civilians were killed, many of them women and children.

"Unfortunately, the location of the tapestry is also the location for the holding of press conferences at the U.N. One such conference was held in January of 2003, during which U.S. Secretary of State Colin Powell announced that America was preparing to invade Iraq. Interestingly, during that conference the Guernica tapestry was concealed by a blue drape, ostensibly to make for a better backdrop for the cameras. And as the world watched on, another Guernica was only just beginning."

Now past the noon-time hour, Honoré thought it best that we enjoy a light lunch in a cafè in Place de Thorigny, during which he told me more about his lifetime of writing: "*La Comédie humaine*, or what you English-only speakers call *The Human Comedy*, consists of 91 interwoven stories, novels or essays, and 46 unfinished books, some only ever existing as titles. The collection portrays French society in the years between the Restoration and the July Monarchy, in other words, from 1815 to 1848. In the 1820s I lacked a general plan for my project, but by 1830 I began grouping my works together. However, it was not until 1842 that I published my *Avant-propos*, my overall conception of *La Comédie humaine*: 'French society would be the real author; I should only be the secretary. By drawing up an inventory of vices and virtues, by collecting the chief facts of the passions, by depicting characters, by choosing the principal incidents of social life, by composing types out of a combination of homogeneous characteristics, I might perhaps succeed in writing the history which so many historians have neglected: that of Manners.'

"However, before I relate to you any of *my* stories, let me, as your personal *raconteur*, begin the tale of Voltaire, for it is this illustrious philosopher that paved the way in France for all that we today call Modernity."

Voltaire in Paris

"In 1694, when Louis XIV was at the height of that military glory which at once dazzled and ruined France, there was born in Paris on November 21st a little, puny, weak, sickly son." So begins *The Life of Voltaire* (1907), written by S. G. Tallentyre, pseudonym for Evelyn Beatrice Hall. François Marie Arouet's father was a prosperous man of position, while his mother was a woman of gentle birth and refinement. He had an older brother, Armand, aged ten, and an older sister, Catherine, aged nine.

However, it would not be the father or the mother, or the brother or the sister, who would most influence the young François Marie. That person would be his godfather, the Abbé de Châteauneuf, who, like other members of his rascal profession, was a "free liver and free thinker, gay, base, and witty." From an early age he instructed the boy in the classics of French literature, and in so doing created a mind well-disposed to free thought. In fact so much so that after François Marie was enrolled in St. Louis-le-Grand in 1704, one of the masters declared: "Wretch! you will one day be the standard-bearer of Deism in France." Needless to say, no truer words were ever spoken, for this young philosopher was soon to espouse the tenets of a natural religion that are independent of any Christian church.

Upon leaving school in 1711, François Marie told his father of his intention to devote himself to writing, upon which the father scolded his son and told him that his career would be in law and that was the end of the discussion. After two years of watching his son enjoy everything but the law, the father shipped him off to The Hague as an attaché to a prominent family. But with his passionate character already established in life, François Marie was soon writing verses and making overtures to the daughter of the household. After a few months, Arouet was sent back to Paris, where he still offered overtures, at least until the daughter married another.

Father Arouet, now at his wit's end, soon sent the young man to a château near Fontainebleau to resume his studies. But it was not the law that François Marie studied at the château, instead it was the many books in the plentiful library. In August of 1715, and with Louis dying, this twenty-one year old poet "hastened to Paris to see the strange things that death would bring about. In his pocket he had a play, *Œdipe*, on which he had now been working for two years. In his soul were the courage, the conscious power, the clear outlook to a future all unwarranted by the present, which are the consolations of genius. Arouet was beginning the world."

As John Morley points out in a critique and biography that is included in the collection, *The Works of Voltaire: A Contemporary Version* (1901), the beginning of Arouet in the world would also soon see the beginning of Voltaire in the world: "It was one of the happy chances of circumstance that there arose in France on the death of Louis XIV, a man with all Voltaire's peculiar gifts of intelligence, who added to them an incessant activity in their use, and who besides this enjoyed such length of days as to make his intellectual powers effective to the very fullest extent possible.... As it was, with his genius, his industry, his longevity, and the conditions of the time being what they were, that far-spreading movement of destruction was inevitable."

After the conclusion of the festivities surrounding the death of the Sun King and the coronation of Louis XV, François Marie once again associated with the members of the Temple, a Parisian collection of wits and freethinkers. Upon reading his *Œdipe* to the group, half the salons in Paris opened their doors to him. Unfortunately, in 1716 a pointed epigram was mistakenly attributed to him, which resulted in his exile to the countryside. The next year other biting verses were mistakenly ascribed to him, though this time there was no exile, only a fairly comfortable one-year stay in the Bastille, one accompanied by good food, good wine and good books. And also while incarcerated, François Marie painted the finishing strokes on his tragedy *Œdipe*, signing it with the *nom de plume* that he chose for himself while in confinement... M. Arouet de Voltaire.

In the fall of 1718 Voltaire returned to Paris from a forced stay at his father's country home, the old man still hoping to change his incorrigible young son. But of course that was never to be, especially after the night of November 18, when the city was witness to the first performance of *Œdipe*. The astounding success of his first play offered two rewards, the remaining salons of Paris opened to him and money would never again be a problem. Over the next four years Voltaire's life was that of a celebrity playwright, and he stayed at one château after another and wrote one play after another, though not always with great success.

However, and according to Tallentyre, there were other ideas flowing through Voltaire's ever-questioning mind concerning the abuses of the Church, with the first of these blasphemous skepticisms appearing in 1722: "The *Epistle to Uranie*, in which he gave, in a few graceful pages, and with the admirable terseness and lucidity which were to be the hallmark of all his writings, the most powerful objections to Christianity. It was his first open avowal of Deism. How long he had cherished that belief and outgrown all others, cannot be told. The whole temper of his mind was rationalistic."

Over the next three years Voltaire continued his writing, his travels and his adventures, always charming some and alarming others, and always calling Paris home. However, in December of 1725 Voltaire was insulted by and then insulted Chevalier de Rohan, who was a member of the haughtiest and most illustrious family in France. According to Morley, history records the following exchange between the two men:

Chevalier Rohan: Who is the young man who talks so loud?

Voltaire: My lord, he is one who does not carry about a great name, but wins respect for the name he has.

A few days after their confrontation some of Rohan's lackeys beat our brave but foolish poet, and so naturally, Voltaire sought revenge. Unfortunately for the young bard, Voltaire's chance at revenge was not to be his this time. For due to the influence of Rohan, he was thrown once again into the Bastille in March of 1726. Not wanting to remain imprisoned for a second year, the irrepressible Voltaire wrote the authorities a pointed letter, one that's included in *Voltaire in His Letters* (1919), edited by S. G. Tallentyre: "... M. de Voltaire demands permission to dine at the table of the Governor of the Bastille and to see his friends. He demands, still more urgently, permission to set out for England. If any doubt is felt as to the reality of his departure for that country, an escort can be sent with him to Calais."

Perhaps not understanding the writer's sarcastic intent, or perhaps hoping to rid themselves of a troublesome miscreant, the authorities granted Voltaire permission to exile himself in England.

Beaubourg

Lying west of The Marais, Beaubourg offers the philosophical investigator a fine museum of modern and postmodern art, two crowded squares for passing the afternoon while people-watching, and many stylish bistros for passing the evening while also people-watching. And while studying the crowds that forever meander through this upscale neighborhood, Honoré continued with his story of Modernity.

Place Georges Pompidou

After investigating the Pompidou Centre - to be reported on later - Honoré and I settled ourselves in Place Georges Pompidou, where my personal philosophical investigator returned to his history of the first Revolution, "The evolution of the French Revolution proceeded through various stages - Estates-General, National Assembly, Constituent Assembly, Legislative Assembly, Convention, and Directory. And at the end of the timeline there arose the only solution out of the crisis, a dictator who was far more severe than the king that had been beheaded by the people.

"However, the pivotal historical event on July 14, 1789, need not have occurred, for a gradual transition from the *ancien regime* to a British-style constitutional monarchy was favored by many of the major participants prior to this ominous beginning of the Revolution. But to begin to understand this historical event, Gustave Le Bon made an important historical observation in his penetrating analysis, *The Psychology of Revolution* (1912): 'The true cause of the disappearance of the *ancien regime* was simply the weakening of the traditions which served as its foundations. When after repeated criticism it could find no more defenders, the *ancien regime* crumbled like a building whose foundations have been destroyed.'

"Mired in a deep economic crisis after years of domestic and foreign financial abuses, in May of 1789 Louis XVI convened the Estates-General, which consisted of the clergy, the nobility, and all the other citizens of France, a group known as the Third Estate. The Estates-General had not met since 1614, and at that time each of the three groups met and voted separately, and then sent one group vote to the King, who counted on the clergy and the nobility to override the Third Estate. But when the Estates-General was held at Versailles on May 5, the Third Estate sought to require that all groups assemble together, which was rejected by the other two parties.

"On June 17, the Third Estate, which had removed itself from the political process at Versailles, voted to become the National Assembly and invited the other two estates to join it. Louis' response was to close the hall where the National Assembly met, after which the group moved to a nearby tennis court and swore to the Tennis Court Oath: 'We swear never to separate ourselves from the National Assembly, and to reassemble wherever circumstances require, until the constitution of the realm is drawn up and fixed upon solid foundations.' The fact is that the removal of the monarchy was never a consideration until it was too late.

"So with growing support from the clergy and the nobility, Louis was on the verge of giving in to the demands of the Third Estate, when on the 9th of July the National Assembly became the Constituent Assembly. Five days later, the Bastille was stormed by the citizen mob of Paris, much to the regret of the Assembly. On August 4, 1789, the Constituent Assembly announced the August Decrees, which ended the rights and privileges of the first and second estates. Then on August 26 the Assembly published *The Declaration of the Rights of Man and of the Citizen*, which over the years of the Revolution went through a number of changes. However, although these were important political ideas, they remained only words.

"During the two-year life of the Constituent Assembly, many changes occurred to end the three tier structure of the *ancien regime*. As regards the Church, it lost its authority to tax crops, its special privileges, and much of its property, where previously it had been the largest landowner. As regards the Nobility, their members also lost much of their property, as well as numerous privileges, with many of them fleeing to other countries as *émigrés*. And as regards Louis XVI, on June 20, 1791, he and Marie-Antoinette fled from Paris in servant's clothes, only to be captured and then paraded in those clothes through the streets of the city the next day.

"In 1791 the Constituent Assembly finally framed a Constitution establishing the nation as a constitutional monarchy, not a republic. France was now controlled by the Legislative Assembly, which consisted of Feuillants, or constitutional monarchists, Girondists, or liberal republicans, and Jacobins, or radical revolutionaries. However, Louis still had the power of royal veto and the right to select ministers.

"Over the one-year life of this new government the nation was pushed further into debt as the various interest groups warred with one another, the result being a constitutional crisis by the following year. On August 10, 1792, the revolutionary Paris Commune, made up mostly of Jacobins, took the royal family prisoners and suspended the monarchy. The Commune soon began a campaign of selected executions, with the Assembly now too weak to put a stop to the events. To address the situation, the Convention met on September 20 to write another constitution establishing a new government. The next day the monarchy was abolished and France declared the First Republic, which marked the beginning of Year One of the French Republican Calendar, as well as the setting into motion of another series of uncontrollable events.

"On January 21, 1793, Louis was executed, with the queen guillotined on October 16, thus setting into motion the war with the other European powers. Also, now began one of the most horrifying events in French history, when the lawyer Maximilien Robespierre took control of the Committee of Public Safety. Along with the Jacobins, he unleashed the infamous Reign of Terror from 1793 to 1794. Records show that at least seventeen thousand people lost their heads to the guillotine, though some historians believe that as many as forty thousand people accused of counter-revolutionary activities may have been executed without trial or died while awaiting trial.

"In June of 1793, the 'enraged ones' took over the Convention calling for increased political purges. They arrested many of the Girondin leaders, which allowed for the Jacobins to gain control of the Committee of Public Safety. The resulting revolutionary dictatorship instigated the assassination of Jean-Paul Marat, as well as the removal of Georges Danton from the Committee. Robespierre, known as 'The Incorruptible', then became the group's most powerful member. He now ordered increasingly radical measures to be used against the government's enemies, both foreign and domestic. Also, in June the Convention adopted the Constitution of the Year I, which allowed, among other rights, for universal male suffrage. But Constitution or not, justice was never to prevail, for Danton was guillotined in the spring of the next year, with Robespierre following him in the summer.

"Due to the excesses of the Reign of Terror, in August of 1795 the Convention adopted the Constitution of the Year III, which took effect the following month. With the Convention now adjourned and a new constitution approved, in September 1795 the Directoire, or Directory, became the first bicameral legislature in French history. It consisted of 500 representatives in the Conseil des Cinq-Cents, or Council of the Five Hundred, and the Conseil des Anciens, or Council of Elders, which consisted of 250 senators. Five directors, named annually by the Elders from a list submitted by the Five Hundred, held the nation's executive power. However, the Directory proved to be as ineffective at governing France as had been the assemblies.

"As noted by Le Bon, faced with enemies on all sides, hostile rulers within, and an insurmountable financial crisis, the end of the government was in sight: 'At the end of the Directory the anarchy and disorganization were such that everyone was desperately calling for the man of energy capable of reestablishing order. As early as 1795, a number of deputies had thought for a moment of reestablishing royalty. The monarchy being impossible, it was necessary to find a general.' That general was of course Napoleon Bonaparte, who in 1799 brought an end to the first French Revolution."

Place Igor Stravinsky

Honoré and I next moved to a bench near the fountain in Place Igor Stravinsky in order to continue our people-watching, as well as for him to talk about the lessons to be learned from the French Revolution. However, no sooner did we sit down than an old man sat next to us. He appeared to be in something of a state, for every few moments he'd mumble a phrase just loud enough for us to hear: "*The Gods are Athirst* (1912)."

So I said to him, "Sir, are you alright? May I be of any assistance?"

He looked at me with sad and weary eyes, and then said, "I apologize for my odd behavior, but I am anxiously waiting for my friend Anatole France to arrive, for he always manages to calm me down when I get like this. But as he appears to be a bit late, perhaps you would kindly listen to my story. My name is Citizen Évariste Gamelin, and before the Revolution I was a painter. 'This humble Secretary of the Sectional Committee could see no disproportion between the immensity of the task and the meagerness of the means for performing it, so filled was I with a sense of the unity in a common effort between myself and all other patriots, so intimately did I feel myself one with the Nation at large, so merged was my individual life in the life of a great People.... I, too, have betrayed the Republic. The Republic perishes. It is just and fair that I die with her. I have been over sparing of blood. Let my blood flow! Let me perish!'"

Citizen Évariste was clearly in a state now, though fortunately, his friend Anatole eventually arrived to first comfort and to then lead him away. And as they walked off, I heard the old man say to the younger one: "Liberty, Equality, Fraternity... or Death."

"There's your first lesson on the Revolution," Honoré said to me. "But let me offer you a second one that is equally associated with death, the much-acclaimed punishment and entertainment apparatus known as the guillotine. Contrary to popular technological myth, the use of guillotine-like machines began long before the French Revolution. Of course prior to the use of the guillotine, the ax or the sword lopped off most miscreants' heads, though all that changed in 1307 when Murcod Ballagh was executed with a primitive form of the guillotine in Ireland. The English-built 'Halifax Gibbet' and the Scottish-built 'Maiden' improved upon the first primitive machines, and over the years their use proved a popular form of civic entertainment.

"The first official guillotine wasn't constructed until 1792, and also contrary to popular technological myth, it wasn't invented by somebody named Guillotine. Actually, the physician Dr. Joseph-Ignace Guillotin is the man who recommended to the French Assembly in 1789 that state-sanctioned murder should be accomplished through humane decapitation by 'means of a machine' and without the traditionally entertaining and rewarding methods of torture. After much debate, and though the compassionate conservatives of Paris preferred the old ways of doing business, two years later the Assembly approved a text stating that 'every person condemned to the death penalty shall have his head severed'.

"The following year, Tobias Schmidt, a German harpsichord-maker by trade, came up with a prototype machine, which enjoyed as an accessory a leather bag in which to dispose of the severed head. His machine was first tried out on sheep and calves, and then on human corpses, with those tests indicating to Tobias a need for the blade to be oblique, not curved or straight. Unfortunately for Nicolas-Jacques Pelletier, the machine worked almost to perfection in April of 1792. Sadly, the demonstration wasn't well received by the crowd, who still preferred time-honored hangings as their chosen form of civic entertainment.

"Not wanting to abandon the idea, and with suggestions from a number of prominent architects, a re-designed guillotine made of red painted wood was soon presented to the citizens for their approval. That technological advance in capital punishment stood about thirteen feet high, with the distance between the uprights set at about sixteen inches. To avoid any problems with swelling in the wood, grooves for directing the 'mouton' or blade were lined with metal to allow it to fall freely. Also, the 'bascule' against which the condemned knelt was tilted in a horizontal position so that a person's neck could be properly placed in the 'lunette', which then closed over the top. Needless to say, this highly sophisticated apparatus proved popular with the masses, as well as with anyone else who enjoyed watching unpopular heads removed from their unpopular bodies.

"That original guillotine design remained in use in France until 1870, when it was replaced by a more humane, though less entertaining form of machine built by Leon Berger, who was an assistant executioner and carpenter. Sadly for the modern-day investigator, the last public execution in France occurred in 1939, though decapitations still continued in private until 1977, when Hamida Djandoubi became the last man to see his head removed from his body.

"Actually, that last statement is somewhat misleading, for though it is true that that was the last *man* to see his head removed from his body in France, a newer machine, 'The Balzac', named for me, is still used on mother-in-laws. For a French mother-in-law to lose her head, a son-in-law must find one other male to sign a letter of complaint against her. Usually that co-complainant is either an ex-husband of his wife or a husband of one of his sister-in-laws. However, in some cases the father-in-law is more than willing to sign the complaint, which then allows the state to discharge its duty for the betterment of society.

"Of course, the beheading of a miscreant forever brought out the frenzied crowds. And just like at games today the festivities always began with the singing of the French national anthem, *La Marseillaise*, composed in 1792 by Claude-Joseph Rouget de Lisle. It was first played at a patriotic dinner at Marseilles, with copies printed for the revolutionaries to sing while marching into Paris. The Convention approved it as the national anthem on July 14, 1795, though Napoleon banned it during the Empire, as did Louis XVIII during the Second Restoration. The song was reinstated as the national anthem after the July Revolution of 1830, though it was banned once again by Napoleon III. Fortunately for lovers of the movie *Casablanca*, the song returned permanently as the anthem in 1879.

"Up to this point, the Revolution appeared a dismal failure except for bequeathing unto the nation a much-beloved national anthem. However, there is a lesson to be learned here, and that concerns *The Declaration of the Rights of Man and of the Citizen*. And though the basic tenets of a citizen's rights were continually crushed during the Revolution, it did imbed in the minds of the French people the importance of a legal framework for governing a Modern society. So please, allow me to recite this most important document to you: 'The representatives of the people of France, formed into a National Assembly, considering that ignorance, neglect, or contempt of human rights, are the sole causes of public misfortunes and corruptions of Government, have resolved to set forth in a solemn declaration, these natural, imprescriptible, and inalienable rights.... For these reasons the National Assembly doth recognize and declare, in the presence of the Supreme Being, and with the hope of his blessing and favor, the following sacred rights of men and of citizens...'

"With these Rights in mind, allow me to refer once again to Le Bon in *The Psychology of Revolution*: 'The outward life of men in every age is molded upon an inward life consisting of a framework of traditions, sentiments, and moral influences which direct their conduct and maintain certain fundamental notions which they accept without discussion. Let the resistance of this social framework weaken, and ideas which could have had no force before will germinate and develop. Certain theories whose success was enormous at the time of the Revolution would have encountered an impregnable wall two centuries earlier.'

"Let us now consider a few questions as regards the first French Revolution, this in order to remind ourselves as to why we must continually study history so as to hopefully avoid repeating similar mistakes in the present. Firstly, what can be said of the lasting influence of the Revolution, at least as regards the philosophy of Modernity? Secondly, how does our understanding of the Revolution guarantee that events as disastrous to society never occur again? Lastly, and this is most important, what can one say about possible future revolutions?"

Café Beaubourg

As the lunch hour was now upon us, Honoré and I meandered around the corner to Rue St-Martin, where we settled into a table in Café Beaubourg. This stylish watering hole and restaurant offers an elegant interior that can only be described as Art Deco sumptuousness, one that appeals to art dealers and modern museum staff alike. And while we enjoyed a light meal and a glass of white wine, Honoré said, "Allow me to tell you the sad story of *Eugénie Grandet* (1833).

"The story of the girl Eugénie is set in the town of Saumur. The father Felix Grandet is enormously wealthy through businesses and inheritance, having been left the estates of his mother-in-law, grandfather-in-law and grandmother. However, Monsieur Grandet is also a very miserly creature, for: '... there, incarnate in a single man, revealed in the expression of a single face, did there not stand the only god that anyone believes in nowadays - Money, in all its power?'

"Naturally, this made the marrying off of his daughter Eugénie a most difficult task, for he wishes to part with as little of his wealth as possible, even if it means sacrificing his daughter's happiness. On Eugénie's birthday, Felix's nephew, the indolent Charles Grandet, arrives from Paris, having been sent there by his now bankrupt father. Eugénie and Charles immediately fall in love, and unbeknownst to her father, she foolishly gives the young man some of her own money. The father is of course too busy increasing his wealth to worry about two love-struck young lovers, or anything else of enduring importance for that matter.

"Charles soon travels overseas to make his way in life, with Felix eventually learning that it was his daughter's money that funded the expedition. And though the family quarrels over this realization, Felix surprisingly reconciles with his wife and daughter. After eight years, Charles returns to France, now wealthy, corrupt and not inclined to marry Eugénie, but another girl of greater standing. Needless to say, after patiently waiting all those years Eugénie is heartbroken. Reluctantly, Eugénie decides to marry another, though he dies young, leaving her to dwell upon the vicissitudes of life. But enough of my stories for the time being, instead, let me return to the continuing story of Voltaire."

Voltaire in England

As John Morley observes in *The Works of Voltaire*, Voltaire's exile in England was the beginning of a great change in the illustrious poet: "He was in the thirty-third year of his age, that earlier climacteric, when the men with vision first feel conscious of a past, and reflectively mark its shadow."

Voltaire enjoyed a productive two-year stay in London, leaving France a poet and returning from England, also a philosopher. And during that sojourn in the land across the Channel, he wrote his first philosophical treatise. *Letters on England* (1733) was a collection of essays covering Voltaire's observations of the English way of life during his forced exile from 1726 to 1728, during which time he came to believe "that the doctrine and history of such unusual people were worthy of the curiosity of a reasonable man."

Firstly, those articles were on the English religious sects: the Quakers, the Anglicans, the Presbyterians, the Socinians, and the Arians or Anti-Trinitarians. Secondly, they were on English civil society, in particular, parliament, government and commerce. Voltaire also wrote on medicine, gravitation, optics, infinity and chronology, as well as on the English scientists and philosophers, such as Francis Bacon, John Locke and Isaac Newton. And lastly, he considered the arts of English tragedy and comedy, the patrons of the arts, the English poets, and the academies.

As it turned out, it was the essay on John Locke that proved to be the most influential in France, for it forced French philosophers to begin divorcing themselves from the century-old Cartesian method of viewing the world. René Descartes believed that our ideas concerning reality are all innate, meaning that they are derived from the intellect rather than through the senses. He made this assertion in his *Meditations on First Philosophy*: "We come to know ideas by the power of our own native intelligence, without any sensory experience."

However, as Voltaire observed in his *Letters*, the English brought forth John Locke to set the mind free from this error in philosophical reasoning: 'Divide mankind into twenty parts: nineteen consist of men who work with their hands and will never know that there is a Locke in the world, and in the remaining twentieth part how few men will you find who are readers! And of those who read, twenty read novels to one who studies philosophy. The number of those who think is exceedingly small, and they are not interested in upsetting the world. It is to the man who rules over minds by the power of truth, not to those who enslave men by violence, it is to the man who understands the universe and not to those who disfigure it, that we owe our respect.'

As Morley points out, it was not only the misconceptions of philosophers that Voltaire's letters addressed, but also those of the theologians: "It was the English onslaught which sowed in him the seed of the idea, and eventually supplied him with the argumentative instruments, of a systematic and reasoned attack upon that mass of doctrinal superstition and social abuse, which it had hitherto been the fashion for even the strongest spirits in his own country to do no more than touch with a cool sneer or a flippant insinuation, directed to the private ear of a sympathizer."

Les Halles

Sitting to the west of the arty Beaubourg is the energetic Les Halles, home to a marvelous fountain, a magnificent forum and a munificent feast. While meandering about this lively neighborhood, Honoré continued the story of modern France, first with the ending scenes of the first Revolution, then with the military exploits of a grand emperor, and finally with the political thoughts of an important philosopher.

Fontaine des Innocents

Wandering up Rue Aubry le Boucher and then Rue Berger, Honoré and I arrived at Square des Innocents, where we enjoyed the appropriately named Fontaine des Innocents, a Renaissance creation moved to this location from another in the eighteenth century. And it was here that my personal philosophical investigator began his lecture for the afternoon, "Coming as no great surprise, the Revolution engendered hostile feelings from the other crowns of Europe, who sent armies to ensure that revolutionary changes didn't find new homes in their countries. During the War of the First Coalition from 1791 to 1798, the French army was remarkably successful in defending France from its aggressors. The battles of the War of the First Coalition also served the Government well, for an enemy from without always turns citizens' heads away from the deprivations at home.

"However, let me backtrack historically to the story of Napoleon Bonaparte, the general responsible for many of the French military successes. Napoleon was born on the island of Corsica on August 15, 1769, a year after the isle was transferred to France from the Republic of Genoa. By 1785 Napoleon was a second lieutenant in the French army, though with the outbreak of the Revolution he returned to Corsica to help bring about the island's independence. And though at times he fought against the French, in 1792 he was promoted to captain by the military authorities in Paris.

"The next year Napoleon published a pro-republican pamphlet that caught the eye of Augustin Robespierre, the younger brother of Maximilien. With their support the captain led the successful siege of Toulon, resulting in his promotion to Brigadier General. However, the following year found him out of favor after the fall of Robespierre. But with the uprising of the Parisian monarchists in 1795, Napoleon successfully helped defend the Convention in the Tuileries Palace. And with the rise of the Directory, the general was given command of the Army of Italy, which he led to victory after victory over the next two years.

"Napoleon's victories continued in Egypt, where he fought both British and Ottoman forces. But after hearing of the series of European defeats in the War of the Second Coalition, Napoleon returned to Paris, where he drafted a new constitution that established the Consulate, with him as First Consul and now the most powerful man in France. In 1800 Napoleon returned to Italy to reestablish French authority, though due to tactical errors he just narrowly avoided defeat. The next year the general turned his troops north to Austria, securing a weak victory and a peace treaty.

"Returning to Paris in 1802, Napoleon instituted some badly needed reforms by centralizing government and education departments, organizing road and sewer systems, and establishing the Banque de France and a new tax code. He also increased his powers within a new constitution, becoming now the First Consul for Life. In the area of civil law, Napoleon created the system known today as the Napoleonic Code, which required that the law be clearly written and accessible to all. Despite the centralization of power by the First Consul, this was precisely what France needed after years of revolutionary unrest.

"After a series of plots against him, on December 2, 1804, Napoleon proclaimed himself Emperor, with Josephine as Empress, thus establishing the First Empire. The following year, Britain, Austria and Russia began the War of the Third Coalition. Despite losing control of the seas at the Battle of Trafalgar, Napoleon's Grande Armee was victorious at the Battle of Austerlitz, which ended the conflicts momentarily. But peace was not to endure, for 1806 saw Napoleon defeat Prussia in the War of the Fourth Coalition, the next year saw the beginning of the ongoing Peninsular War in Spain and Portugal, and in 1809 the War of the Fifth Coalition ended with another uneasy peace.

"In 1812 Napoleon finally gained evidence that Russia was violating the Continental System, the Emperor's enforced Europe-wide commercial boycott of Britain. Napoleon's decision to invade Russia resulted in a dubious victory in Moscow, his loss of control in France, and a ruinous retreat during a harsh Russian winter that ended with the deaths of most of his four hundred thousand troops. In addition, he returned to France to face the War of the Sixth Coalition, now consisting of Britain, Prussia, Austria, Russia, Sweden, Spain and Portugal.

"In April of 1814 his generals forced Napoleon to abdicate to the island of Elba off the coast of Italy, though before leaving he addressed his still faithful officers in the courtyard of Fontainebleau: 'Soldiers of my Old Guard, I bid you farewell.... Do not regret my fate. If I have consented to survive, it is to serve your glory. I intend to write the history of the great achievements we have performed together. Adieu, my friends. Would I could press you all to my heart.'

"Not understanding the meaning of the word 'defeat', after ten months of exile Napoleon escaped back into France in March of 1815. With a thousand soldiers from his Old Guard, he marched to Paris, gathering an army along the way. Once again Emperor, at least for the next hundred days, Napoleon led his troops to a final defeat against Britain and Prussia at the Battle of Waterloo on June 18. His final exile was to the island of St. Helena off the coast of Africa, where he died on May 5, 1821, thus bringing to an end the life of this extraordinary Frenchman."

Forum des Halles

Continuing up Rue Berger, Honoré and I arrived at Forum des Halles, the site of lovely gardens and pavilions, cultural centers devoted to art and poetry, and stylishly cosmopolitan fashion shops, some above and some below ground. And as we browsed about the stores, Honoré told me a different story about Modernity, a tale that lays hidden well beneath, but remains forever the scaffolding for, the hustle and bustle of contemporary society, "Although the chaotic world of pre-modernity, the *ancien régime*, the first Revolution and the first Empire distracted almost all minds of a common bent, from the sixteenth century onward there was unwavering progress in the sciences, mathematics, probability and statistics, advances that prepared the way for the Industrial Revolution. And though these achievements occurred throughout Europe and Britain, the French contributed their share not only through individual efforts, but through the collecting and organizing of knowledge by the Encyclopédists":

René Descartes (1596-1650) revolutionized mathematics by combining Euclidean geometry with algebraic analysis, creating in this way a new branch of knowledge called Cartesian or analytic geometry. Descartes' work was the basis for the later development of the calculus, and he applied his method to problems in mechanics and optics. This mathematical method is today the fundamental approach in physics and engineering, as well as the foundation of most fields of modern geometry. He also developed the convention of representing the unknowns in equations by x, y and z, and the knowns by a, b and c.

Pierre de Fermat (1601/7/8-1665) developed mathematical ideas that later resulted in the infinitesimal calculus, as well as methods for finding maxima and minima of curves as is applied in the differential calculus. He, along with Blaise

Pascal through correspondence, also laid the foundations for probability theory. Fermat's most famous contribution to mathematics was in number theory, in particular, his Last Theorem, which he claimed to have proven, despite the fact that the methods for proving it were unknown in his day. "Fermat's Last Theorem" states that no three positive integers a, b and c can satisfy the equation $a^n + b^n = c^n$ for any positive integer value of n greater than two.

Blaise Pascal (1623-1662), along with laying the foundations for probability theory with Fermat, made contributions in the science of fluids, the construction of calculating machines, and in the mathematical field of projective geometry. His most famous contribution in mathematics is what's known as "Pascal's Triangle," a convenient method for representing binomial coefficients, in other words, the coefficient of the x^k term in the polynomial expansion of the binomial power $(1 + x)^n$. His triangle also offers a representation of the Fibonacci numbers, 1, 1, 2, 3, 5, 8, 13..., where the next number in the sequence is always the sum of the previous two.

Abraham de Moivre (1667-1754) linked complex numbers to trigonometry in his celebrated formula, *(cosx + isinx)^n = cos(nx) + isin(nx).* He also made contributions to probability theory in his text *The Doctrine of Chances: a method of calculating the probabilities of events in play,* the first published book to cover games of chance. Included in his probability text is the de Moivre-Laplace theorem, which showed that a binomial distribution can be approximated by a normal distribution. And in a paper, *Annuities upon Lives,* he applied the normal curve to mortality rates.

Jean le Rond d'Alembert (1717-1783) made scientific contributions in fluid mechanics, the nature of refraction, and the laws of motion. In mathematics he produced the ratio test for determining whether a series converges or not, as well as a somewhat flawed proof of the fundamental theorem of algebra. And in probability theory he defined the d'Alembert system, the game strategy of decreasing one's bet the more one wins and increasing one's bet the more one loses.

Antoine-Laurent de Lavoisier (1743-1794) is considered the "father of modern chemistry," making scientific contributions in chemistry and biology. He named both of the chemicals oxygen and hydrogen, and as well predicted the existence of silicon and established that sulfur was an element. He also helped construct the metric system, drew up the first list of elements, reformed chemical nomenclature, and discovered the law of conservation of mass.

Pierre-Simon Laplace (1749-1827) made advances in mathematical astronomy in his influential book *Celestial Mechanics*, which transformed the geometric study of classical mechanics to one based on calculus. He also devised the Laplace transform used in mathematical physics, developed the nebular hypothesis of the origin of the solar system, and postulated the existence of black holes and gravitational collapse. And in statistics he developed the Bayesian interpretation of probability, a method that involves specifying a prior probability, which is then updated by new data.

After telling me about just a few of the French mathematicians and scientists from the sixteenth to the eighteenth centuries, Honoré continued, "So as we see, the fundamental basis of Modernity, which is in large part the discovery and creation of scientific and mathematical knowledge, proceeded without hindrance throughout the social turmoil in the years between 1500 and 1815. What occurred next in history would continue this progress at a much more accelerated pace, with advances not just in theoretical knowledge, but in the application of that knowledge in the creation of new technologies during the Industrial Revolution. And in the nineteenth century there would also be the establishing of new fields of study, namely, economics and the social sciences."

Bistro d'Eustache

Across Rue Berger from Forum des Halles, sits the lively and popular Bistro d'Eustache, which offers good food, good wine and good jazz, both classic and gypsy. And with the dinner hour upon us, Honoré and I found ourselves enjoying all that that bistro offered on a warm evening. But as the crowds began to thin, my dinner companion said, "Let me now tell you the tragic story of my deceased friend, *Père Goriot* (1835).

"This tragic tale begins in the home of the elderly Mme. Vauquer, who has kept a rooming-house, the Maison Vauguer, in the Rue Nueve Saint Genevieve for the past forty years. The Maison Vauguer is home to seven permanent inmates, as well as to a couple birds of passage, though at dinner the dining room also sees several lost souls from the neighborhood, which makes for a total of eighteen men and women.

"When my retired and widowed friend first moved into Maison Vauguer in 1813, he was addressed respectfully by one and all as Monsieur Goriot, with Mme. Vauguer even plotting a matrimonial scheme as regards her well-to-do lodger. Of course he immediately rebuffed her designs, which elicited in her a vengeance of grand proportions. For you see, '... the human heart may find here and there a resting-place short of the highest height of affection, but we seldom stop in the steep, downward slope of hatred.'

"After that day, Père Goriot, which was his newly designated name within the rooming-house, became the butt of spiteful reproaches made all the more severe after the visitation of two mysterious young women, who were the self-centered daughters of my friend. And from that point, life remained in a steep decline for old Goriot, as he moved into cheaper accommodations within Maison Vauguer and as he sold off all of his beloved memories.

"Another boarder in the rooming-house was Eugène de Rastignac, a law student more interested in understanding the social "rules" that govern life in Paris than in the social 'laws' that govern life in Paris. Seeing his chance to rise in society, Rastignac first pursued Mme. Restaud, one of the two daughters of Goriot, and then the other, Mme. de Nucingen. Goriot set Rastignac up in an apartment so that his daughter Delphine could visit him there, and also in the hope of living upstairs to be near her. But the day that he was to be happy once more, he took to his deathbed. Goriot called for his daughters until the very end, but neither came to say goodbye to their loving father. In the end, his final home was but a pauper's grave.

"Rastignac visited that last resting place for the burial: 'I gazed into the grave, and the tears I shed were drawn from me by the sacred emotion, a single-hearted sorrow. When such tears fall on earth, their radiance reaches heaven. And with that tear that fell on old Goriot's grave, my youth ended. I went a few paces further, to the highest point of the cemetery, and looked out over Paris and the windings of the Seine. There lay the great world that I had longed to penetrate. I glanced over that humming hive, seeming to draw a foretaste of its honey, and said magniloquently: We'll fight this out, you and I.'

"Rastignac eventually became a successful lawyer, as well as a cultured man of Paris. And needless to say, he was always invited into every salon and every bedroom of this jaundiced city. Sadly though, just like old Goriot, he never found happiness in this metropolis of misguided intentions. But I've gone on far too long with this terrible tale and now feel the need to continue a happier one, the ongoing story concerning Voltaire."

Voltaire in Cirey

After more than two years in England, Voltaire was finally given permission to return to Paris, where he once again enjoyed the popularity and the acclaim that came with each of his new plays. Regrettably, prior to leaving for London in 1726, his vane desire for that popularity and that acclaim allowed him to half-close his eyes to the many injustices taking place in France. But even with his eyes near shut, he still observed much about the court of Louis XV: "It is a dreadful bore to be here, but it is very advantageous - the cage is so exquisitely gilded that one must try not to see the bars through the gold." However, a new side of Voltaire began to emerge during those years abroad. He was now steadfastly devoted to encouraging progressive efforts in politics, the sciences and philosophy, as well as to championing the freedoms that are necessary for giving birth to all of those efforts.

Voltaire's transition from court favorite to court provocateur came to light upon the death of Adrienne Lecouvreur, who was the greatest actress of her day and a brilliant woman that died horribly in his arms at the age of thirty-eight. But because she had lived her life on the stage, as well as on her own terms, she was denied a priest, absolution and a Christian burial. As a consequence, she was taken out of the city at night and "thrown in the kennel" like a dog. Voltaire was so incensed by this treatment that he asked an important question of his countrymen: "Shall I ever cease to see the light-minded Frenchman sleeping under the rule of superstition? Is it only in England that mortals dare to think? Men deprived of burial here to whom Greece would have raised altars. In London she would have had a tomb among geniuses, kings and heroes. Ye gods, why is my country no longer the fatherland of glory and talent?"

As unpopular as those words were in some quarters, the denunciations were nothing compared to the onslaught of accusations that was unleashed in 1734 upon the appearance of his *Letters on England*, published as *Lettres philophiques* in France. The publisher was immediately thrown into the Bastille and an order of arrest was soon issued in Voltaire's name, despite the fact that he claimed to know nothing about the book that was being publicly denounced and burned throughout Paris.

So Voltaire fled to the château of Madame du Châtelet and her husband in Cirey-sur-Blaise, a small town located in the region of Champagne to the northeast of Paris. It was a convenient and safe place to reside, for if the authorities were not currently looking for him, then he could easily visit his beloved city of Paris. And if the authorities were looking for him, then he could easily slip across the border to Belgium or to Prussia. But how did Voltaire know of this refuge in the first place?

In 1706 there was born a daughter Émilie to the Baron de Breteuil, who was the Principal Secretary and Introducer of Ambassadors to Louis XIV. She grew up learning at a very early age Greek and Latin, and song and dance, and mathematics and science. Introduced to the court at Versailles when only sixteen, she quickly developed a taste for all things of splendor, about which Voltaire once wrote: "Émilie's tastes are impeccable. What she sees she wants, and her eyesight is remarkably keen."

Émilie's superior intelligence caused almost all women and most men to avoid her, a result of her being born into a particular time and a particular place not conducive to admiring intelligent women. As Tallentyre wrote in *The Life of Voltaire*: 'There have been few women in any age devoted from all eternity to the exact sciences, impassioned for learning for learning's sake, capable of that keen delight in the discovery of a new truth which is like the delight of the sportsman when he has run his quarry to earth. There were very few such women even in the eighteenth century. But there were some: and Émilie de Breteuil was one of them.'

Émilie married the Marquis du Châtelet at the age of nineteen, and like many such arrangements of that Age and Class, the husband and wife had very little in common and so lived separate lives. She gave her military husband three children, but she gave her first three lovers much more. And though denied entry into the coffeehouses of Paris due to her unfortunate choice of sex, she would clandestinely enter wearing fashionable men's clothes so as to join in on the many discussions of science, mathematics and philosophy.

In the spring of 1733 Émilie met Voltaire, eleven years her senior, though the two already knew a great deal about each other through mutual friends. He knew that she was "a philosopher with a passion for metaphysics - a being at once excitable and sensual, who united to an entire lack of the moral sense, intellectual passions the most pure and sincere that ever raised a woman above the pettiness, the backbitings, and the meannesses common to her sex." The two became lovers almost immediately, with the love-struck poet soon writing verses to his new love.

Needless to say, her attraction for Voltaire was also immediate, with their need for each other surviving for the next fifteen years, mostly behind the doors of the Château de Cirey. The final stroke that sent Voltaire to Cirey was the censorship of the *Letters on England*. Of course he didn't leave Paris without a fight, as indicated in Tallentyre's collection, *Voltaire in His Letters*: "... A great library is like the City of Paris, in which there are about eight hundred thousand persons: you do not live with the whole crowd: you choose a certain society, and change it. So with books: you choose a few friends out of the many.... The man of taste will read only what is good, but the statesman will permit both bad and good."

After Voltaire finally took up residence in the château in 1734, he immediately went about the business of renovating the rundown home and gardens, of collecting well over twenty thousand books for the château's library, and of building a scientific laboratory for his and Émilie's common interests. From that first year on their days were filled with labors of the intellect and labors of the home, and even their many guests were forced to entertain themselves until a late dinner hour, perhaps all the while enjoying Voltaire's little poem dedicated to his lover and friend:

A traveler, who never lies,
Passes by Cirey, admires it, contemplates it;
At first he believes it is only a palace;
But he sees Émilie. "Ah," he says, "it is a temple."

Despite the occasional and sometimes secretive jaunts to Paris to oversee his many plays, Voltaire's first few years of life in Cirey were occupied with a history, *The Century of Louis XIV* (1751), and works on philosophy, such as *Treatise on Metaphysics* (1734) and *Discourses on Man* (1738). He also wrote an irreverent poem about Joan of Arc, titled *La Pucelle d'Orléans* (1762), or *The Maid of Orleans*, which many consider unworthy of him:

Near the end of 1736 a short poem, *Le Mondain* attracted firstly the attention of the solons of Paris and then the government censors because of its irreverent attitude towards the teachings of the Church. To avoid trouble with the authorities, Voltaire was forced to leave Cirey for a few months stay in the Netherlands and Belgium, where he oversaw the printing of his *Elements of Newton's Philosophy* (1738), a book undoubtedly coauthored by Émilie given her superior mathematical abilities and scientific knowledge.

Not only is it amazing when a new idea surfaces to enter the heads of men and women, but it is equally amazing when an old idea is extinguished from the haze of their minds. This had already been the case in the *Letters on England*, where Voltaire overthrew René Descartes' theory of innate ideas in favor of John Locke's view that all of our ideas come through the senses.

According to Tallentyre, for a second time Voltaire destroyed the prevailing Cartesian orthodoxy of the day in the *Elements*: "With what a passion of zeal those two people set themselves to seek truth for truth's sake - to seek truth whether it agreed with the fashionable belief and the textbooks or whether it did not - to find it, and to give it to the world!... The censor prohibited the work with its dangerous and terrible anti-Cartesian theories when it appeared. But in ten years' time, the Cartesian theories were proscribed in the schools of Paris and the Newtonian taught everywhere in their stead. Voltaire hardly ever won a finer victory."

As more evidence of Émilie's exceptional abilities in the sciences, in 1737 a competition was announced by the Academy of Sciences in Paris. Both Voltaire and Émilie submitted original papers to the Academy, his on heat and hers on light, though she was forced to submit her paper without his knowledge. And though neither of them won the award, Émilie's paper was considered better than the winning one by many French scientists. In fact, if not for her being a woman, as well as for favoring a Newtonian and not a Cartesian approach to her description of light, she would have won the competition.

Outside of trips to oversee his publisher in Brussels, Voltaire seldom left Cirey until 1741, when he made a short visit to Paris, one that was followed by a longer stay until August of the next year. During those months of 1742 he saw his play, *Fanaticism, or Mahomet the Prophet*, win accolades from the intellectuals and condemnations from the Church. And later in the same year his *Mérope* achieved the same success as *Mahomet*, though it wasn't enough to allow him to occupy an open chair in the French Academy the following year.

For the remainder of 1742 and for much of the next year, Voltaire and Émilie were often away from Cirey and sometimes apart, he in Brussels or Prussia, she in Paris. They were back home by the spring of 1744, with him soon busy on a play for the wedding celebration of Maria Theresa of Spain in the autumn. "It is not necessary to say that Voltaire took immense trouble over this *bagatelle*, because he always took immense trouble over everything. All his works are as good as he could make them. He called his play *The Princess of Navarre*."

Voltaire and Émilie arrived in Paris for the wedding festivities in September, and by January of the next year they were in Versailles. Voltaire's literary and social successes over 1745 captured for him the post of Historiographer of France, and eventually a Chair in the French Academy. "On April 25, 1746, the greatest literary man of the age, who was fifty-two years old and a member of almost every other Academy in Europe, was at last formally elected to the Literary Society of his own country." And in December of the following year, Voltaire was made Gentleman of the Chamber to Louis XV.

However, two months prior to that, in October of 1747, Voltaire and Émilie were invited by the Queen to Fontainebleau. And while there, Émilie was given permission to play cards at the Queen's table, where she immediately lost a small fortune. Alarmed by the situation, Voltaire whispered into his companion's ear in English: "Don't you see you are playing with cheats?" Unfortunately, another player at the table overheard and understood his words, forcing the two of them to return quickly to Paris and then into hiding until the Court forgot the incident.

An ordinary couple might have been done in by this incident, but not Émilie and not Voltaire. In Paris, the clever Émilie immediately designed a financial scheme to get her out of debt. As to Voltaire, he spent several months in hiding in a darkened room of the duchesse du Maine's Chateau de Sceaux, which sits southwest of the capital. While hiding there, Voltaire produced four of his most beloved masterpieces: *Zadig* (1747), *Scarmentado* (1756), *Micromégas* (1752), and *Babouc* (1746). And as Tallentyre noted concerning these ageless philosophical tales: "Everything that makes a story immortal is his own in those matchless *contes*. Charm, wit, delicacy, an exquisite lightness of touch, the finest taste in satire, humor, variety, epigram, gaiety - with that ever-present undercurrent of biting meaning - almost all the Voltairian gifts are here."

Though the gambling episode at Versailles blew over after a few months, another one was brewing by January of 1748, when Voltaire wrote some complimentary poems to Marquise de Pompadour, the mistress of the King. They fell into the wrong hands, which forced Émilie and him to return immediately to Cirey. And for the next month Voltaire and his companion of fourteen years happily spent their days in what they both loved best - reading, researching and writing.

In February Voltaire and Émilie paid a visit to the former King of Poland, Stanislas, and his mistress, Madame de Boufflers, who were living in Luneville, located to the east of Cirey in Lorraine. Also at the miniature Court was the Marquis de Saint-Lambert, "one of most picturesque figures of the century. Poet and soldier, handsome, haughty and cold, with just enough disdain in his perfect manner to make every woman adore him and long to thaw that flawless ice - he had almost every quality which makes riches superfluous."

Although Saint-Lambert was the lover of Madame de Boufflers, Émilie was filled with a passion for him that could not be resisted, especially by such a complicated woman. Of course it must be remembered that for many of the last fifteen years, Voltaire treated Émilie as only a philosopher might, as a deeply loved intellectual friend. But despite being a mathematician and a scientist of extraordinary ability, she was still a woman, one now in her forties. So it's understandable how she fell head over heels in love with a dashing officer, one ten years her junior.

The affair that began during those several months in Luneville, about which Voltaire was unaware, continued briefly in Cirey while Voltaire was in Paris. In Commercy, another Court of Stanislas, the liaison renewed itself in July. And with Voltaire soon leaving for Paris to oversee his play *Semiramis*, the still undetected affair continued for many months in both Luneville and Commercy. "The discovery of their secret was of course only a matter of time. One night early in that October of 1748 at Commercy, Voltaire walked into Madame du Châtelet's apartments, unannounced as his habit was, and there in a little room at the end of the suite, lighted by only one candle, he found the handsome young soldier and his clever, foolish, elderly mistress talking upon something besides poetry and philosophy."

All the parties involved immediately exchanged bitter and accusing words, though surprisingly, Émilie later went to Voltaire's room and reminded him that she was a woman who still needed to love and be loved by someone. To this he responded as only a philosopher could: "Madame, you are always right. But if things must be so, do not let me see them." And the next day Saint-Lambert apologized to Voltaire, to which he replied: "*Mon enfant*, I have forgotten all. It was I who was wrong. You are at the happy age of love and pleasure. Make the most of both." Voltaire, ever the philosopher, even wrote a few lines to Émilie's paramour in the next year.

Later in October the trio traveled amicably back to Luneville, where Voltaire continued work on his *Age of Louis XV*. In December of 1748 he and Émilie returned to Cirey, where she learned that she was with child, and needless to say, it was not Voltaire's. Acting quickly, Émilie summoned her husband home from his regiment. For appearances sake, she remained near to him for several weeks, thus assuring that their two inheritances stayed within the family.

Whether or not her husband believed the child to be his cannot be said, and that question remains a matter of historical speculation. However, and judging from a distance of a few centuries, the entire episode does not speak highly of anyone concerned with it. But as must be admitted, Voltaire "shared the vices of the social conditions he condemned, and was himself in some sort a part of that system which set itself above decency and duty and which he knew to be fatal to the good of mankind."

By February of the next year, Voltaire and Émilie were back in Paris, though in late June the two returned to Cirey for a fortnight's stay. The two then followed the Court between Luneville and Commercy throughout the summer and into September, when Émilie gave birth to a baby girl. Sadly, she died a week later, as did her daughter, though historians disagree as to whether the child died a few days before or after her mother. In the aftermath of her death, the eight volumes of love letters and other correspondences between Émilie and Voltaire were either lost to history or burned by Saint-Lambert, with historians also uncertain about the circumstances.

Upon that death at Luneville in 1749, Voltaire could only write: "It is not a mistress I have lost but half of myself, a soul for which my soul seems to have been made." And Émilie, her thoughts about her death were spoken of by her many years before: "It's rare to admit it, but we all secretly like the idea of being talked about after our death. In fact, it's a belief we need." Of course the story of the great love affair between Voltaire and Émilie never came to an end for him until his death many years later, but he did leave a loving *Ode* to her:

I shall await you quietly,
In my meridian in the fields of Cirey;
Watching one star only,
Watching my Émilie.

Opéra Quarter

Lying to the northwest of Les Halles, the Opéra Quarter presents three architectural wonders in the Opéra de Paris Garnier, La Madeleine and the Palais de la Bourse, two stylish shopping arcades in Les Galeries and the shops around the Hôtel des Ventes, and one exceptional watering hole, Harry's New York Bar. As with every other area of Paris, the many squares offer perfect places to people-watch and perfect places to continue the ongoing investigation of Modernity.

Place de la Opéra

After taking the Metro to Opéra station the next morning, I joined Honoré in Café de la Paix for coffee and croissants. From the outdoor tables the philosophical investigator enjoys a wonderful view of the comings and goings in Place de l'Opéra, as well as the fine sight of Opéra de Paris Garnier, with its mixture of architectural styles designed by Charles Garnier for Napoleon III.

As we began the day while people-watching, Honoré continued with his lessons on French history, this time offering a few historical stories, which is forever the habit of a true *raconteur*, "With the defeat of Napoleon in 1815, Louis XVIII made his second return from exile to reestablish Bourbon rule, though generally the mood of France was not for a resurrection of the *ancien regime*. Instead, political power was in the hands of the Chamber of Deputies, which consisted of three competing and contentious parties. The political extremes, or ultras, supported a strong monarchy, while the independents, or liberals, supported a return to the ideals of the Revolution. And the middle party, the constitutionalists, or moderates, supported a constitutional monarchy similar to the British model.

"French history is often best viewed and understood through the writings of its literary men, with this particular period colorfully described in a novel by Alexandre Dumas, *The Count of Monte Cristo* (1845). It is the story of Edmond Dantès, who at the age of nineteen is a merchant sailor in Marseille engaged to Mercédès, a most beautiful young woman. On his final voyage with his soon to be deceased captain, the ship stops briefly at the island of Elba. On the return voyage and as the captain approaches death, he asks Edmond to deliver a letter from Napoleon to a faction of Bonapartist sympathizers in Paris.

"Upon his return home and for various malevolent reasons, three supposed friends send a letter to a deputy public prosecutor accusing him of treason. The prosecutor immediately sees through the plot, though when he discovers that the captain's letter refers to his own father, he sends Edmond to the prison Château d'If off Marseilles. Edmond might have died there except for a fellow inmate, an Italian priest and intellectual jailed for his political views. Through the efforts of his beloved Abbé Faria, over many years he becomes a well-educated man, knowledgeable in history, languages, science and philosophy.

"Just before he dies, the Abbé tells him the location of a treasure hidden on the island of Monte Cristo. Upon his friend's death, Edmond manages to escape, and then travels to the island and finds the fortune. In disguise he returns to Marseilles and not only learns from one of his former friends about the plot that sent him to prison, but also that his father is dead and that Mercédès is married to one of his supposed friends. As well, he learns that his other two friends and the prosecutor are now wealthy and influential citizens in Paris. And though it would take some time, Edmond knows that he will exact revenge.

"After ten years and now known as the Count of Monte Cristo, he organizes a ruse in which he saves the son of the friend that married Mercédès. To return the favor, the young man introduces the Count to Parisian society. Although recognized by no one but Mercédès, and with damning knowledge about the three involved, he exacts revenge on all the perpetrators of the plot to imprison him. And though it would not be with Mercédès, the Count eventually finds happiness and peace with another woman.

"You are probably wondering what is learned from the story of Edmond's life. Most importantly, human justice in the form of revenge is not for humans, for the innocent as well as the guilty are also punished and ruined in this world. As regards happiness, we must not envy others, but must appreciate what we have and do some good with it. Lastly, it is only through the strong emotion of love that we find true comfort in life.

"Continuing on with our historical voyage, after the death of Louis XVIII in 1824, his younger brother, Charles X, a monarch decidedly in favor of the now-antiquated view of the divine right of kings, ascended to the throne. During his reign of six years the country experienced a revival of its Catholic roots, laws instituted to favor the seminaries over the universities, and various restrictions placed on the press and publishers. Needless to say, this return to the days before the Revolution polarized the country, with events coming to a head in 1830. The July Revolution overthrew Charles X, allowing for the ascent of his cousin, Louis Philippe III, Duke of Orléans, to the throne.

"Perhaps this period of French history is best viewed and understood through the writings of Victor Hugo, in particular, his novel *Les Misérables* (1862). The story of the parolee Jean Valjean is the tale of one man's redemption from the instincts of the brute, and the replacing of those impulses by ones of love and compassion. The story begins in 1815 in Digne, with Jean recently released from prison, but shunned by society. Jean is taken in by a local bishop, who gives him shelter. However, after stealing the bishop's silverware, he takes the priest's advice and finally repents of his sins.

"Six years later and under an assumed name, Jean is now a wealthy factory owner and the mayor of his adopted town, Montreuil-sur-Mer. Through a series of incidents he rescues Fantine, a mother searching for her lost daughter Cosette. Sadly, she dies before finding her, though Jean vows to never stop searching for her. But after his identity is discovered, Jean is arrested and sentenced to death.

Managing to escape, he eventually finds Cosette, and the two of them flee to Paris.

"Another eight years pass, with the July Revolution two years in the past and anti-Orléanist civil unrest now taking over Paris. The grown and beautiful Cosette is in love with the student Marius, who works to save Jean from extortionists demanding money. All are caught up in the student uprising of 1832, with Marius and Jean joining the rebellion. And though Marius is injured, he eventually recovers and marries Cosette. On the other hand, Jean, now tired of life, takes to his deathbed surrounded by his adopted daughter and son-in-law, and then dies peacefully.

"Rather than divine right, the bourgeois monarchy of Louis-Philippe was based on the concept of 'popular sovereignty'. All the laws mandated by Charles and pertaining to the Church, the schools and the press were quickly rescinded, with new suffrage rights doubling the number of voters. In the Chamber of Deputies a two party system prevailed, with the ultras supporting a stronger monarchy and the republicans supporting a weaker one. By the 1840's the two competing parties were both politically weak, which allowed for almost a decade of stability until the Revolution of 1848.

"The uprising overthrew the constitutional monarchy of Louis-Philippe, who abdicated to Britain, bringing about the Second Republic. Suffrage was immediately extended to all nine million French males, though surprisingly, in the April election the conservatives and moderates were the big winners in the Chamber of Deputies. This forced the June Days civil war, which was brief and bloody, and which involved mainly the workers of Paris. The most democratic constitution in Europe was completed six months later, with France now headed by a popularly elected president serving a four-year term. The voters chose for their first president Louis-Napoleon Bonaparte, the nephew of the great emperor of the First Empire. Forever unable to make up their minds, within three years the people demanded and were awarded the Second Empire in 1851, with Napoleon III as emperor.

"The authoritarian years of Napoleon's regime lasted from 1852 to 1859, and though civil liberties were reigned in, France did experience a great resurgence in the areas of economic growth and foreign policy. With both domestic and international stability seemingly assured, the next eleven years of Napoleon's reign were far more liberal. The decade of the 1860's saw advances in worker rights, the enlargement of public education, and the extension of freedoms to the press and to political assemblies. Unfortunately for these progressive movements, France was goaded into the disastrous Franco-German War, which resulted in the capture of the emperor, a bloodless revolution in September of 1870, and the besieging of Paris.

"Lastly, perhaps this period of French history is best viewed and understood through the writings of Emile Zola, in particular, his twenty-volume collection *Les Rougon-Macquart*. The first novel, *The Fortune of the Rougons* (1871), begins with Zola's purpose for writing the decades-long story: 'Historically the Rougon-Macquarts proceed from the masses, radiate throughout the whole of contemporary society, and ascend to all sorts of positions by the force of that impulsion of essentially modern origin, which sets the lower classes marching through the social system. And thus the dramas of their individual lives recount the story of the Second Empire...'

"After her defeat in the Franco-German War of 1870, which resulted in the signing of the costly Treaty of Frankfurt, the French government formed itself into the Third Republic under the leadership of Adolphe Theirs. The Parisian members of the National Assembly soon rebelled against Theirs and formed the Commune of Paris, a loose confederation of workers' groups. But in the Bloody Week of May, the forces of the government killed twenty thousand Communards, thus putting an end to the first French socialist movement.

"France of the 1870's again saw a never-ending battle raged between the monarchists and the republicans, though internal quarrels within both groups allowed for great divisions in the National Assembly. Georges Clemenceau led the most radical wing of the republican faction, and he stood for a strong central government and foreign policy, as well as for a complete rejection of monarchism and clericalism. However, it was the more moderate republican wing of the Assembly that governed France until the end of the nineteenth century."

Harry's New York Bar

Honoré was in a thirsty mood this particular morning, so he decided that we should next stop in at the famed Harry's New York Bar, located down Avenue de l'Opéra and around the corner on Rue Daunou. Sent over from New York and rebuilt in 1911, Harry's has enjoyed the likes of such imbibers as Sinclair Lewis, F. Scott Fitzgerald, Ernest Hemingway and Humphrey Bogart. It's also reported that it was in the "Ivories" Piano Bar that George Gershwin composed *An American in Paris*, probably while enjoying a properly mixed gin martini.

The year 1911 was a wonderful year for gin martinis, for it was in that year at the Knickerbocker Hotel in New York that the head barman, Martini di Arma di Taggia, mixed a drink consisting of equal parts of gin and vermouth, as well as a splash of orange bitters and an olive. Ever since those simpler times the martini has become just about anything a barfly wants it to be, and a certain private investigator has even come up with a few libations of his own using gin, a splash of dry vermouth and the following choice of stuffed olive: *Martini Americano* (pimento), *Martini Mexicano* (jalepeno), *Martini Italiano* (garlic), *Martini Greeko* (anchovy), and *Martini Germano* (blue cheese).

As a note to the lover of martinis, there are three well-known problems concerning those wonderful elixirs. The first problem relates to the proper amount of vermouth in a dry martini, about which Winston Churchill said: "I would like to observe the vermouth from across the room while I drink my martini." The second problem is mentioned in a James Thurber line: "One martini is alright, two are too many, and three are not enough." And the third concerns a physiological malady commonly referred to by the ladies as the "Tini Wieni," but enough said on that embarrassing matter.

While enjoying a much-needed dry gin martini, Honoré returned to one of his favorite subjects, the investigation of Modernity, "We have spoken of the great advances in mathematics, the sciences and philosophy that occurred from the sixteenth century onwards, as well as the increased rates of those advances. However, despite the scientific progress in physics, chemistry and biology, in the nineteenth century there was one area of study just beginning to be born, Sociology, the study of man in society.

"The founder of that discipline was the philosopher Auguste Comte, who also originated the doctrine of 'positivism'. His social theories resulted in the concept of the 'religion of humanity', which greatly influenced religious and secular humanist organizations during the century. Comte's general theory was best explained in 1848 in his introductory remarks from *A General View of Positivism*: 'Positivism consists essentially of a Philosophy and a Polity. These can never be dissevered; the former being the basis, and the latter the end of one comprehensive system, in which our intellectual faculties and our social sympathies are brought into close correlation with each other. For, in the first place, the science of Society, besides being more important than any other, supplies the only logical and scientific link by which all our varied observations of phenomena can be brought into one consistent whole.'

"Comte also offered an account of social evolution in his conception of the *Law of Three Stages*, the idea that society and all its sciences develop first through a 'theological stage', then through a 'metaphysical stage', to end in a 'positive stage'. The theological stage explains the world in terms of personified deities: first through 'animism' or 'fetishism' in which inanimate objects contain spiritual essences, then through 'polytheism' and the worship of many gods, and finally through 'monotheism' and the worship of one supreme god.

"The metaphysical stage explains the world through abstract ideas, ones that are often mistakenly believed to be positive, as well as through the belief that abstract powers and forces determine the events in the world. Lastly, the positive stage offers scientific explanations based on observation, experiment, and theory, these days most often of a mathematical nature. Since the world is best explained through a scientific method that establishes cause and effect relationships, positivism is a way of looking at the world using only intellectual concepts.

"Though now considered an obsolete theory, Comte also proposed a hierarchy of the sciences, from simpler to more complex areas of knowledge, based on historical development. His order of progress was mathematics, astronomy, physics, chemistry, biology, psychology and sociology. And it was through the science of society, the 'Queen science', that all human social ills would eventually be remedied... as optimistic a belief as ever there was one.

"Of course, it wasn't just the sciences that were advancing, but also the analysis of the social and political nature of democracy, a system of government that in the nineteenth century was spreading to all corners of the world. Of major importance in this endeavor was the French government sending Alexis de Tocqueville and Gustave de Beaumont to study the American penal system in 1831. When finished late in the year, they returned to France and submitted their report the following year.

"However, it wasn't the penal system report that shined a fresh light on the nature of democratic societies, but Tocqueville's two-volume *Democracy in America*, published in 1835 and 1840, respectively. And though Tocqueville covered many aspects of democracy, his observations 'concerning the philosophical approach of the Americans' are still of fundamental importance in understanding the American form of democratic thought: 'I think that in no country in the civilized world is less attention paid to philosophy than in the United States. The Americans have no philosophical school of their own; and they care but little for all the schools into which Europe is divided, the very names of which are scarcely known to them.'

"Tocqueville's observation that 'Americans have no philosophical school of their own' would be out-moded within forty years. For in 1878 there appeared an essay by Charles Sanders Peirce, *How to*

Make Our Ideas Clear, which laid the foundation of a new school of philosophy, an American one. This new philosophy was best explained by the philosopher and educator John Dewey in his book *Philosophy and Civilization* (1931), in particular, in the chapter *The Development of American Pragmatism.*

"Although Pierce's ideas influenced many American thinkers, Pragmatism could hardly be considered a new school of philosophy until William James generalized those ideas. The third philosopher of the new American school, as well as its most influential, was John Dewey, who explained his conception of Pragmatism, which he called 'Instrumentalism': 'American thought continues European thought. We have imported our language, our laws, our institutions, our morals, and our religion from Europe, and we have adapted them to the new conditions of our life. The same is true of our ideas.... If I were asked to give an historical parallel to this movement in American thought I would remind you of the French philosophy of the Enlightenment. What interested them was the application of scientific method and the conclusions of an experimental theory of knowledge to human affairs, the critique and reconstruction of beliefs and institutions.'"

Place de la Madeleine

With the lunchtime hour upon us, Honoré and I meandered west along Rue Daunou, Boulevard des Capucines and Boulevard de la Madeleine to eventually arrive at Place de la Madeleine. The square is home to the impressive church La Madeleine dedicated to Mary Magdelene, the childhood home of Marcel Proust, a beautiful flower market, and the "millionaire's supermarket" known as Fauchon. After picking up a few overly expensive food items and an over-priced bottle of wine, we landed on a bench near the church trees and enjoyed a wonderful Parisian picnic.

Once lunch was finished, Honoré said, "To pass a little more time in this wonderful spot, let me tell you the story of *Cousin*

Bette (1846). This story is one of desire and infidelity, jealousy and treachery, and love and faithfulness, in other words, a representative story of contemporary Parisian society: 'Paris is a meeting-place, swarming with talent, for all the forceful vigorous young men who spring up like wild seedlings in French soil. They haven't a roof over their heads, but they're equal to anything, and set on making their fortune.... for only in Paris exists the endless concubinage of luxury and want, of vice and sober virtue, of repressed desire and ever-renewed temptation...'

"The tale begins with the beautiful Adeline Hulot, wife of the wealthy Baron Hector Hulot. Mme. Hulot is being pressured into an affair with the businessman Célestin Crevel, though to his surprise this saintly woman resists his advances. Of course the Baron knows nothing about these goings-on. Also complicating the situation is that the Hulots'·daughter, Hortense, is looking for a husband and their son, Victorin, is married to Crevel's daughter Celestine.

"Living in a tiny apartment elsewhere in Paris is Mme. Hulot's cousin, Bette, an unmarried spinster lacking in physical beauty and filled with resentment about her life. In the apartment above hers she discovers an unsuccessful Polish sculptor, Wenceslas Steinbock, attempting suicide and she nurses him back to health, developing over time a maternal fondness for the young man. She also makes friends with Valérie, the wife of a government clerk, and the two form bonds of affection and protection. Valérie attempts first to improve Bette's appearance, but with no success.

"Baron Hulot is soon rejected by the courtesan Josépha, who favors Crevel and his larger fortune, which causes the Baron to meet and fall in love with Valérie. Along with the debts accrued by spending money on Josépha, Baron Hulot increases his arrears by continuing his lavish ways with Valérie. Realizing his predicament, with his uncle he quickly devises a way to embezzle money from an overseas government department.

"Hortense soon meets Wenceslas, and much to the embitterment of Bette, Hortense weds Wenceslas. Having lost Steinbock, Bette decides to take vengeance on the entire Hulot family, using as her means all that she has learned about them over the years. Cousin Bette and courtesan Valérie soon swindle money from both Baron Hulot and Crevel by playing each against the other, and as well, Valérie draws Steinbock into her bed. And when any of the dupes complain, the temptress simply plays the wounded lover. Hortense next learns of her husband's infidelity, leaves him and returns to live with her mother Adeline.

"However, despite her infidelities to her husband and her three lovers, Valérie is secretly in love with a Brazilian Baron, Henri Montès de Montéjanos, with whom she becomes pregnant, though all five men are told that each is the father. In the meantime, Baron Hulot's brother discovers all about the infidelities and the overseas scheme, and so makes arrangements for repayment prior to his death. Shamed, Baron Hulot leaves his family and disappears into Paris, with his wife Adeline working for a Catholic charity as she searches for her husband.

"In the end, Valérie loses her child at birth, loses her husband soon after, and then marries Crevel for his money. Outraged by this turn of events, Baron Montès poisons both of them and they die a horrible death. On the other hand, Adeline eventually finds her husband and brings him back to the family, and Wenceslas returns to his wife Hortense. After seeing the now reunited Hulot family, Bette takes to her death bed, followed soon thereafter by Adeline. The story ends with the aged Hulot marrying the kitchen maid Agathe, who is, needless to say, a much younger woman.

"This heartbreaking tale offers a man the important lesson that he should remain faithful to his loving wife, and as well, that he should devote his time in life to a loftier vision than the pursuit of common pleasures: 'The entire detachment from all worldly concerns of true artists, and their devotion to their work, stamp them as egoists in the eyes of fools, who think that such men ought to go dressed like men about town performing the gyration that they call their social duties.... Such men, who have few peers and rarely meet them, grow accustomed to shutting out the world, in their habit of solitude. They become incomprehensible to the majority, which, as we know, is composed of blockheads, the envious, ignoramuses, and skaters upon the surface of life.' And the man who understood this life-long commitment to a loftier vision more than any other was Voltaire, whose story I shall now return to."

Voltaire in Prussia

Though fraught with emotional pain after the death of Émilie, Voltaire continued with his work, first in Cirey and then in Paris, where he wrote two new plays, *Rome Sauvée* and *Oreste*, both successfully staged in the capital by early 1750. However, also making the rounds were two satirical pamphlets, *Voice of the Sage and the People* and another, with both attacking the injustices of the Church.

With Louis only too happy to see the back of his troublesome poet, and rather insisting that he go, in June of 1750 Voltaire finally took up King Frederick of Prussia's offer of a long stay, though this was not the first meeting of the philosopher and the king. Voltaire and Prince Frederick had been exchanging letters since 1736, and the first letter to him in August summarizes the hopes that Voltaire had for the Prince who would soon become King Frederick the Great.

However, it wasn't until four years later that they finally decided to meet in person. But there was one stumbling block, and that was Émilie. Always jealous concerning her Voltaire, "she must be first - everything! Her women's instinct told her to mistrust Frederick, and she did mistrust him. Then the mistrust grew to dislike, dislike to hate, and hate, war to the knife." And on the part of Frederick, he always offered compliments to his friend's lover, while also working to come between the two.

After a little subterfuge by the newly crowned King Frederick, Voltaire finally met his friend for three days in September of 1740 at Moyland Castle, located across the French border in North Rhine Westphalia. And with Émilie in Paris preparing for Voltaire's return to the city, the two met again in Remusberg in November, this time at one of the gayest courts in all of Europe. But return to Émilie he must, for as he knew so well, "men serve women kneeling: when they get on their feet they go away."

Voltaire at first viewed Frederick as one of Plato's philosopher-kings, though that delusion came to an end in December, when the King that so loved peace invaded Silesia with his troops. Although disappointed in his friend, Voltaire visited Frederick again for a few days in September of 1742 at Aix-la-Chapelle. And in August of 1743 he once again made a visit, though this time in Berlin and Bayreuth, and this time under rather different circumstances.

Through his political advisors, Louis XV earlier informed Voltaire that he needed to know whether the Prussian king would side with France over the rights of Maria Theresa concerning the Hapsburg territories. Our budding diplomat even went so far as to draw up a series of questions for Frederick to answer, but "the fact was that where Voltaire was but a brilliant amateur, Frederick was the sound professional. Voltaire was not above trickery, but Frederick tricked better. His answers to that famous series of questions are evasive, or buffoonery."

After leaving Frederick briefly, Voltaire was back in Berlin in October of 1743 for a few days, and eventually back in Paris to report on his diplomatic mission. The two were not to see each other again until July of 1750, when Voltaire joined Frederick at his palace in Potsdam near Berlin. Within a month the sovereign offered him the post and salary of Chamberlain, and then for the remainder of the summer and throughout the autumn Voltaire lived in a whirl of majestic celebrations in Potsdam and Berlin. However, the relationship between Voltaire and Frederick was never a good or profitable one for either the philosopher or the king.

Unknown to Tallentyre when writing his biography, while on a visit to Paris in 1744, Voltaire began an on-again off-again affair with a new mistress, his niece Marie-Louise Denis, who was his junior by eighteen years. During his lifetime, the real nature of Voltaire's relationship with Marie-Louise was a closely guarded secret. Positive evidence of the affair was missing until 1957, when Theodore

Besterman discovered and published a series of very explicit love letters between Voltaire and his niece.

By November of 1750, the serious problems between Voltaire and Frederick were on the rise. And after one particular episode, nothing could stop the inevitable conclusion to their friendship. The philosopher and the usurer Hirsh concocted a plan whereby they purchased illegal notes, though the deal went flat by the next month. Voltaire was forced to take Hirsh to court in February of 1751, with the legal proceedings sounding as if their business was concerned with something other than illegal notes. And though Voltaire won the court case, everyone knew what the contract had really been about, including Frederick, who now kept a close eye on his philosopher guest.

But two can play at that game, so Voltaire made certain that his confidantes at the Court told him everything that was discussed by the King. One such tidbit of gossip was given to him by La Mettrie, who told him that Frederick said: "I shall want him a year longer, at the outside: one squeezes the orange and throws away the peel." Needless to say, this wounded and angered Voltaire.

In December of 1751 Voltaire's *The Century of Louis XIV* finally appeared, and it was a historical flower that first took bud when the author was still in his early twenties. Of course it was immediately prohibited in France, though that didn't stop the book from becoming a bestseller there and in every other country in Europe. Also during this time Voltaire was beginning his *Philosophical Dictionary* (1764), and "further fanning the flame, by innumerable suggestions, of that light-bringer of the eighteenth century, that torch in a darkness which could be felt, the *Encyclopédie* of Diderot and d'Alembert."

The straw that finally broke Frederick's back came in the form of Voltaire's confrontation with the mathematician and scientist, Maupertuis, who several years earlier was the tutor and lover of Madame du Châtelet, though he was now the President of the Berlin Academy. After several more run-ins with this most serious and dull man, Voltaire decided to respond to him by publishing a satire of

Maupertuis' more nonsensical thoughts in the acclaimed *Diatribe of Doctor Akakia* (1752).

As Tallentyre wrote concerning this invective: "There is no more scathing and burning satire in literature. Voltaire made Maupertuis a byword and a derision, the sport of fools, the laughing stock of Europe, a buffoon, a jest, a caricature, such that men seeing, stopped, beheld open-mouthed, and then laughed in convulsions." In this scathing lampoon, Voltaire satirically refers to Maupertuis as Plato.

By the end of 1752 Frederick demanded to know whether or not Voltaire wrote the *Akakia*, but of course his guest denied any knowledge of that offensive satire. But despite his denials, all of Europe knew who wrote that invective. Of course so did Frederick, who received the following letter on the first day of January, 1753, asking that his guest be allowed to leave the court: "... Your Majesty may rest assured that I shall remember nothing but the benefits conferred on me.... I flatter myself that out of so much kindness you will keep at least some feeling of humanity towards me: that is my sole consolation, if consolation I may have."

Voltaire received from Frederick an equally famous response, one leaked to the popular press in the middle of March: "He can leave my service when he feels inclined, but he must have the goodness, before he goes, to return to me the contract of his engagement, the key, the cross, and the volume of poetry which I have confided to him: I could wish that he had only attacked my works, which I sacrifice willingly to those who desire to belittle other people's reputations: I have none of the vanity and folly of authors, and the cabals of men of letters seem to me the depth of baseness."

So the time was right for Voltaire to flee, and flee southwest he did to Leipzig. There he published a new addition of the *Akakia*, including this time two supplements, as well as a threatening letter that he received from Maupertuis. Voltaire remained in Leipzig for several weeks and then fled to Gotha, where he stayed until the end of May, after which, he journeyed to Frankfurt. Here his flight to freedom was cut short, for Frederick sent an official to restrain his former guest until that possibly embarrassing volume of poems was returned to him.

The volume was finally delivered into the hands of the official in early July after over a month's stay in Frankfurt, so Voltaire was given permission to travel on to Mainz, which sits on the Rhine and out of the control of Frederick. Near the end of the month, Voltaire traveled along the Rhine to Mannheim. And in the middle of August he crossed over the French border to Strasbourg, where he remained until leaving for Colmar in early October of 1753.

Voltaire waited along the border for Louis to forgive him one more time and so allow him to return to France, though the publication of a pirated edition of *Essay on the Manners and Spirit of Nations* (1756) sealed the fate of the homeless philosopher. And as Tallentyre noted concerning this incendiary paper: "The *Essay on the Manners and Spirit of Nations* is of all Voltaire's works the one which has exerted the most powerful influence on the mind of men. It prepared men for freedom. It was the first history that dealt not with kings, the units, but with the great, panting, seething masses they ruled, which took history to mean the advance of the whole human race - a general view of the great march of all nations toward light and liberty."

Although his words seem commonplace to us today, in his *Essay on the Manners and Spirit of Nations* Voltaire struck at the very power-structure of eighteenth century France: "... It must once again be acknowledged that history in general is a collection of crimes, follies, and misfortunes, among which we have now and then met with a few virtues, and some happy times, as we sometimes see a few scattered huts in a barren desert."

Tuilleries Quarter

Extending from the Louvre to Place de la Concorde, the Tuilleries Quarter offers half a dozen museums and galleries, another half a dozen squares and gardens, and a multitude of famous historic buildings. While meandering about this very active, though fascinating quarter, Honoré continued with his history of Modernity, this time covering the story of France from the beginning of the twentieth century to the end of the Second World War.

Jardin du Palais Royal

After finishing lunch in Place de la Madeleine, and given the debilitating effects of two gin martinis and half a bottle of white wine each, instead of walking, Honoré and I took the Metro from Madeleine to Palais Royal/Musée du Louvre. We then walked across Place du Palais Royal to the Palais Royal, formerly Palais-Cardinal and originally home to Cardinal Richelieu, who bequeathed it to the Crown upon his death in 1642. Over the years its gates have opened for monarchs and revolutionaries alike, and after the restoration of the Bourbons even Alexandre Dumas was employed in one of its offices. Today the palace is home to the Constitutional Council and the Ministry of Culture, while nearby is the Bibliothèque Nationale de France, home to six million books and other materials.

Continuing on to Jardin du Palais Royal, Honoré and I found a pleasant garden bench, where after a slight doze he carried on with the story of France, "In the early years of the twentieth century, the Bloc Republican governed France and ushered in the so-called *La Belle Époch*, remembered later as 'the good old days'. During this period the General Labor Federation, with its devotion to the ideals of revolutionary syndicalism and its use of general strikes, helped bring about a unified Socialist Party. It soon withdrew from the Bloc

Republican, which paved the way for a centrist government under the leadership of Georges Clemenceau.

"As the First World War loomed on the horizon, a conservative movement trumpeting French nationalism gained strength over the fear of increasing German military might. The socialists openly opposed this faction, due mainly to their belief that an international workers' movement could prevent another war. This of course proved not to be the case in 1914, nor did it prove to be the case during the following three decades.

"Though there were many events that contributed to the inevitability of the war, it was the assassination of Austrian archduke Francis Ferdinand on June 28, 1914, that put France on the course to open conflict with Germany. After negotiations between the powers failed, Germany declared war on France on August 3. The French immediately formed a national union Cabinet, which assigned command of the impending war to General Joseph Joffre. In France, as in the rest of Europe, the assumption was that the war would last only a few weeks, at most a month. This mistaken belief proved to be disastrous for all sides, as well as to the many millions of lives lost during the conflict.

"The first major advance of the war was from the German army, which in late August marched into France through Belgium and threatened to surround Paris. Fortunately, Joffre was able to stop the German advance, with the enemy settling into positions in northeastern France, a situation that remained almost unchanged until the end of the war in 1918. For France, the first major advance of the war was the Battle of Verdun, with French troops under the command of General Philippe Pétain. The battle lasted from February to June of 1915, with a loss of a quarter of a million men on both sides.

"The remaining three years of the war were essentially a stalemate, with the French holding the front in the south and the Allies holding it in the north. And in Paris, Joffre was replaced in 1916 by General Robert Nivelle, who was replaced by Pétain the next year. By then the morale of the troops, as well as of the civilian population, was at a low, at least until the command of the nation was handed over to the elderly Georges Clemenceau, who infused a new spirit to hold out for victory.

"In March 1918 the Germans attempted one last assault, though with France and the British now under the command of General Ferdinand Foch, the drive was checked and an armistice signed on November 11, thus bringing the First World War to an end. But victory came at an enormous cost, for out of the eight million men France mobilized, over one million died and one million were left crippled for life. In addition, much of northeastern France was left unfit for agriculture or industry, a condition that lasted until the middle of the next decade.

"For many European intellectuals, the First World War marked the end of Modernity. All the grand ideas concerning science, democracy and philosophy that Voltaire and other thinkers spent their lives propagating resulted in the most destructive war the world had ever seen in its history. The belief in modern progress was shattered, and this psychological loss was eventually replaced by a philosophy of the individual. With another world war looming on the horizon, Existentialist writers began developing their thoughts over the next two decades. Jean-Paul Sartre, in particular, wrote on those troubling times in his *Roads to Freedom* trilogy: *The Age of Reason* (1945), *The Reprieve* (1945), and *Troubled Sleep* (1949).

"Change was in the air, first in the outbreak of the Spanish Civil War in July of 1936 and then with Adolf Hitler's crossing of the Austrian border in March of 1938. But the calm before the real storm lasted only six months, until September, when Premier Édouard Daladier, along with Prime Minister Neville Chamberlain of the United Kingdom and Prime Minister Benito Mussolini of Italy, flew to Munich to negotiate an agreement with the German Chancellor.

"Word came on Thursday, September 29, 1938, when the four European powers signed the Munich Agreement, an accord printed in every paper the following morning. With the war almost upon them, on that fateful morning Chamberlain returned to London proclaiming 'peace for our time'. And in Paris, with the crowds cheering, Daladier whispered to his aide: 'The God-damned fools!'

"Hitler invaded Poland on September 1, 1939, and two days later France declared war on the Third Reich. 'The Phony War' resulted in no major conflicts in Europe until April of 1940, when Germany invaded Denmark and Norway. The following month, the French army, under the command of General Maurice Gamelin, along with the armies of allied nations, failed to stop the Germans from taking the Low Countries and northern France. Quickly defeated, France surrendered to Germany on June 22.

"The war in Europe came to a close in May of 1945, with millions of lives lost or crippled for life. But for many intellectuals the victory would not resurrect the modern European mind, but only isolate it further in the limiting ideas of the postmodern world. And as for America, she also left Modernity behind in favor of Postmodernity... precisely in the split second of the deadly flash over Hiroshima."

Jardin des Tuileries

Returning to Rue Saint Honore, Honoré and I walked past Place André Malraux, home to the Comédie Française, where in his plays Moliere laughed at the absurdities of the world he lived in centuries ago, one not that much different than our own. Continuing on to Rue des Pyramides, we turned left and walked to Place des Pyramides, and then crossed Rue de Rivoli to Jardin des Tuileries. Extending along the Seine from the Louvre to the Arc de Triomphe, the gardens were built in the seventeenth century for Louis XIV on the grounds of the long-gone Palais des Tuileries.

While we enjoyed life from the vantage point of a park bench, Honoré continued his story of Modernity: "Throughout the last two decades of the nineteenth century, socialist and Marxist politicians received increasing political support from the urban working class. However, the natural inclination of the French to support Socialist causes was evident from the beginning of the first Revolution, when Pierre-Sylvain Marechal addressed to the people of France his *Manifesto of the Equals* (1796): 'People of France, the moment for great measures has come. People of France, open your eyes and hearts to the fullness of joy. Recognize and proclaim along with us the Republic of Equals.'

"However, amongst members of the trade unions, there now emerged a more radical movement, revolutionary syndicalism, as championed by Pierre-Joseph Proudhon. His 1840 book *What is Property? An Inquiry into the Principle of Right and of Government* had as its goal the complete abolition of capitalist forms of production in favor of a confederation of trade unionists and industrial workers: 'If I were asked to answer the following question: *What is slavery?* and I should answer in one word, it is murder, my meaning would be understood at once.... Why, then, to this other question: *What is property!* may I not likewise answer, it is robbery, without the certainty of being misunderstood, the second proposition being no other than a transformation of the first?'

"In the twentieth century, the French inclination for Socialist thought and action was sustained by Georges Sorel in his 1950 book *Reflections on Violence*: 'Socialism tends to appear more and more as a theory of revolutionary syndicalism - or rather as a philosophy of modern history, in as far as it is under the influence of this syndicalism. It follows from these incontestable data, that if we desire to discuss Socialism, we must first of all investigate the functions of violence in actual social conditions.'

"Lastly, Guy Debord spoke to the masses of people in his 1967 book *The Society of the Spectacle*: 'The revolutionary organization can be nothing less than a unitary critique of society, namely a critique which does not compromise with any form of separate power anywhere in the world, and a critique proclaimed globally against all the aspects of alienated social life.... It must struggle constantly against its deformation in the ruling spectacle.'"

Place de la Concorde

With the dinner hour now upon us, Honoré and I sauntered west through the gardens to Rue St Forentin, and then crossed over to Place de la Concorde. This magnificent and historic square began life as Place Louis XV with a statue of the king, though it later became Place de la Révolution, with the monarch replaced by the guillotine. In two and a half years that busy little machine beheaded over eleven hundred weary souls, including Louis XVI, Marie-Antoinette, Danton and Robespierre. It eventually became Place de la Concorde, and today sports the Luxor obelisk, two fountains and eight statues honoring French cities.

After settling into an outdoor table in a local café, and while enjoying a light meal and white wine, Honoré began another one of his tales, "Between 1837 and 1843, I wrote *Lost Illusions*, a story in three parts that begins in the provinces, then shifts to Paris, and finally returns to the provinces. The first part, 'The Two Poets,' introduces Lucien Chardon, an impoverished but ambitious writer who has penned a historical novel and a collection of sonnets. He lives in the provincial town of Angoulême with his widowed mother, his sister Ève and his best friend, David Séchard, who all believe that Lucien is destined to be a great literary man. On the other hand, David is a scientist, though he is also a poet in the sense that he too seeks creative truth.

"Madame de Bargeton is the leading figure of Angoulême provincial society, though in her heart she desires a different style of life. Longing to meet her, Lucien is introduced to Bargeton. Given their respective needs, it is not surprising that the two fell madly in love with one another. Unbeknownst to Lucien, his friend David and his sister Ève have also fallen in love. However, David is reluctant to commit and slow to proceed. Despite these difficulties, David eventually marries Ève. With the highest of accolades now thrust upon Lucien by Angoulême society, the poet develops an exalted sense of himself.

"One wanting fame and the other society, Lucien and Bargeton flee to Paris together to confront their futures: 'Society, which in these days bids all her children to the same table, awakens all ambitions in the dawn of life. It deprives youth of its graces, it vitiates generous sentiments, mingling selfish calculation with all things. Nobility of soul does not always carry with it nobility of manners. The manners of good society, when they are not a gift of birth, an acquisition sucked in with the milk, or transmitted in the blood, are the result of education, which accident often seconds by native elegance of form, distinction of feature, or tones of the voice.' "However, allow me to continue this tale later when it moves on to Paris, for at this moment I prefer to return to the ongoing story of Voltaire."

Voltaire in Geneva

After calling into question the entire social, political and religious structure of Europe, and with two kings banning him from their countries, Voltaire searched for a new home. He considered exiling himself in England, "where one thinks as a free man," or in America amongst the religiously open-minded Quakers of Pennsylvania. But neither of those places would be his final destination, and after thirteen months in Colmar, Voltaire arrived in Lyon in November of 1754. In the middle of December he moved on to Geneva, and "when he settled in Switzerland Voltaire took a new lease of his life. He entered upon its last, greatest, noblest, and calmest epochs." Amazingly, at the age of sixty Voltaire's best was yet to come.

In those days Geneva was the home of Calvinists, "who believed, with all the morbid intensity of their founder, that enjoyment was sinful, musical instruments had been invented by the devil, and play-acting was the abomination of desolation." But Voltaire had already rejected the Catholic Church of France, and since my enemy's enemy is my friend, he was welcomed into the city. He immediately bought two homes, Les Délices, located in the city, and Monrion, located at the top end of Lake Geneva near Lausanne. And he later purchased a home within Lausanne, this one known as Chene.

Just as Voltaire settled down to a life of quiet contemplation and intellectual pursuits, his secret and religiously irreverent poem *Pucelle,* or the *Maid of Orleans,* was printed in Paris, but with many errors. Needless to say, Voltaire denied authorship, even as the publication was being cast to the flames in Paris and Geneva. By August of 1755 *The Orphan of China* was playing to packed-houses in the French capital, though of course it would never see the stage in the Swiss capital.

Also in that month Voltaire wrote one his most famous and condemning letters, this one to the philosopher Jean-Jacques Rousseau concerning his *Discourse on the Origin of Inequality among Men* (1755), known to many critics as "The Essay against Civilization." Rousseau's contention in the essay, one dedicated to the Republic of Geneva, was that the life of the savage was nobler than the life of the civilized man. Needless to say, Voltaire held little regard for this philosophical nonsense, and he responded to Rousseau in a celebrated letter: "... No one has ever been so witty as you are in trying to turn us into brutes. To read your book makes one long to go on all fours. Since, however, it is now some sixty years since I gave up the practice, I feel that it is unfortunately impossible for me to resume it."

In November of 1755 came word of the Lisbon disaster, the earthquake that took place on All Saints Day. The churches and cathedrals of Lisbon, which in those days was the fourth largest city in Europe after London, Paris and Naples, were filled for the day when the first earthquake hit, and it immediately collapsed buildings throughout the city. Then the waters of the Atlantic rose in a giant surge, what scientists today call a "tsunami," and that upwelling of the sea destroyed the city's coastal areas. Forty minutes later an aftershock hit, and with the accompanying fires, the final death toll was estimated to be between forty and seventy thousand people, with nine thousand buildings leveled to the ground.

This was the first earthquake to destroy a modern European city, though of course scientists and historians were already aware of the incredible destruction that those natural disasters brought to rural parts of Europe and remote regions of the world. But the social aftermath of the earthquake is what alarmed Voltaire, for the causes of the disaster engendered widespread disagreement amongst the intellectuals of eighteenth century Europe.

There were four opinions concerning the catastrophe, the first from the churches being that the earthquake was delivered by God to punish the people of Lisbon for their sins of materialism and immorality. Then there was the deist position attributable to the German philosopher Gottfried Wilhelm Leibniz, who wrote earlier in the century that since God created the physical and moral laws of the world, and since God was all wise and all good, then this is "the best of all possible worlds." Because of this, the universe can never be understood by considering isolated events, but only by understanding the world as a whole, which is only possible by God. Therefore, "theistic optimism," or the blind acceptance of this "best of all possible worlds," is the only justifiable position as regards such events as the Lisbon earthquake.

The third position on the disaster reflected aspects of the previous two, and it came from Jean-Jacques Rousseau. As an unabashed optimist, he firmly believed that this was indeed "the best of all possible worlds," but because of Man's inherent sinfulness, people would forever suffer from natural disasters. To make his point, he asked: "How many unfortunate people have perished in this disaster because of one wanting to take his clothes, another his papers, another his money?" According to Rousseau, though these catastrophes are always inevitable, people can mitigate the effects by living a more righteous life.

As a man of reason and science, Voltaire's position could not have been more opposed to those other three. Although this philosopher believed firmly in a God who created the physical and moral laws of the universe, his God had not created "the best of all possible worlds." No, He only made one in which men might work together to attain such a possibility. For Voltaire believed that in taking well-reasoned actions to mitigate the effects of catastrophes, as well as the effects of injustices, the world of today is slowly transformed into not the best, but perhaps the better world of tomorrow.

In response to this philosophical and theological disagreement, Voltaire wrote his *Poem on the Lisbon Disaster; Or an Examination of the Axiom, All is Well* (1756). As Tallentyre wrote: "It contains a statement of almost all those searching problems which every thinking man, of whatever belief or unbelief he be, has to face at last: What am I? Whence am I? Whither go I? What is the origin of evil? What end is accomplished by the suffering and sorrow I see around me?" In the next year there appeared Voltaire's *Poem on Natural Law*, another reflection on this journey called Life.

Although his reputation as the "The Innkeeper of Europe" was really earned at his next home, even at Délices Voltaire constantly played host to the traveling intellectuals and socialites of Europe. Jean le Rond d'Alembert arrived in August of 1756 for a stay of five weeks, during which time the philosopher and his editor spoke about the *Encyclopédie*, a work that was nothing less than "the Guide to the Revolution, the first great public invitation to all men to drink of that knowledge which enfranchises the soul."

Voltaire spent the year 1757 and the first half of the next staging plays old and new in the privacy of his homes, enjoying the company of a multitude of famous visitors, and writing *The History of Peter the Great* (1759). He also contributed articles to the *Encyclopédie*, with the last half of 1758 filled with a new controversy concerning that monumental effort. An article written by d'Alembert on Geneva appeared at the end of the previous year, and it called into question the Calvinist beliefs of the city. The accusation, or as Voltaire thought, the compliment, was that the pious pastors of Geneva actually preached Deism. In addition, at the request of Voltaire, d'Alembert included in his article an opinion concerning the need for a theater in Geneva.

The many aspects of this controversy produced a reaction from Rousseau, who wrote a series of essays on the subject that helped fuel the fires that were soon burning the *Encyclopédie*. Against this intolerance and censorship, Voltaire wrote a series of refutations. Unfortunately, the entire episode proved too much for d'Alembert, and he eventually left his work on the *Encyclopédie* to retire to his studies in mathematics. Sadly, Voltaire's letter offering moral support to the beleaguered Philosophe came to no avail and Diderot was left to edit the great project alone.

Champs-Elysées

The Champs-Elysées offers numerous old palaces and museums, a historic and panoramic monument, and one of the most celebrated and stylish avenues in any city in the entire world. It also presents a multitude of café's for watching the world pass by, for listening to the continuing story of France after the Second World War, and for returning to the ongoing investigation of Modernity.

Grand Palais

Arriving the next morning by the Metro at Champs-Elysées-Clémenceau, I met Honoré on the Champs-Elysées and we enjoyed a short walk across Place Clémenceau and then down Avenue Winston Churchill before searching for an outdoor café offering a morning coffee and croissants. Our short tour took us first by the Grand Palais, home to temporary art exhibitions, the Petit Palais, home to permanent art collections, and finally to Pont Alexandre III, the most architecturally stunning bridge in Paris.

Retuning to the Champs-Elysées, Honoré and I walked up to the cafés and chose a perfect outdoor table to both people-watch and to listen to his modern French story, "After suffering through the First World War, enjoying the Jazz Age of the Twenties, and then suffering through the Depression and the Second World War, France established the Fourth Republic in 1946. And though he led the French provisional government after the war, Charles de Gaulle retired from political office until 1958, when he became President of France under the Fifth Republic.

"The 1958 French Constitution set up a bicameral legislature, with the nearly six hundred deputies of the National Assembly directly elected in constituencies for five-year terms and the over three hundred senators of the Senate elected for six-year terms by an electoral college made up of regional or department administrators.

Much like the United States, bills dealing with the civil, electoral and fiscal running of the country originate in either of the two parliamentary institutions, with both the lower and the upper house required to pass a bill by a majority vote before it enters into law.

"The lion's share of political power is consolidated in the President of France, who is directly elected by the people to a five-year term. The remainder of the power resides in the Government, which consists of the Prime Minister of the National Assembly and the Council of Ministers, all of which are appointed by the President. The President also has the power to dissolve the National Assembly and call for an election, and in addition, he is allowed to introduce bills for consideration to the Assembly. And though there is no complete separation of powers between the executive and legislative branches of the government, the judiciary is independent of the other two branches.

"Although political power in France is highly centralized, the nation is divided into twenty-two 'regions', with each one consisting of two to eight local administrative 'departments', which number ninety-six in the whole of the country. Each department is governed by a General Council, which consists of thirteen to seventy 'councillors' who are elected by local 'cantons'. At the lowest level of government are the 'communes', which are headed by a mayor and number over thirty-six thousand throughout the whole of France.

"Today in France the political Left is represented by a coalition of the French Socialist Party, the French Communist Party, the Green Party and other liberal groups, while the political Right is represented by a coalition of the Union for a Popular Movement and other conservative groups. As of the 2012 presidential election, when François Hollande narrowly defeated Nicolas Sarkozy, the French government has been controlled through a coalition headed by the French Socialist Party.

Avenue des Champs-Elysées

After our morning coffee and croissants, Honoré and I meandered up the Avenue des Champs-Elysées, or the Elysian Fields, all the while enjoying the coquettish attire of the competing *tarts de jour* who frequent the stylish shops along this famed boulevard. And as we strolled, Honoré continued with his story of the modern world, "Once again, the tale of Modernity lays hidden well beneath, but remains forever the scaffolding for the hustle and bustle of contemporary society. From 1815 onward technological advances brought about the Industrial Revolution, a change that completely altered modern life, as did progress in the sciences, mathematics, probability, statistics, and philosophy":

Augustin-Louis Cauchy (1789-1857) began the project of formulating and proving the theorems of the infinitesimal calculus, even defining continuity in terms of infinitesimals. He also proved many significant theorems in complex analysis, and as well initiated the study of permutation groups in abstract algebra. Highly influential in his own time, his work covered almost all areas of mathematics and mathematical physics.

Pierre-Joseph Proudhon (1809-1865) was an economist, socialist and philosopher, and the first politician to call himself an "anarchist." His most famous work was *What is Property? Or, an Inquiry into the Principle of Right and Government*, in which he coined the phrase "Property is Theft!" He instigated the discussion of a Socialist utopia by supporting workers' associations, co-operatives, and the nationalization of land and workplaces. And though unsuccessful, he also attempted to create a national bank funded by taxes levied on capitalists and stockholders.

Évariste Galois (1811-1832) was the first mathematician to determine a necessary and sufficient condition for a polynomial to be solvable by radicals, which laid the foundation for Galois theory, group theory, and the field of Galois connections. Along with being the first to use the term "group" in mathematics, his approaches to solving problems were later applied by other mathematicians outside the areas considered by him.

Jules Henri Poincaré (1854-1912) was a mathematician, physicist, engineer and philosopher of science. He made contributions to pure and applied mathematics, mathematical physics, and celestial mechanics, and as well formulated the Poincaré conjecture and the assumptions concerning what later would lay the foundation for the theory of special relativity. His research on the three-body problem introduced the concept of a chaotic deterministic system, which years later would establish the field of modern chaos theory.

David Émile Durkheim (1858-1917) is considered the academic father of Sociology, establishing the discipline and guidelines of social science in *Rules of the Sociological Method*. Much of his work addressed his concern with how modern societies maintain their stability, especially as regards the ending of traditional religious systems and the introduction of new social institutions. He also extended the positivist ideas of Auguste Comte, and as well, coined many now well-known terms such as "collective consciousness."

Henri-Louis Bergson (1859-1941) was a prominent philosopher during the first half of the twentieth century, though much of his work was highly criticized outside France. His central thought in *An Introduction to Metaphysics* was that immediate experience and intuition are more important than rationalism and science for understanding reality, an idea that greatly influenced the writer Marcel Proust. And in *Creative Evolution* he introduced the term *élan vital*, or "vital force," though his thoughts on explaining evolution were dismissed by most of the scientific community.

André Weil (1906-1998) made significant contributions to number theory and algebraic geometry, and showed the important connections between those two once distinct areas of mathematical study. He also helped establish the collective pseudonym "Nicolas Bourbaki," a group of mainly French mathematicians who wrote works on modern mathematics with the goal of founding the discipline on set theory.

Jean Alexandre Eugène Dieudonné (1906-1992) made advances in abstract algebra, functional analysis, and both classical and formal groups. Along with Weil, he was involved with Nicolas Bourbaki, becoming one of the initial members, known as "normaliens," chosen for the group. He also wrote on the history of mathematics, mainly in the fields of functional analysis and algebraic topology.

Claude Lévi-Strauss (1908-2009), as one of the three fathers of modern anthropology, contributed to the fields of anthropology and ethnology. His most important ideas were concerned with the relationship between the "savage" mind and the "civilized" mind, which he argued had the same structures and underlying patterns as in all human activities. His thoughts positioned him as one of the central figures in the founding of Structuralism, with his ideas greatly influencing academics in the humanities, sociology and philosophy.

René Frédéric Thom (1923-2002) made contributions in the field of mathematical topology early in his career, and then moved on to the area of singularity theory in geometry. However, later in his life the academic community, including those outside mathematics, and the general public took an interest in his work as the founder of catastrophe theory, a field of study that investigates how small changes in the initial conditions of a dynamic system lead to dramatic changes in the long-term stability of the system.

Benoit B. Mandelbrot (1924-2010) developed the "theory of roughness" in nature, with his goal being to create a mathematical formula for measuring the overall "roughness" in such objects as mountains and coastlines, plants and animals, and galaxies and clusters. His work established the field of fractal geometry, and he coined the term "fractal" for the general public in his celebrated work *The Fractal Geometry of Nature*. He also defined the Mandelbrot set, with its computer-generated image becoming the first visualization of a fractal.

"As we see once again, the discovery and creation of scientific and mathematical knowledge proceeded without hindrance throughout the social turmoil and chaos in the years after 1815. These intellectual advances were fundamental to the progress of Modernity, which is today dependent upon theoretical knowledge for technological evolution and social stability. What occurs in the remaining years of the twenty-first century will also maintain this progress, with both advances in theoretical knowledge and the application of that knowledge to the creation of new technologies and social systems. And there will also be the establishing of new fields of study, with the present offering only hints of that unknown future."

Arc de Triomphe

Now at Place Charles de Gaulle at the western end of the Champs-Elysées, Honoré resolved that I should catch my first bird's-eye view of Paris. So we made our way to the second most famous monument in the city, the Arc de Triomphe, built to commemorate Napoleon's greatest victory, the 1805 Battle of Austerlitz. Although he promised his soldiers that "you shall go home beneath triumphal arches," the monument wasn't completed until 1836, well past the time for a victory lap. Nevertheless, the fifty-meter arch is today the customary starting point for all victory celebrations, which means hardly any French soldiers ever parade under it, though every now and then troopers from Germany make up for that domestic lack of manful fortitude.

The customary method for getting to and from the Arc de Triomphe is to first take any of the stairs that lead down to the tunnels, and to then walk under the avenues. However, there's a quicker way to accomplish this task. And that's to wait for a lull in the traffic and to then sprint across about seventeen lanes, all the while keeping a watchful eye for oncoming vehicles. This more precarious method of getting to and from the monument also has one other distinct advantage, and that's that urban investigators get to observe firsthand the operating dynamics of modern mass transit systems.

The view from the platform atop the Arc de Triomphe is one of the best in Paris, especially for investigators interested in a bird's-eye view of the operating dynamics of modern mass transit systems. For surrounding the arch is the world's most chaotic roundabout, one that offers approximately one fender bender every two minutes. No less than twelve avenues radiate from the center of Place Charles de Gaulle, and ten of those streets are named after such well-known historical figures as de Friedland, Hoche, de Wagram, Mac-Mahon, Carnot, Foch, Victor Hugo, Kleber, d'Iena and Marceau.

After enjoying the bumper-car chaos for awhile, and while looking back along the Champs-Elysées, Honoré said, "Let me now return to the second part of *Lost Illusions.* 'A Great Man from the Provinces in Paris' takes place in the grand city that spreads out before us. Once in Paris, Madame de Bargeton is instructed that if she wishes to succeed in Parisian society she must first sever all of her ties with Lucien, much to the young man's surprise and disappointment. Now destitute, Lucien takes on his mother's more distinguished-sounding name 'de Rubempré,' hoping that it might improve his chances of becoming a famed poet

"With Bargeton now taking up with Sixte du Châtelet, Lucien takes up with Coralie, a high-class actress-prostitute who falls in love with him. But Lucien also prostitutes himself as a literary journalist, quickly turning his back on the liberal press and writing witticisms for the royalist newspapers. This act of betrayal is an affront to his higher-minded journalist friends, who band together to destroy Coralie's theatrical reputation. However, Lucien also quickly loses interest in the courtesan. This final betrayal causes Coralie to take to her deathbed.

"Hoping to still assume by royal warrant the surname "de Rubemprés," Lucien forges his brother-in-law's name on three promissory notes, losing any remaining personal integrity in the process. On the other hand, Bargeton marries du Châtelet, who has been appointed prefect of the Angoulême region. With this marriage, all her previous sins are absolved. Now in abject disgrace and a literary failure, Lucien stows away in the Châtelets' carriage for the journey back to Angoulême.

"With the second part of the story now at an end, what lesson is to be learned from this piece of the tale?: 'Genius is a horrible disease; every writer bears in his heart a monster, like a tapeworm in the stomach, devouring the feelings as soon as they unfold. Which will conquer, - the disease or the man. Surely the man must be great indeed to keep his balance between his genius and his nature. Talent grows, the heart withers. Short of being a colossus, or of having the shoulders of a Hercules, he must end without a heart or a brain.' Before moving on to the third and final part of my tale, let me once again return to the continuing story of Voltaire."

Voltaire in Ferney

Near the end of 1758 Voltaire began negotiations for the purchase of two new properties, Ferney and Tourney, both of them located in Burgundy a few miles from Geneva. As Tallentyre points out, it would be in Ferney that: "... if one offended France, which was only a question of time, what more simple than to drive into Geneva. Voltaire at first thought it would be a sort of supplement to his first Swiss home. But as all the world knows, Ferney soon supplanted Delices in its master's affections, and became the literary capital of Europe."

Voltaire did not take up permanent residency in Ferney until 1760, though by that year the ever-busy philosopher had already renovated much of the château, developed the grounds and farms, and had in his employ sixty to seventy persons on a regular basis. His only permanent attendant was his niece Marie Louise Denis, who had been with him since leaving Prussia. However, age had changed this once beautiful woman and she was now by no means an easy person to live with on a daily basis.

According to Tallentyre, even from the beginning the home of "The Innkeeper of Europe" was open to visitors: "Half the genius - and but too many of the fools - of Europe came to worship at the shrine of the prophet of this literary Mecca. Nearly all great men have had one place dedicated to them - Florence to Dante, Corsica to Napoleon, Stratford to Shakespeare, Weimar to Goethe, and Ferney to Voltaire."

Literary-wise, the year 1759 brought forth a new book, the *History of Peter the Great*, as well as the first of many pamphlets taking aim at the Church and the Monarchy. In Paris Voltaire's plays were still staged to great approval, and they forever mocked those who would stand in the way of intellectual progress. And that year also saw the first editions of Voltaire's second attack on "theistic optimism" in *Candide*, a book that became his greatest literary legacy.

The year 1759 was also the one in which Voltaire greatly intensified his confrontation with the Church. In February the *Encyclopédie* was suspended, and as noted by Tallentyre, it was that intolerant act that forced Voltaire into greater attacks against the *ancien régime*: "... he framed his battle-cry and formulated the creed of all the philosophers, and the aim and the conviction of his own life, into one brief phrase - 'Écrasez l'infâme.'... 'l'infâme' was that spirit which was the natural enemy of all learning and advancement; which loved darkness and hated light because its deeds were evil... He flung down the glove at last and declared upon 'l'infâme' an open war..."

The *modus operandi* of Voltaire's open war on "l'infâme" took many forms, not the least of which were in his plays staged to bring into light the abuses of the Church and the battles of the philosophers. One such play, *Socrates* (1764), is the retelling of Plato's story of the events leading to the death of the famed Athenian gadfly. Although the action in the play takes place in the Athens of old, the characters are far more representative of eighteenth century France.

The story concerns the philosopher Socrates, his wife Xanthippe, and their disagreement over the marriage of Aglaea, a young woman raised by Socrates. However, the plot is undoubtedly connected to a real life episode. While at Ferney, Voltaire adopted Mademoiselle Marie Corneille, the great-niece of the famed dramatist Pierre Corneille, and arranged for her marriage. So from the beginning the audience understands that the character of Socrates is indeed Voltaire, and that his philosophy will be forthcoming throughout the play.

An event now occurred that was far more ominous than anything transpiring in Paris, and it was the one that changed Voltaire's legacy forever. In the eighteenth century, Toulouse, which lies to the west of Ferney in central France, was not a pleasant city to live in if one was not a reverent Catholic. On October 13, 1761, Jean Calas, a Protestant shopkeeper, and his family were enjoying their supper in the house above his shop. The sixty-three year old Jean was anything but a religious zealot, and as regards the choice of a religion, he "supposed the matter to be one in which each must judge for himself."

The family consisted of the father and mother, as well as four sons and two daughters. The eldest son, Mark Anthony, was for many years a troubled youth, and on that fateful evening he took his life with the help of a rope. A doctor and the police were summoned, and given the commotion, a crowd soon gathered outside the home. "It had the characteristics of most crowds - perhaps of all French crowds - it was intensely excited, it was exceedingly inventive, and it would follow a leader like a sheep."

A rumor soon spread throughout the crowd that the Huguenot Jean had killed his troubled son after finding out that the boy wished to convert to the Catholic Church, a rather absurd belief given that the eldest son was quite prejudiced against Catholicism. Within three weeks the city's intolerant priests made the dead boy into a religious martyr, and they also made Jean and the rest of his family into a band of murderous zealots.

The family of prisoners spent the next five months chained by the feet in separate dungeons, after which, on March 9, 1762, and without the least bit of evidence, Jean was tried and found guilty of his son's murder. The next day Jean's bound body was first stretched until every limb was drawn from its socket, with water then forced into his mouth until his body was twice its normal size. The executioner finally strangled the tortured man, and he died still proclaiming his innocence to the world. In the aftermath, Jean's wife retired in sorrow to the Toulouse countryside, while the two daughters were tossed into a convent, with the sons escaping to Geneva.

When Voltaire heard about the horrific events surrounding the Calas family in March of 1762, he was at first unaffected by the case. Within a month Voltaire was consumed by the affair, sending agents to Toulouse to gather information, as well as to other parts of France and Switzerland to take the remaining family members to safety. At his expense, Madame Calas was taken to Paris, where he arranged legal advisors for her and also encouraged his associates to petition the government to begin an investigation into the entire sordid affair.

However, Voltaire soon discovered that this was not the only abuse by the Church. To the east of Toulouse is the small city of Castres, which in the year 1760 was also the site of a gross religious intolerance. In March, the respectable Protestant family Sirven found that the local bishop took their feeble-minded youngest daughter to a convent. Believing it was her choice, father Sirven agreed to his daughter's wishes to convert to Catholicism.

After going mad in the convent, and after being whipped by the not so understanding nuns, Elizabeth returned home with horrific marks on her body. In December of 1761 the daughter went missing once again, though this time she wasn't discovered in a convent, but at the bottom of a well. Despite the lack of any evidence whatsoever, the local Catholic magistrates found father Sirven guilty of killing his youngest daughter. And after hearing about this shocking episode, Voltaire also took up this cause. In August of 1762, Voltaire published and circulated *The Story of Elizabeth Canning and the Calas Family.*

The story of the Calas family was soon the talk of Europe, with the slow investigation proceeding towards a just end. In 1763 Voltaire's *Treatise on Tolerance* was clandestinely passed around the intellectuals in Paris, and in the next year it was forbidden to even send a copy of it through the mail for fear that it might infect someone with its revolutionary ideas. And as noted by Tallentyre: "To Voltaire the cause of Calas was the cause of Tolerance, that Tolerance which was the principle and the passion of his life."

The *Treatise on Tolerance* "was what may be called the fruit of the Calas case, fruit of which men today may still eat and live, the pamphlet of two hundred pages which advanced by many years the reign of justice, of mercy, and of humanity." It is "the work of a man without whom Calas would never have been avenged, and "l'infâme" been left unchecked till the Revolution." For Voltaire, the *Treatise on Tolerance* establishes his opposition to religious and philosophical intolerance.

Returning to the father Sirven, he escaped a hanging when Voltaire brought the family to Lausanne in April of 1762. Three years later Voltaire, having concluded the Calas case, took up this second one in the name of Tolerance. That case took nine years, though like Calas, in the end the father was found innocent of any wrongdoing. And of great help to Voltaire in this second case, as well as to the Sirvens, was the publication of *An Address to the Public concerning the Parricides imputed to the Calas and Sirven Families.*

Despite the court decisions, the Church failed to change its intolerant ways. In early August of 1765, in the northern French town of Abbeville, two large crucifixes, one on a bridge and the other in a cemetery, were vandalized, greatly upsetting the town's citizens. In September three young men, all between eighteen and twenty years old, were formally arrested for the crimes. One of the boys, d'Étallonde de Morival immediately fled to Prussia, while another youth, Moisnel, went mad.

In February of the next year, the third young man, Jean Francois Lefebre, Chevalier de la Barre, was found guilty of the offenses. His sentence was firstly to have his tongue torn out with hot irons, next, to have his right hand cut off, and lastly, to be beheaded and then slowly burnt to death over a fire. After all of this, "the body was thrown to the flames with *The Philosophical Thoughts* of Diderot, the *Sopha* of the younger Crebellion, two little volumes of Bayle, and *The Philosophical Dictionary*" of Voltaire. Not to let matters rest, in July of 1766 Voltaire published another essay, *An Account of the Death of Chevelier de la Barre*, though it took a final essay, *The Cry of Innocent Blood*, published in 1775, to finally bring justice to the affair.

The latter 1760's and early 70's saw Voltaire intercede in Geneva's ongoing disputes between the members of the councils, the bourgeoisie, and the Natives, a large group of descendants of foreigners that settled in the city. As well, Voltaire encouraged both artistically and financially in the careers of a number of protégés, and of course he remained forever the "Innkeeper of Europe."

Never without energy, Voltaire took the plight of the peasantry to heart by hiring them to work on his lands and in his homes at the best of wages, and also by organizing and financing local industries, such as silk-weaving and watch-making. This farsighted man, one who fully realized that revolutions are always bred in the stomachs of the poor, believed that "true philosophy makes the earth fertile and the people happier. The true philosopher cultivates the land, increases the number of the ploughs, and so of the inhabitants. Occupies the poor man, and thus enriches him. Encourages marriages, cares for the orphan. Does not grumble at necessary taxes, and puts the laborer in a condition to pay them promptly."

Voltaire's fight for tolerance and reason is exemplified in his many works, one being his *Questions on the Encyclopédie* (1770): "Government must be a very great pleasure, since so many people want to get involved in it. We have many more books on government than there are princes in the world. God forbid that I should educate kings, their esteemed ministers, their esteemed manservants, their esteemed confessors, and their esteemed tax collectors! I understand nothing about it, I respect them all. It would be very strange that with three or four thousand volumes on government, there should be anyone left who does not fully understand the duties of kings and the art of being a leader."

According to Tallentyre, as regards the *Philosophical Dictionary* (1764), it wasn't just the body of Chevelier de la Barre that was thrown onto the fire: "The first volume of that blasphemous collection of articles appeared in July of 1764, and within a year the hangman in Paris was publicly destroying it.... If an article is too daring even for the *Encyclopédie*, put it in the *Dictionary*. The *Dictionary* had room for everything.... The *Philosophical Dictionary* has well been said to be the whole of Citizen Voltaire."

Forever concerned about the ongoing battle between the certainties of religion and the uncertainties of philosophy, Voltaire addressed that war in his essay on "Philosophy" in the *Dictionary*: "Follow philosophy as you please, but agree that as soon as it appears it is persecuted. Dogs to whom you present an aliment for which they have no taste, bite you. We have always seen philosophers persecuted by fanatics."

Lastly, a selection from the *Treatise on Tolerance* (1763) illustrates Voltaire's fight against religious and philosophical intolerance: "This essay on tolerance is a humble request made on behalf of humanity before the forces of power and discretion. I have tried to sow a seed from which one day there might be gathered a harvest. For the rest, we depend on the fullness of time and the spirit of reason which is beginning to spread enlightenment everywhere."

The last years of life for the Hermit of Ferney were filled with many visitors, some political battles and a few literary projects. But

Voltaire was now getting too old and too infirmed. With the death of Louis XV in 1774, there arose the possibility of Voltaire returning to his beloved Paris for the first time in twenty-eight years. Then on February 5, 1778, and now in years over three and eighty, and carrying a new play, *Irene*, he set out in a carriage for the capital... the faraway capital that he'd dreamt of for so long.

Chaillot Quarter

Once the village of Chaillot, the western-most quarter on the Right Bank of Paris is now home to a stunning modern palace, over a dozen museums and galleries, a countless number of elegant cafés, and perhaps most importantly, the home of my personal philosophical investigator, Honoré de Balzac. And while enjoying a glass of champagne in the garden of his home, Honoré first concluded his thoughts on the search for Modernity and then sent me on my way to meet other philosophical investigators.

Palais de Chaillot

After returning through the tunnel back to the Champs-Elysées, Honoré and I entered the Metro and caught the train heading from Charles de Gaulle-Etoile to Trocadéro. We then walked down to Palais de Chaillot, a 1937 Neo-Classical architectural wonder consisting of two curved wings, with two tall pavilions overlooking the main square. The buildings are home to four museums, a theater and a film library.

On the river side of the palace are the two gardens in the Jardins de Trocadéro, which we admired on both sides of us while making our way to the fountains. After finding a bench from which to enjoy the spouting waters and the Eiffel Tower on the Left Bank, an old man dressed in a robe approached us and sat down. He then began a strange but fascinating story, "It's so beautiful and peaceful here that I often visit to simply reflect upon the history of my life with my good friend Anatole France. My name is Mael, and I was once a holy man living on *Penguin Island* (1908). But I can see by the puzzled look on your faces that you have never heard of my island, so let me tell you the story of that odd little kingdom.

"Similar to other holy man, my sole duty on Penguin Island was to bless all the men, women and children that I should come upon.

Unfortunately for me, there were no men, women or children on the island, so: '... having previously blessed the water that fell from the cascades and recited the exorcisms, I baptized those whom I had just taught, pouring on each of their heads a drop of pure water and pronouncing the sacred words. And thus for three days and three nights I baptized the birds.'

"As you well know, blessings are appropriate only for Man. Once He heard about it, the Lord became concerned about the matter and consulted his associates. After consulting with his heavenly contingent, the Lord came upon an unusual solution to His problem. An archangel delivered the message to me, so: '... I, having wept and prayed, armed myself with the mighty Name of the Lord and said to the birds: *Be ye men!*' After giving Penguinia the blessings of civilization, such as clothing, property and taxation: '... I noticed with sadness that since they became men the inhabitants of this island acted with less wisdom than formerly.'

"One of the more astonishing aspects of Penguinia was the accelerated pace of history, for within a short period of time the island entered into what we humans might call the Middle Ages. Just as in human history, so in Penguin history, the island matured to the Renaissance. And once again similar to Man, following the Renaissance came the Reformation. With science and learning Penguinia became a modern island, with all the trappings of political Revolution. From revolution to republic to democracy, the island progressed as did human history. Then there arrived the accusations in the press as regards the true rulers of Penguinia. Once the breaking point was reached, there were riots and destruction: 'The Fall of Empires and the transmission of dominions astonish us and remain incomprehensible to us, because we have not discovered the imperceptible point, or touched the secret spring which when put in movement has destroyed and overthrown everything.'"

Place du Trocadéro

After saying goodbye to the old priest, Honoré and I returned to the far side of the palace and then made our way across Avenue Paul Doumer to Place du Trocadéro, home to several elegant cafés. Once seated at an outdoor table, a man approached and asked if he might join us as the cafe was quite busy with the lunchtime crowd. We agreed, and then ordered our meals and a glass of wine, after which, the gentleman introduced himself, "My name is Jacques Barzun, and though born in France, after the First World War my family took me to America to be educated, first in a preparatory school and then at Columbia University.

"With my undergraduate years behind me, I continued my education at Columbia as a graduate student. Upon receiving my doctorate, I joined the faculty as a professor of history, over the years founding the discipline of 'cultural history'. Though I published books, papers and popular articles over a wide range of topics, from baseball to music to education, I am most well-known for my final work *From Dawn to Decadence: 500 Years of Western Cultural Life, 1500 to the Present* (2000), written and published in my nineties."

The food and wine finally arrived at our table, and while enjoying lunch, Jacques continued, "My book begins with some apprehensions I have concerning the current state of affairs in Western cultural life: 'Our culture is in that recurrent phase when, for good reasons, many feel the urge to build a wall against the past. It is a revulsion from things in the present that seem a curse from our forebears.... This passion to break away explains also why many feel that the West has to be denounced. But we are not told what should or could replace it as a whole.... Our distinctive attitude toward history, our habit of arguing from it, turns events into ideas charged with power. And this use of the past dates precisely from the years that usher in what is called modern times.' Gentlemen, I must now be going, but I thank you for allowing me to bend your ears during our meal, for 'the finest achievement of human society and its rarest pleasure is Conversation.'"

Maison de Balzac

With one stop remaining on our agenda, Honoré and I walked along Avenue Paul Doumer to Rue B Franklin, and then followed that street west to Place de Costa Rica. Crossing the square, we continued along Rue Raynouard to number 47, the location of Honoré's home, now Maison de Balzac. For the next few hours he gave me a tour of his residence while investigating collections of his works in the study and library, an assortment of book stamps that includes the diners at Madame Vacquer's home, several busts of Honoré by Augustine Rodin, and the amazing wall chart, "Genealogy of Personages in *La Comédie humaine.*"

The tour over, Honoré took me out to a garden that overlooks the River Seine below and the Eiffel Tower off in the distance. Once I was seated at a table, he excused himself for a moment to arrange some celebratory champagne for the two of us. On the table was a half-completed puzzle, with many of the remaining pieces blank. So with a little time on my hands, I attempted to fit a few of the pieces into what was already finished in the puzzle. However, every time I did so some of the pieces changed shape, some of the already fitted ones separated from the puzzle, and as well, new pieces arrived on the table, seemingly out of nowhere. To add to the confusion, there was no box cover to give me an idea as to what the puzzle looked like, so I was at a complete loss as to how to fit any of the pieces together.

Honoré soon returned with a bottle of bubbly and two flutes, and next poured us both a glass. He then said, "I see that you tried to fit some pieces of the puzzle together without knowing what the picture looks like. As you discovered, this is no ordinary puzzle. Instead, it represents a metaphor for the puzzle, maybe the conundrum, or perhaps the mystery of contemporary Modernity. To explain this concept better, let me give you several examples of other older puzzles, ones offered to us through the study of art, literature, history and philosophy.

"As my first example I will present *The School of Athens*, painted between 1509 and 1511 by the Italian Renaissance artist Raphael.

This fresco in the Apostolic Palace of the Vatican shows Plato and Aristotle atop a set of stairs in a massive open-air structure, with the ancient Greek philosophers, such as Socrates and Diogenes of Sinope, standing or lying on both sides of and below them.

"When Raphael painted this magnificent masterpiece he had no idea that the Renaissance was coming to an end, or probably that anything called the Renaissance even existed in Italy. This was because he was living through his own contemporary times, now known as the High Renaissance, a term applied by historians many centuries later. And he could not have known that pre-Modernity was in its death throes, nor that Modernity was slowly ushering itself into Western consciousness. However, what he did realize in his vision of the puzzle was that something was changing, what it was he knew not, though today we now know it to be the evolution from a society governed by tradition, monarchy and religion to one governed by science, democracy and philosophy.

"My second example will be Voltaire's writing of the *Treatise on Tolerance*, published clandestinely in 1763, and thereafter tossed onto the sacramental fires. The great Philosophe could not possibly have known that the world he was passing through was on its deathbed, and that the abuses of the Church and the Monarchy had only one more generation before they would be tossed into the dustbin of history. And he could not possibly have known that the world he was passing through would be replaced by the Modern one, where the need for tolerance is guaranteed by France and every other Western nation. No, like us, all he experienced was a sense of uncertainty in his own times, a period that a future generation of historians would call 'The French Enlightenment'.

"For my third example concerning the puzzle of contemporary Modernity, I will use 'An Inventor's Tribulations', the third part of *Lost Illusions*. With the action now back in Angoulême, David Séchard invents a new and cheaper method of paper production, and it is a process that will greatly increase the spread of knowledge. Unfortunately, Lucien's forgery of his brother-in-law's signature bankrupts David, and the discoverer is forced to sell his invention to business rivals. David's only consolation is his supportive wife.

"To end this long story, Lucien, now suffering from a lack of any will to live, considers suicide. In the last scene of the tale, a sham Jesuit priest intervenes to stop the suicide and offers to take Lucien back to Paris, where the poet will once again confront the capital. Whether Lucien would be successful or not, only a future account would tell, though that story would involve the priest.

"Clearly, the aspect of *Lost Illusions* that pertains to the puzzle of the times that I lived in was the impact of the Industrial Revolution on society. Of course, when I wrote this book I did not have any idea that the Industrial Revolution was underway in Europe. I only saw that new inventions and technologies were springing up in every area of manufacture. The puzzle of those times was as blank as the one sitting on this table right now, with its pieces forever changing shape, separating from the puzzle, and new pieces seemingly arriving out of nowhere. For you see, there has never been a box cover to offer an idea as to what any contemporary puzzle looks like, for that cover is only pictured by historians decades, perhaps even centuries in the future.

"But allow me to give you another example, the mural *Guernica*, painted in 1937 by Pablo Picasso. This impressive masterpiece was created by the artist in response to the bombing of the Basque Country village, Guernica, in northern Spain, by German and Italian warplanes. In reply to this barbarous act perpetrated by the Spanish Nationalists on innocent civilians, the Republican government commissioned Picasso to create a large mural for the Spanish display at the 1937 World's Fair in Paris.

"In painting this mural, Picasso would not have known that another world war was on the horizon, or that most of the first half of the twentieth century would be defined years later by historians as one of economic and military devastation on a worldwide scale. No, he merely added a piece to the half-completed puzzle of *his* contemporary conception of Modernity, with future historians left to decide whether or not it fit. As it turned out, he correctly defined the tragedies of war and the suffering it inflicts upon individuals, with that piece of the twentieth century puzzle remaining to this day.

"Let me see, I offered you three examples of the metaphor of the puzzle of Modernity: one from art, one from literature, and one from history. All three illustrations show that every individual at any moment in history lives in a world where the puzzle of his own contemporary times is only partially-completed, with much of it remaining blank. Even then, that completed portion of the puzzle undoubtedly changes or falls away as scientific, political and economic events modify the future course of history. This has been especially so for the last five hundred years, with progress in the various fields of knowledge continually increasing at faster rates and with each field heavily dependent upon advances in all the others.

"To clarify this point, let me say that you probably imagine that right now you're holding a glass of champagne in your hand. But in fact, what you are really holding is a Modern system of interconnected relationships. The flute was first designed by a graphic artist well-versed in using computer systems to produce a mathematically aesthetic object. After that, the material for the flute was produced by a scientist with knowledge of the physical and chemical properties of glass. Next, a mechanical engineer designed a machine that, using liquid glass, shaped the flute, which was then put in a cardboard box designed by a technologist with knowledge of the bio-chemical nature of pulp. A company manager trained in the area of production processes then organized his labor so as to optimize, probably using a complex cost/benefit analysis model, the final product. The boxes of glasses were finally loaded onto a truck or railcar for delivery to stores, with both means of transportation heavily dependent upon the modern science of petro-chemical and electrical engineering.

"On the other hand, the champagne required a vintner with an extensive knowledge of the science of oenology, which requires a wide-ranging understanding of soil and climate conditions, as well as a broad familiarity with the biological aspects of the primary and secondary processes in wine fermentation. Once ready, the wine was poured into specially designed bottles using a mechanical assembly-line process that required the same knowledge-bases as did the production of the flutes. Next, the bottles were stored in climate-controlled rooms until the wine was ready for consumption and then shipped off to stores to sit alongside the champagne glasses. And needless to say, a market for both products is required to sell them, which is dependent on both national and global economic systems designed to guarantee the stability of trade and industry. Of course, I have only mentioned the main features in the production of any good as it would take me forever to list all the interconnected relationships of economic and technological factors that today join with each other throughout the modern world to bring you this afternoon... a refreshing glass of champagne.

"With that said, tomorrow you will begin a series of excursions in and around Paris, ones that offer investigations into Modernity and its relationship with a concept known as 'Postmodernity'. You will then meet up on the Left Bank with another philosophical investigator, and this guide will instruct you in the area of existential investigations. But before we part for the day, there is one final example of the metaphor of the puzzle of Modernity, this from the area of philosophy. So let me offer you the final chapter in the story of Voltaire, the Philosophe that historians now know completed the puzzle of the eighteenth century French Enlightenment."

Voltaire in Paris

As Voltaire's carriage made its way northwest through Dijon and the rest of Burgundy, word spread that the most honored man in France was on his way to the capital. Then, after a week on the road, he arrived at the Hotel de Villette on the tenth day of February. The next day Voltaire welcomed over three hundred visitors to his room, and that was only the beginning of a never-ending river of admirers that flowed into the hotel over the next few months. One and all came to visit with the great philosopher: the members of the Academy, the writers of the *Encyclopédie*, the friends of a long life, the priests hoping to convert him at the end, the most famous woman in France, Marie-Antoinette, and a certain American, Benjamin Franklin.

Whenever he was well enough to leave the hotel to visit the Academy as the new President or to watch his play *Irene* being staged at the Comédie Française, the crowds would gather to witness the man who forever proclaimed "Écrasez l'infâme" in championing their liberties. But the procession took its toll on him, and by the middle of May he took to his bed. For several weeks Voltaire suffered in the throes of approaching death, surrounded only by close friends and nurses. Then, "at a quarter past eleven on the evening of Saturday, May 30, 1778, in the eighty-fourth year of his life, died François Marie Arouet de Voltaire."

The next day the body of Voltaire was secretly taken over a hundred miles from Paris to the Abbey of Scellières, located in Romilly-on-Seine in Champagne. "Only a small stone marked his resting-place, with the bald inscription 'Here lies Voltaire'. After all, he needed no epitaphs. He had avenged the oppressed and enlightened the ignorant." Voltaire's passing was mourned and eulogized by Frederick of Prussia, Catherine of Russia, the members of the Academy, and of course by the people of France.

For thirteen tumultuous years, Voltaire rested peacefully in Champagne. Then in July of 1791, the ashes of the most beloved philosopher in France were transferred to the old Church of Saint-Geneviève in Paris, which the National Assembly had recently renamed the Panthéon. And the procession that carried Voltaire's remains across Paris brought forth the entire city, for one and all wanted to offer one last farewell to the man that had paved the way for the Revolution. So what can one possibly say to sum up the life of a person such as Voltaire?:

There are of course those who denounce Voltaire for his lack of religion, as well as those who denounce him for not lacking it enough. As for the latter, one must remember to consider him in the context of the very religious times and places that he lived in throughout his long life. And as for the former, perhaps it is best to let the philosopher speak for himself on the matter of religion: "To worship

God, to leave each man the liberty to serve Him in his own fashion, to love one's neighbors, enlighten them if one can, pity them when they are in error, to attach no importance to trivial questions which would never have given trouble if no seriousness had been imputed to them. That is my religion, which is worth all your systems and all your symbols."

S. G. Tallentyre ended her magnificent biography *The Life of Voltaire* with some thoughts on the metaphysical beliefs of the great philosopher: "At last, after sixty years of superhuman effort, he had cleared the place and made it ready for the planting of the Tree of Liberty. Whoso sits under that tree today in any country, free to worship his God as he will, to think, to learn, and to do all that does not entrench on the freedom of his fellow men - free to progress to heights of light and knowledge as yet unseen and undreamt - should in gratitude remember Voltaire."

Without a doubt, Voltaire is one of the most eulogized men in history, evidenced by the writer Victor Hugo, who delivered the oration, *Voltaire* (1878), on the one-hundredth anniversary of Voltaire's death: "He died immortal. He departed laden with years, laden with works, laden with the most illustrious and the most fearful of responsibilities, the responsibility of the human conscience informed and rectified.... He was more than a man. He was an age."

Of course the intellectuals of the twentieth century would not forget Voltaire, in particular, Clarence Darrow in his essay *Voltaire* (1916): "Voltaire marks the closing of an epoch, his life and his work stand between the old and the new.... Among the illustrious heroes who have banished this sort of cruelty from the Western world no other name will stand so high and shine so bright as the illustrious name of Voltaire."

However, perhaps the importance of the great philosopher is best conveyed by the words of John Morley in *The Works of Voltaire*: "Voltaire was the very eye of eighteenth-century illumination. It was he who conveyed to his generation in a multitude of forms the consciousness at once of the power and the rights of human intelligence.... Voltaire was ever in the front and center of the fight."

The Postmodern Investigator

Parisian Culture

Parisian culture offers an investigator so much to experience: the sensuous beauty of the French language, the gastronomical pleasure of a world-renowned cuisine, the sumptuous varieties of exquisite wine, an almost uncountable number of art museums, the melodious sounds of the second home of Jazz, and the chic offerings of the fashion world. It's all here, and it's all on offer in this most fascinating city.

Parisian Language

At the end of each day of meandering around the Right Bank with Honoré, we'd usually have dinner together. However, if he was busy on another case, I'd head out on my own and do as Will suggested: "enjoy the sights and sounds, and the foods and wines, of the most beautiful and interesting, and the most historical and philosophical, city in the world." Unfortunately, sometimes my lack of command in the French language proved to get in the way of my enjoyment, as I suspect it does for most Americans who visit Paris.

But as it turns out, the best place to learn French, or some vulgarization of it, is in an American-style sports bar. Fortunately, I was staying in Montmartre, which offers many such pubs, especially along Rue des Abbesses. Of course the best time to hit any pub is during Happy Hour, which in France is known as "Heure Heureux." And once inside I'd take the heat off the day with a quick *bière française*, which is the most common of the French lager or "blonde" styles. I'd then settle into a *brune*, or what English-speaking folks call "ale" for the remainder of my stay.

One such bar, Pub Dream Team, offered not only sports from around the world, but also a few American TV shows. And since back home I'd memorized every episode of *The Simpsons*, or *Le Simpsons* as it's called in France, I was able to continue with my attempts at becoming fluent in the French language. As a warning though, the French have tossed in a few variations of America's favorite show, with Homer's dubbed in "Doh!" arriving at the ear as an almost inaudible bass. Also as a warning, "The Crepes of Wrath," the episode in which Bart is sent to France as a foreign exchange student only to end up working for two corrupt winemakers, has been banned by every French television network.

Another way to become fluent in French is to talk to other English-speaking travelers and share whatever command each one has of the language. For example, one late afternoon during Heure Heureux I ran into a fellow American who was going about the messy business of translating his first travel book, *No Worries, Mate*, into French. And despite the fact that he had a fine volume for translating English into French, one that also accommodated the reverse linguistic action if ever required, he was still confused as to how to translate the title, the subtitle, his name and the dedication to his travel book:

No Worries, Mate
A Manly Adventure in the Land Down Under

Ken Ewell

Dedicated to America's greatest travel writer,
Mark Twain,
and to the cordial folks who call Australia home.

Fortunately, the title of his travel book turned out to be quite an easy exercise in translation, and he came up with *Aucun Inquietudes, Amis* on his first go round. The "s" at the end of the second word was added of course to indicate the plural of that particular term, and it's an addition that's both straightforward and sensible, at least to folks knowledgeable in the French language. Naturally, he left off all those troublesome apostrophes and other wearisome marks that the French are so prone to putting over their letters. He was convinced that those linguistic omissions would eventually become the norm once his first travel book was available to the French-speaking peoples.

As it turned out, the subtitle of his travel book posed a formidable obstacle to his task of translating the book into French. The problem, of course, was the lack of any word in the French language for the term "manly." So rather than confuse the good people of France, or any of its dominions, with a concept that's obviously completely foreign to them, he chose to leave the entire phrase in English.

The translation of his name into French at first proved a difficult chore, mainly because his dictionary didn't offer translations of personal titles. Fortunately, there was a helpful bartender in the pub that afternoon. So the translator wrote down his name on a napkin, handed it to the bartender while pointing to himself, and motioned for him to write down the French translation of his name. As the bartender was quite amenable to this exercise, and as he knew quite a bit of English himself, he quickly wrote down the writer's name in French. That translation was "Etranger Cochon," which had quite a pleasant ring to it.

Unfortunately, the translation of the dedication proved to be the most time-consuming aspect of his Heure Heureux project. But despite the difficulty of the chore, his quite admirable result was "D'dicateure a Chien-Imperial's ecrivan voyageur grandest, Marque de Twainette, et a un cordial gens (et gans) qui cri Australie demeure." And though it's clearly a very fine translation, perhaps a few explanations are in order.

"D'dicateure" is his own free-style translation of "dedicated," using the common linguistic addition "eure" that often appears at the end of French words. And though "Chien-Imperial's" appears to indicate the Chinese Emperor's instead of "America's," the bartender in the pub guaranteed him that it was most definitely accurate in this context. Moving on, the expression "ecrivan voyageur grandest" appears in the reverse order of the English words for "greatest travel writer," the reason for this being that the French enjoy mixing up their words for no apparent reason.

Naturally, his translation "Marque de Twainette" should be clear to even those who know very little of the French language. Moving on again, since "gens" refers only to "men," he added et gans in parentheses. Needless to say, a translator should always error on the side of caution. Finally, "qui cri Australie demeure" is a fairly straightforward translation, at least for those readers fluent in the French language.

So the final translation of the title, the subtitle, his name and the dedication of his first travel book ended up the following list of superb French and English expressions:

Aucun Inquietudes, Amis
A Manly Adventure in the Land Down Under

Etranger Cochon

D'dicateure a Chien-Imperial's ecrivan voyageur grandest,
Marque de Twainette,
et a un cordial gens (et gans) qui cri Australie demeure.

Coming as no surprise, that writer hopes to finish his translation of his entire travel book someday, for learning a new language is always an enjoyable and rewarding experience.

One final word on French translation and that concerns Jacques Barzun, who years ago translated *The Dictionary of Accepted Ideas* (1913), by Gustave Flaubert. Translating French text is difficult, even in the best of cases, but when the text was written in the past, in this case the latter nineteenth century, the translator must first understand how the language differs with present-day French. In addition, he or she must also understand the cultural and historical context of the text, as well as the personal psychology of the writer.

Barzun explains his method in the introduction of his translation: "The task of the translator can thence be inferred as more than usually arduous. To give anything like the impression of the original, he must be just as natural and fully as quick. Yet he must jump the language barrier from cliché to cliché while carrying from one culture and background to their counterparts what "everybody knows" - or doesn't know. He is continually beset by dilemmas, tempted by lesser advantages, threatened by ambiguities. Whether to take the obvious but factually different equivalent; whether to make clear what the English requires if any meaning is to emerge, even though the French is content with a vagueness that is wholly intelligible;... whether to render identical expressions identically throughout, at the cost of one misfit out of three; whether to omit or reinvent - these and a multitude of other questions arise at every turn, sometimes two or three abreast in one definition."

Parisian Cuisine

Though it's all well and good to hear French words emanating from the old quiche-hole, it's far more enjoyable to taste a slice of quiche heading down that hole in the opposite direction. Of course as the world knows, the peoples that have taken the art of eating quiche, or anything else for that matter, to its highest state of perfection are the French. And when in Paris, the place to begin an exploration of French cuisine is the place where Honoré took me for dinner on my first night in town, namely, Le Procope.

On my own one night, and after being seated at a small table by the *maître d'*, I looked at the menu and immediately realized that I hadn't the foggiest idea what to order. Needless to say, in Paris all the dishes on the menu are in French, which hadn't been a problem on my visit with Honoré, for he arranged the entire meal. But after the waiter came to my table not once, but twice, and then a third time without receiving an order, I gave thought to ducking out the way I came in.

Fortunately, sitting at a table nearby was an older Parisian gentleman who must have taken note of my gastronomic predicament. And being an agreeable man, he leaned over and introduced himself to me, "My name is Jean Anthelme Brillat-Savarin. Won't you please join me at my table so that I might help you with your choices tonight?"

I quickly moved over to his table and said, "I thank you, monsieur, for you must have noticed that my lack of French meant that I would undoubtedly go hungry tonight. By the way, my name's Sam and I'm a private investigator from San Francisco."

"Welcome to Paris, Sam," he said, "and please call me Jean. It gives me great pleasure in helping travelers enjoy our wonderful French cuisine, in fact so much so that many years ago I wrote a book, *The Physiology of Taste* (1825), which described my *Meditations on Transcendental Gastronomy.*"

Just then the waiter arrived at our table and Jean told him, "Let me see, for the entrée I think that my friend and I would enjoy a pistachio-studded Beaujolais sausage, one that's served with warm potatoes and a Julienas wine vinegar dressing, and one that's best accompanied by a glass of Beaujolais. After that we'll have your excellent Odeon French onion soup, which is an exquisite consommé topped with melted Gruyère cheese and best complimented by a glass of Pinot Noir."

Before continuing with further selections, Jean sent the waiter off to the kitchen with the first orders, after which he considered his next choices for our dinner, "For the main course I believe that a prime cut of beef fillet, one covered in pepper and flambéed with Armagnac brandy, would please us greatly, as would a glass of Cabernet Sauvignon. And lastly, for desert I recommend the crepes flambéed, which are topped with Grand Marnier and best enjoyed with a glass of that wonderful French elixir."

Once the first dish arrived I began a meal I'll not soon forget, though of course it wasn't just the food and the wine that made the feast so enjoyable. No, it was also the company, with Jean spending most of the meal telling me about his famous book. While enjoying the pistachio-studded sausage, Jean meditated on the senses, on bouquet, on taste, on appetite, on thirst, and on digestion. Once the French onion soup arrived, his meditations dwelt on rest, on sleep, on dreams, on the influence of diet, on obesity and its treatment, on thinness and fasting, and on exhaustion. During the main course of beef fillet, Jean meditated on food in general, on cooking, on the theory of frying, on drinks, on hunting luncheons, and on restaurateurs. And lastly, while enjoying the crepes flambéed, his meditations were on gastronomy and its tests, on gourmandism and gourmands, on the pleasures of the table, on death, and on the end of the world.

After our meal ended the waiter cleared the table, and as there was no one waiting to be seated, Jean ordered another bottle of wine for the two of us. Just then a gentleman arrived at our table and said, "Jean, it's so good to see you again."

"Hello, Jean-Robert," Jean responded, "it's wonderful to see you again too. This is my American friend, Sam, who The Professor is introducing to French cuisine. Sam, this is my friend Jean-Robert Pitte, who must join us for a glass of wine."

"An excellent idea, Professor," Jean-Robert said, "but let me tell your friend something about myself, for I too am a writer of things gastronomic." After taking a sip of wine, our new companion continued, "Let me summarize for you my essay 'The Rise of the Restaurant', which is included in the collection *Food: A Culinary History from Antiquity to the Present* (1999), edited by Jean-Louis Flandrin and Massimo Montanari: 'If most restaurants in France are permanent rather than itinerant operations, it is probably because France was the birthplace of what we now call the restaurant, which gradually replaced an older variety of eating establishments. This happened toward the end of the eighteenth century.'

"Prior to the rise of the restaurant, and when not at home, people ate mainly in taverns or cafés. The food was seldom of much gastronomic appeal, as the best chefs worked in the homes of the aristocracy, at least until a lawsuit opened the doors. Restaurants now sprang up throughout Paris, with the dishes listed on a framed piece of paper and the diner given a check of the items ordered at the end of the meal. This slowly continued up to the downfall of the aristocracy in 1789."

Just then the chef came out from his kitchen and made his way to our table, "Good evening, Jean and Jean-Robert, it's been far too long since we last dined together."

"Hello, Henri," Jean said, "This is my friend, Sam. I know you're busy in the kitchen, but could you join us for a glass of wine?"

"Of course," Henri responded, "there's always time for a glass of wine with old friends." Then looking at me, Henri continued, "Let me introduce myself to you, I am Henri-Paul Pellaprat. At an early age I was apprenticed into the restaurant trade, and after the First World War I entered the Cordon Bleu. In 1935 I published *L'Art culinaire moderne*, which in your country goes by the title *The Great Book of French Cuisine*. And if I am not mistaken, both of my friends, Julia Child and Jacques Pépin, learned how to cook in the French fashion using my collection of recipes.

"My cookbook covers the four styles of French cooking. The first is *la haute cuisine*, which is 'the most elaborate and sophisticated cooking', as well as 'one of the greatest achievements of France'. The more common type is *la cuisine bourgeoise*, which is 'middle-class cooking, the triumph of both Cordon Bleu holders and housewives', and also the approach to cooking in my kitchen here in Le Procope. Then there's *la cuisine regionale*, 'the provincial cooking of France, unique in the world because of the diversity, richness, and originality of its countless local dishes and specialties'. And finally, the last style is *la cuisine impromptue*, or 'impromptu cooking which, using whatever is at hand, is the simplest and the quickest type of cooking'. Of course no matter the style, a good chef must always attend to the needs of his guests."

Henri then got up and said "I must get back to my kitchen, but please enjoy your wine."

"I too must be on my way," Jean-Robert added, "but I hope to join the both of you for dinner in the near future."

With our other guests gone, Jean offered a parting salute to the Gastronomers of the Old and New World, just as he did in his celebrated book: 'The Temple of Gastronomy, chief ornament of the capital of the world, will soon lift toward the skies its mighty porticoes; you will make it echo with your voices; you will enrich it with your talents; and when the academy promised by the oracle establishes itself on the two un-shifting cornerstones of pleasure and of need, you, enlightened gourmands, you, most agreeable of table guests, will be its members and its aides.'"

With his gastronomic thoughts concluded, Jean and I left Le Procope and then parted ways outside. While walking to the Metro to catch the train back to Montmartre, I decided to set a few culinary goals for myself. And though most goals that are set when not at home are invariably forgotten, I did manage to pick up Henri-Paul's classic work, *The Great Book of French Cuisine*, as well as two equally classic cookbooks, Julia Child's *Mastering the Art of French Cooking* (1961/1970) and Jacque Pépin's *Essential Pépin* (2011). And perhaps one day I'll get around to opening them up and cooking a meal, for in Paris I was given to understand that the way to a woman's heart is through her French stomach.

Parisian Wine

Although the traveler to Paris occasionally splurges on a fine meal at Le Procope or some other restaurant offering traditional French cuisine, on most days his stomach probably just happily enjoys the breads, the cheeses and the meats that abound in all the neighborhood markets of this market-laden city. And needless to say, a good bottle of wine helps wash down the day's market-fare. So when standing in front of the wine section of a local vino shop, it's important to keep in mind the four grades of French wine:

Appellation d'Origine Contrôlée (AOC): Fine wines are of the highest quality and are produced under the most restrictive rules.

Appellation d'Origine Vin de Qualité Supérieure (AOVDQS): Fine wines are of a higher quality, but are produced under less restrictive rules than AOC wines.

Vin de Pays: Daily-consumption wines are of a high quality, but are produced under less restrictive rules than AOVDQS wines.

Vin de Table: Daily-consumption wines are of a medium quality and are produced under few restrictive rules.

Though the top two grades of French wine are quite pricy, the latter two grades are probably well within the budget of any philosophical investigator. And even after eliminating the brands in the top two categories, there are still many wines to choose from, even in the smallest of vino shops. But no matter the choice, expensive or cheap, red or white, enough of any wine will always remind one of the wise old saying, *in vino veritas*:

Red Wines

Cabernet Franc: Grown in Bordeaux, and the aroma is of strawberry and blackberry.

Cabernet Sauvignon: Grown in Languedoc-Roussillon, the Loire Valley, Provence and the South-West, and the aroma is of blackberry and violet.

Carignan: Grown in Languedoc-Roussillon and Provence, and the aroma is of black fruits, black pepper and licorice.

Cinsault: Grown in Languedoc and Provence, and the aroma is of red fruits.

Gamay: Grown in Beaujolais, and the aroma is of strawberry, cherry and spice.

Grenache: Grown in Languedoc-Roussillon and the Rhone Valley, and the aroma is of red fruits, lavender and thyme.

Merlot: Grown in Bordeaux, and the aroma is of blackcurrant and blackberry.

Mourvèdre: Grown in the Rhone Valley, and the aroma is of black fruits and licorice.

Pinot Noir: Grown in Burgundy and Champagne, and the aroma is of cherry, blackcurrant and licorice.

Syrah: Grown in the Rhone Valley, and the aroma is of raspberry, black pepper, licorice and violet.

White Wines

Chardonnay: Grown in Burgundy and Champagne, and the aroma is of apple, linden and almond.

Chenin Blanc: Grown in the Loire Valley, and the aroma is of apple, cinnamon and quince.

Clairette: Grown in Languedoc-Roussillon and Provence, and the aroma is of peach and apricot.

Muscadelle: Grown in Bordeaux, and the aroma is of acacia.

Pinot Gris: Grown in Alsace, and the aroma is of dried fruits, wood and spice.

Sauvignon: Grown in Bordeaux and the Loire Valley, and the aroma is of melon and mineral.

Sémillon Blanc: Grown in Bordeaux and the South-West, and the aroma is of honey, lemon and linden.

Ugni Blanc: Grown in Corsica, Languedoc and Provence, and the aroma is of banana.

Viognier: Grown in Languedoc-Roussillon, Provence and the Rhone Valley, and the aroma is of apricot, violet and apple.

Parisian Art

Along with good talk and good food and good wine, the Parisian also enjoys good things to look at, especially if they hang or stand in any of the numerous art museums that call Paris home. Now if stuck for time, there are only four must-see museums in Paris: Musée du Louvre, Musée d'Orsay, Centre Georges Pompidou and Musée Picasso. And if really stuck for time, the first and foremost museum to visit is The Louvre.

Before moving on, it should be noted that there are two main reasons for visiting the most famous museum in the world. The first is that if an investigator of Paris doesn't visit The Louvre, everyone back home will consider him an uncultivated dunderhead, assuming that they don't already. On the other hand, the second reason for visiting this museum is to garner some obscure facts concerning some obscure artists, with that information useful in making folks back home look like uncultivated dunderheads, assuming that they don't already.

Moving on, for those who've never been to Paris or for those who haven't been since 1988, the entrance to the museum is now a huge glass pyramid that reminds one of a huge glass pyramid. And after standing in line for seventeen hours, I entered that huge glass pyramid and immediately descended to the lower level, where a number of options presented themselves to me. My first option was to remain on the Lower Ground Floor, where I could wander through exhibits of Egyptian Antiquities, Greek Antiquities, Etruscan Antiquities, Roman Antiquities, Oriental Antiquities, Sculptures, Islamic Art, the History of the Louvre, and the Medieval Louvre.

On the other hand, my second option was to rise to the Ground Floor, where I could wander through more exhibits of Egyptian Antiquities, Greek Antiquities, Etruscan Antiquities, Roman Antiquities, Oriental Antiquities, and Sculptures. My advice to any first-time visitor to The Louvre is to skip both of those floors, for the only stuff that anyone will ask about back home sits on the First Floor and the Second Floor.

With all of that in mind, I made my way up to the First Floor, which is home to more exhibits of Egyptian Antiquities, Greek Antiquities, Etruscan Antiquities, and Roman Antiquities, though I resolutely avoided any of those unnecessary diversions. Instead, I sought out the more useful stuff for making folks back home look like uncultivated dunderheads, namely, the Paintings, Prints, Drawings, and *Objets d'art*, whatever that means. And before going on, there's another word of advice. Since the Second Floor is home to only more Paintings and Drawings, the sensible visitor to The Louvre needn't even bother climbing the stairs, unless he's in need of a little exercise.

Remaining on the First Floor, my first order of business was to have a gander at probably the most famous painting in the world, that being Leonardo da Vinci's *Mona Lisa*. Of course that's no easy chore, for 99.99% of the folks in The Louvre on any given day are crowded around this famed work of art. But by combining a little cunning with a little pushing and a little shoving, I was eventually able to behold that famed work of art. And how disappointed I was, for though I fully expected the *Mona Lisa* to take up an entire wall of the museum - what with all the exaggerated talk about it - the fact of the matter is that that famed work of art is no bigger than a large postage stamp.

Although I walked away from the Mona Lisa with diminished expectations as regards the remainder of The Louvre, I did learn a few things while wandering about the other paintings on the First Floor. The first lesson was that unlike some things in life, as regards paintings, bigger *is* better. And the second was that I came to fully understand the difference between the erotic and the pornographic - I can afford pornography. In addition, I learned that a parent is a fool to take children to a museum, for brats spend the entire time pleading to leave, knowing full well that they're undergoing cruel and unusual punishment. Furthermore, a parent should never bring adolescents to The Louvre, for any well-intended cultural experience is completely lost on those worshippers of McCulture. Of course that can probably be said for most adults as well, including private investigators.

The next must-see museum is The d'Orsay, home to works of art from the middle of the nineteenth century to the middle of the twentieth. However, only two floors are worth bothering with, those being the Pre-Impressionists on the ground floor, and the Impressionists and Post-Impressionists on the fifth floor. The other floors are devoted to Academism, Naturalism, Symbolism and Art Noveau, though if the budding art connoisseur attempts too many floors, he'll end up suffering from SAF, or "Severe Art Fatigue." Needless to say, I know this for a fact. Actually, when you get right down to it the only section worth seeing is the one devoted to the works of Claude Monet, who's pretty much the poster boy for the Impressionist movement.

After visiting the two floors devoted to the Impressionists, I was about ready to head outside when I noticed a sign for a special exhibit, one devoted to Pablo Picasso and Édouard Manet. Apparently, Picasso was so overwhelmed by Manet's "Lunch on the Grass" that he painted a zillion and one crazy looking pictures of it. The budding art connoisseur may remember this painting as the one where a couple of fully-clothed dudes are having a picnic, while nearby two busty babes frolic in the nude. I mean really, what are you waiting for guys? Clearly, these two bountiful dames aren't going to say no.

The third must-see museum in Paris is the Musée National D'Art Moderne, otherwise known as The Pompidou, which is an inside-outside building. By that I mean that what's usually on the inside of a building, such as elevators and pipes, are for some strange reason on the outside of this one. Once inside The Pompidou, or was I really on the outside, I first tried to figure out the meaning of two paintings, one solid black and the other solid white. After considering them from an aesthetic point of view for a minute or two, I came to the conclusion that the first one was of a black cat in the dark and the second was of a white dog in a snowstorm. Needless to say, the titles of those two works indicated that the artist hadn't considered my two aesthetic interpretations.

In one room I discovered that one of the paintings was hung upside-down, so I tried to turn it right-side up. Unfortunately, one of the staff members, a gal that clearly had little understanding of modern art, rushed over and abruptly told me to cease and desist. In the next room I accidently knocked over a piece from one of the sculptures, and so immediately tried to put it back up. Once again a staff member came over, this time preventing me from cleaning up after myself. And in another room I came upon a five-foot red vagina, which actually had an arousing effect on me, one observed by the security guard that had been assigned to trail after me.

After spending the better part of an hour trying to elude the security guard, I ended up in the Christian Boltanski room. This narcissistic jackass had created a room filled with photos of his self, old bill slips and even used movie tickets. In other words, a room filled with a load of old rubbish from his self-centered life, crap that any sensible person would have tossed out years before. And get the pretentious title of the room: "The impossible reconstruction of his own life."

Actually, the best piece of art in The Pompidou is in the crapper. For after experiencing a case of the runs in the toilet, a result of either all that modern art or the tuna sandwich I ate for lunch, I went over to wash my hands. Now the piece of art I'm referring to is the Dyson hand dryer, invented by the same guy who sells the vacuum cleaners on American TV. This is by far the best hand dryer ever invented, though like all other hand dryers, it doesn't dry hands as well as good old paper towels.

For those visitors with plenty of time on their hands, Paris offers a ridiculous number of museums to satisfy the tastes of even the most discriminating of art connoisseurs, over 150 at last count. So after visiting three of those must-see museums, with Musée Picasso being closed, I discovered that I had no interest whatsoever in any art before the Revolution, nor did I understand why anyone else would have such an interest. On the other hand, since the artistic movements from the late eighteenth century onwards seemed to hold my interest, I jotted them down along with their approximate dates and some of their more famous French artists:

Neoclassicism (1780-1800): Jacques-Louis David, François Gérard, Anne-Louis Girodet, Pierre-Paul Prud'hon, Jean-Antoine Houdon

Romanticism (1800-1850): Antoine-Jean Gros, Théodore Géricault, Eugène Delacroix, Paul Delaroche, François Rude, Antoine-Louis Barye, Jean Auguste Dominique Ingres

Realism (1840-1880): Honoré Daumier, Jean-François Millet, Charles Méryon, Gustave Courbet

Impressionism and Post-Impressionism (1860-1910): Édouard Manet, Claude Monet, Camille Pissarro, Pierre Auguste Renoir, Paul Gauguin, Edgar Degas, Auguste Rodin, Georges Seurat, Paul Cézanne, Émile Bernard, Maurice Denis, Paul Sérusier, Édouard Vuillard, Toulouse-Lautrec

Symbolism (1880-1900): Gustave Moreau

Expressionism (1900-1910): Henry Julien Rousseau

Fauvism (1900-1910): Henri Matisse

However, while meandering about the many museums of modern French art, I discovered that I became physically disoriented and mentally disturbed when confronted by pieces of any period later than Fauvism. After experiencing this on a number of occasions, I decided that at some point near the beginning of the twentieth century the world of modern French art evolved into a confusing, if not a completely perplexing period. And to usher in the century in proper fashion, art-wise, modern art immediately offered a few new art movements:

Cubism (1900-1920): Pablo Picasso, Georges Braque

Dada (1910-1920): Marcel Duchamp

Surrealism (1920-1940): Salvadore Dali, Joan Miró, André Masson

Needless to say, in these postmodern times the dropping of the word "surrealism" in urbane conversations is mandatory at any cultured and sophisticated social gathering. But just as the word "art" is little understood by private investigators, the same can also be said for the word "surrealism." Fortunately, there was a Frenchman, one André Breton, who some years ago attempted to get at the meaning of the word in his essay *Manifesto of Surrealism* (1924). And after a confusing start composed of mainly verbal diarrhea, Andre finally got down to a few basic and really quite obvious definitions:

After making his definitions completely clear to even the most dim-witted of private investigators, Breton went on to describe the "surrealist" approach to artistic endeavor: "Language has been given to man so that he may make Surrealist use of it. To the extent that he is required to make himself understood, he manages more or less to express himself, and by so doing to fulfill certain functions culled from among the most vulgar.... He is not worried about the words that are going to come, nor about the sentence which will follow after the sentence he is just completing."

Needless to say, this is not the recommended method for writing anything that might make any sense whatsoever to anyone whatsoever. Of course, that didn't stop Breton from arriving at a few conclusions concerning his obscure method: "This world is only very relatively in tune with thought, and incidents of this kind are only the most obvious episodes of a war in which I am proud to be participating....

Surrealism is the "invisible ray" which will one day enable us to win out over our opponents.... Existence is elsewhere."

After enjoying this well-written and illuminating essay on the concept of "surrealism," and now thoroughly understanding that "existence is elsewhere" implies that existence is anywhere away from this perplexing notion, there are only two additional French art movements to consider before moving on to other artistic matters:

Abstract Expressionism (1950-1960): Jean Dubuffet

New Realism (1960-1970): Yves Klein, Arman, Martial Raysse, Raymond Hains, Jacques de la Villeglé, Niki de Saint Phalle, Gérard Deschamps, Christo

To be perfectly honest, this private investigator has never had the slightest clue as to what is "good" or "bad" art, or even what is or is not "art." I realized this one evening a few years back when a dinner conversation got on to the subject of "The Gates," the exhibit in NYC's Central Park by the above-mentioned Christo and his partner in crime, Jeanne-Claude. As I pointed out to everyone at the table, it seemed to me that this was a case of two postmodern hucksters putting drapes up throughout the park, after which, everyone walked around under the impression that they were experiencing a day of art.

Well, I asked everyone at the dinner party as to why they thought that hanging drapes in a park amounted to art, while doing the same thing at home amounted to merely home improvement. Needless to say, my skeptical attitude provoked quite an outcry, with one and all taking me to task for my insensitive and ill-informed views of what was clearly a major advance in aesthetics. The prevailing attitude was that if it's called "art," then it must be, and no one, especially me, had the right to say otherwise.

Naturally, my insensitivity and ignorance remained with me for some time, at least until the day I came upon a book, *The End of Art* (2004), by Donald Kuspit, who had a number of interesting thoughts on postmodern art, or as he called it, "postart." So as it turns out,

I'm not the only amateur art critic to question the validity of those stylized and questionable park improvements, as well as many other concepts that pass themselves off as "art" these days: "Contemporary culture must satisfy mass taste, which means that its form must not be too complex and its meaning must be transparent. It must bring us together in the crowd rather than help us become individuals, which may alienate us from one another."

But perhaps the end of art is not necessarily inevitable, and perhaps art is only taking a long respite from its very old tradition of inspiring people and societies. At least this is what I came away with after reading the aesthetic thoughts of the philosopher John Dewey, in particular, the chapter "Art and Civilization" in his book *Art as Experience* (1934): "... the question of the place and role of art in contemporary civilization demands notice of its relations to science and to the social consequences of machine industry. The isolation of art that now exists is not to be viewed as an isolated phenomenon. It is one manifestation of the incoherence of our civilization produced by new forces, so new that the attitudes belonging to them and the consequences issuing from them have not been incorporated and digested into integral elements of experience."

Parisian Jazz

Although America is the birthplace of jazz, there was once no better home to enjoy it in than Paris, as evidenced by the 12 CD collection, *Jazz in Paris*, which includes extensive historical and pictorial information: "Jazz chose Paris as one of its haunts, and set up home there for a while; in so doing, it transformed the city completely. In the Twenties, it was how Montmartre became Harlem-on-Seine.... During the Occupation, the world's most beautiful avenue [Champs-Elysées] provided its own resistance by offering excellent jazz in its nightclubs, and other venues staged concerts frowned on by the authorities. All these places preserved their good habits after the Liberation... by which time jazz had... descended into the cellars of Saint-Germain-des-Prés..."

Of course most of the old jazz haunts are long gone, though the most famous, Le Bouef sur le Toit, still sits just off the Champs-Elysées, though not at its original location. After the First World War and in the Twenties, Le Bouef was home to the first sounds of Parisian jazz, and they're remembered today at the entrance to the restaurant. There are photographs of the Surrealist poet Jean Cocteau, who'd read poetry while backed by his jazz group - a Beat thirty years before the Beats. Jean was also a popular artist of the day, and his drawings of Pablo Picasso and Igor Stravinsky still hang outside the restaurant. This consummate jazz aficionado also hosted what may well be the first jazz festival, as evidenced by a poster announcing the event.

The Champs-Elysées also once offered jazz at Les Ambassadeurs, with the famed American singer Josephine Baker headlining every night. And during the years of the Great Depression, that most famous of Parisian thoroughfares offered jazz at The Blue Note and The Mars Club. Those were the venues made famous by the guitarist Django Reinhardt and the violinist Stephen Grappelli, and they were also the second homes of Charles Delaunay, the editor of *Jazz Hot*, the first Parisian magazine devoted to jazz. Jazz spread throughout post-war Paris, especially to Montmartre, where the clubs Harlem-on-Seine, Le Grand Duc and Brick Top opened after the war, with Gus Viseur on accordion at Petit Jardin, the Django Reinhardt and Stephen Grappelli Quintet at Le Hot Club de France, and Louis Armstrong playin' and diggin' the scene.

Unfortunately, the Second World War completely stopped American jazz musicians from visiting Paris, and it also somewhat stopped the Parisian musicians from following the new sound in jazz, Bop. After the war, Saint-Germain-des-Prés became the center of jazz in Paris. In those long gone days, Le Caveau des Lorientais and Le Tabou were cellar-clubs offering Bop, which was soon being played not only by American visitors, but by Parisians such as the trumpet player Boris Vian and Henri Renaud, a pianist and modern jazz aficionado. And the legendary Sidney Bichet, the American sax-man who'd been playing since the Twenties with the likes of Louis Armstrong, now presented his New Orleans sound at the Club du Vieux-Colombier.

Just as in America, the sound one and all now longed to hear was Bop, with Miles at the forefront of the Parisian movement. And also as in America, it was a time when jazz met films, especially in Louis Malle's *Ascenseur pour l'echafaud* or *Lift to the Scaffold* or *Elevator to the Gallows*. It was the story of a love affair and murder gone wrong, and set to scenes of Parisian loneliness amidst the haunting refrains of Miles' horn.

Though Miles played all over Paris, his main club in Saint-Germain-Des-Prés was Club Saint-Germain, where he enjoyed the company of the young and beautiful actress Juliette Greco, who also sang at the Rose Rouge. This wonderful singer, whose voice tugs at the heartstrings while evoking images of love-struck Paris, lost her own heart to Miles, and she spoke of those far off times many years later in the May 24, 2006, edition of *The Guardian* newspaper: "Like every young person of my generation, I immersed myself in jazz.... The first time Miles Davis came to Paris, it was at the Pleyel, a crumbling place.... So I met this man, who was very young, as I was. We went out for dinner in a group, with people I didn't know. And there it was. I didn't speak English, he didn't speak French. I haven't a clue how we managed. The miracle of love."

As is clear from Juliette's wonderful memories, the jazz connoisseurs listening to Miles included numerous postwar celebrities, many in the vanguard of the Existentialist movement that was already spreading its wings over America. In fact, it was at one of the clubs that Juliette, Anne-Marie Cazalis and Annabel Buffet, all of them dressed in solid black, were asked what they called themselves. They responded "existentialists," which coined the word for a new generation of hipsters. It must be said, those bebopping gals were the original *Sex in the City*, albeit with class and intelligence and taste.

As the Fifties progressed, the Parisian jazz scene spread throughout the city, both on the Rive Gauche and the Rive Droite. The last venue for jazz was the Olympia, which in its time showcased Art Blakey, Milt Jackson, Gerry Mulligan, Horace Silver, John Coltrane, Count Basie, Ella Fitzgerald, Cannonball Adderley, Dizzy Gillespie, Oscar Peterson, Thelonious Monk, Miles Davis, Stan Getz, Duke Ellington, and many other legendary names in jazz. Sadly, though perhaps inevitably, in the Sixties a new sound spread around the world, with jazz becoming a beloved memory in the history of music.

Parisian Fashion

Given that Paris is a renowned fashion capital of the world, I made my way one afternoon to the most popular department store in the capital, Printemps, located at 64 Haussmann Boulevard. Of course the Champs-Elysées offers the latest in chic fashions, as do other boulevards in the city. But for a private investigator on a private investigator's budget, Printemps is definitely the place to go.

The first place I visited was Printemps Homme, the men's store located in one of the three buildings that make up Printemps. Fortunately, I only needed one item of apparel that day, an American style baseball cap, preferably with the word "Paris" emblazoned across it. Unfortunately, the quite rude salesman that I approached about this item displayed a rather indignant attitude as regards my request, and he could only respond, "I'm sawve, ser, but we haf no basseebull cups at Printemps."

Realizing that the likelihood of procuring a cap that day was minimal at best, I next made my way to Printemps Mode, the women's store, to have a look around. I meandered about the building for quite some time until finding the only department that held much interest for me, the French lingerie section. But after trying on a few items to see how I looked in stylish women's under-things, I was asked to leave posthaste... and not in a friendly fashion either.

Now having given up any hope of ever achieving success in my urban shopping experience, I visited the third building, Printemps Beaute/Maison, or the Beauty/Home Store. And fortunately, in this main building Printemps offers precisely what a private investigator needs in the form of several restaurants and bars that tender good food and wine: Brasserie Printemps, Café Be, Cojean:, Ladurée, Le World Bar, Le Déli-Cieux, Pouchkine, and Pouchkine Terrace.

After enjoying a few brews and some pub grub at Le World Bar, I made my way to the 9th Floor, home to the Panoramic Terrace, which offers the best views of Paris in the downtown area. As it turned out, the day of my visit was Thursday, when Printemps stays open for shoppers until late in the evening. And while enjoying a chilled glass of bubbly and the unbelievable views, a gentleman approached me and said, "Excuse me, sir, but did you enjoy your urban shopping experience today?"

"Well, not really," I replied, "but why do you ask?"

"Let me introduce myself," he responded. "My name is Jean Baudrillard, but please call me Jean. I am a sociologist by trade or what some in France call a writer on postmodern issues."

"Glad to make your acquaintance, Jean," I said. "My name's Sam and..."

"Yes, the San Francisco private investigator that Honoré told me about," Jean interjected. "I was told that I might find you here today. The reason I wanted to speak with you concerns my views on fashion that I wrote about in one of my books, *Symbolic Exchange and Death* (1976): 'The astonishing privilege accorded to fashion is due to a unanimous and definitive resolve. The acceleration of the simple play of signifiers in fashion becomes striking, to the point of enchanting us - the enchantment and vertigo of the loss of every system of reference.... Fashion exists only within the framework of [post]modernity, that is to say, in a schema of rupture, progress and innovation.'

"But perhaps I speak too quickly, for in saying this I must first describe how fashion evolved through three stages. During the 'pre-modern stage', which lasted until around 1500, rank was evidenced by standards in dress. Only the most privileged of classes could display a sense of fashion, mainly due to the cost of materials.

"However, with new technological and social developments during the 'modern stage', there came a corresponding reduction in the cost of materials. Subsequently, the mass production of clothing produced some similarities in style amongst various social classes, especially amongst women. And with the industrial revolution creating a new mass society, social roles became more dependent on work rather than lineage. Of course, in the higher social groups there still remained a system of status differentiation in clothing between the rapidly-declining aristocracy, the 'old money' class, and the rapidly-rising capitalists, the 'new money' class.

"The 'postmodern stage', which began around 1950 or so, overturned most of the conventions in modern fashion, mainly through the rejection of traditional styles, the relaxation of norms, the emphasis on diversity, and the variability of styles. This evolution in fashion, from production to seduction, is characterized by excess, as well as by the rejection of the modern concepts of objective reality, absolute meaning, shared morality, and rational truth: '... there is no possible subversion of fashion since it has no system of reference to contradict - it is its own system of reference. We cannot escape fashion, since fashion itself makes the refusal of fashion into a fashion feature.... the alternative to fashion... lies in a deconstruction of both the form of the sign of fashion and the principle of signification itself...'"

Jean stopped there, so I asked, "What is it that you mean by 'sign' and 'signification'? I've never heard such words before concerning fashion, or concerning much else for that matter."

"Do not worry about that right now," Jean replied, "for you will soon run into another philosophical investigator that will answer all your questions." With that, Jean left me to enjoy from atop Printemps the panoramic view of the City of Light, with those lights now coming to life.

Parisian Pleasures

Taking Honoré's advice, my first day-trip was to the most popular destination outside of Paris proper, the legendary Versailles, once home to the most flamboyant king in the history of France, Louis XIV, aka, "The Sun King." And throughout that pleasurable journey, I pondered on the words of Roland Barthes from his book *The Pleasure of the Text* (1973): "The pleasure of the text:... it can say: 'never apologize, never explain'. It never denies anything: 'I shall look away, that will henceforth be my sole negation.'"

The Misanthrope

Once onboard the train that takes the multitude of travelers to the Mecca of French palaces, I settled into a somewhat comfortable seat in the Moliere car and closed my eyes to hopefully enjoy forty-winks before arriving at my final destination. Unfortunately, after only five of those winks, several young people began a rather noisy conversation on the subject of misanthropy. Now having given up any hope of enjoying any more winks whatsoever, I decided to search for the club-car, where I could at least procure a much-needed cuppa java.

As I was leaving, I heard in back of me the following thoughts on the subject of love: "Love, generally speaking, is little apt to put up with these decrees, and lovers are always observed to extol their choice. Their passion never sees aught to blame in it, and in the beloved all things become lovable. They think their faults perfections, and invent sweet terms to call them by.... Thus a passionate swain loves even the very faults of those of whom he is enamored."

Zadig

As it so happens, the waits to get into and through Versailles are a monumental test of one's patience. There are lines for everything, and not just for the entrance tickets, but also for the crappers, which are filthy beyond redemption, as if they haven't been cleaned since the time of "The Sun King." And once in the palace, the visitor to Versailles meanders aimlessly from one room to another *ad infinitum*. However, there are only two rooms worth a show of patience. The first is the Hall of Mirrors, which all have a load of scratches on them, and the other is the Hall of Battles. Now that latter hall celebrates all the French victories throughout history until Austerlitz in 1805, and then the hall remains mute over the next two hundred years for some reason. Is it possible that France hasn't won even one battle in that long length of time?

Tiring of the throng of visitors bumping and elbowing each other to gaze at all of Louis' stuff, I finally called it quits and went to the palace café for some lunch. It was of course busy there too, but I managed to get a grilled sandwich and a soda, and then searched for a place to sit. And while sharing a table with an older couple, one clearly from Babylon, the man struck up a conversation with me, "Good day, sir, my name is Zadig. My wife and I have been traveling for many years, and are now in Paris to visit our good friend Voltaire. Perhaps if you have a little time, I could tell you something about our journeys thus far in life." After nodding my head in agreement, Zadig began his *Oriental Tale of Destiny*.

"I will start with my proposed marriage to a well-placed Babylonian woman, who, after I defended her honor in a fight, left me and married another. So I instead married a more common woman, though after she tried to cut off my nose, I cut off my wife. Now tired of life in the city, I retired to the country and to some '... happiness in the study of nature.... Nothing is happier than a philosopher who reads in this great book that God has put under our eyes. The truths that he discovers are his own, he nourishes and elevates his soul. He lives at peace.'

"Unfortunately, while walking near a woods one day I was accused of stealing both the king's horse and the queen's bitch. Naturally, I was fined a goodly amount of money. But after proving my innocence in those crimes and having no money returned, I returned to Babylon and turned myself over to philosophy, and then surrounded myself with the most learned of men and the most beautiful of women.

"Unfortunately, an envious man told the king that I had insulted him in a poem, though by good luck my life was saved by the intervention of the king's parrot. After that, I became the king's minister. Unfortunately, my desire to please Queen Astarte, caused the two of us to fall passionately in love with one another, which forced me to flee to Egypt in order to save both of our lives. I set my course by the stars and '... marveled at these vast globes of light which to our eyes appear to be only feeble sparks, whereas the earth, which is in fact only an imperceptible point in nature, appears to our cupidity as something so great and so noble. I then visualized men as they really are, insects devouring one another on a little atom of mud.'

"I was brought back to earth from the universe by my thoughts of Astarte, as well as by the cries of a woman being beaten by a man. Unfortunately, after I killed her lover she wished only to tear my heart out, so I continued on to an Egyptian village. Once there I was sold into slavery and taken by a merchant to Arabia, where my knowledge and wisdom won for me great acclaim and great esteem.

"Unfortunately, after arguing that widows should not die on the funeral pyre, I was sentenced to burn over a slow fire myself. But one of the widows that I saved also saved me in return, which impressed the merchant, so he took her for his wife. During their honeymoon the merchant sent me to the isle of Serendib, where I helped the king find an honest treasurer and a faithful wife. Unfortunately, this angered so many thieves and trollops that I left the island to once again find my beloved Astarte.

"Unfortunately, I was soon set upon by thieves. But when their lord observed that I fought bravely against his men, he brought me into his castle. On leaving I first wandered along a river and then through a meadow, and eventually discovered, to my surprise, my beloved Astarte. She told me the story of how her husband was killed, how she was placed in a harem, how she escaped to Arabia, how she was captured by that lord, how she was sold into slavery, and how she eventually ended up in that meadow.

"We then swore our love for each other, after which I arranged with her insalubrious master that she be allowed to return to Babylon. In return for his generosity, I made the insalubrious master healthy once again. And before leaving I told him '... that people are always healthy with sobriety and exercise, and that the art of making intemperance and health live together is an art as chimerical as the philosopher's stone, judicial astrology, and the theology of the magi.'

"But our love was not yet to be, for after Astarte was received once again as the queen of Babylon, the people demanded that she marry a man both courageous and wise. Unfortunately, after I defeated in combat all the other aspirants for the queen's hand, I was tricked by one of them and run out of the city. By good fortune, the Angel of Destiny, who was in the guise of a hermit, told me to return to Babylon, where I answered the riddles on time, life, justice, the sovereign good and the art of ruling. And after I married my beloved Astarte, and after I became the King of Babylon, the '... empire enjoyed peace, glory, and abundance. It was the earth's finest century. It was governed by justice and love.' Unfortunately..."

Madame Bovary

At that point I'd heard just about enough of this poor man's rather unfortunate existence, and so I bid adieu to him and his wife. I made my way outside and discovered to my pleasant surprise that the most enjoyable aspects of Versailles are the grounds that surround the palace, despite the fact that the benches are all dirty and that none of the fountains work. But these are trifles when lying in a rowboat under clear blue skies, all the while enjoying a glass of white wine.

Unfortunately, while enjoying the warmth of the sun as it beat its way into my marrow, and while also enjoying a wonderful nap brought on by the effects of the wine, I was rudely interrupted by what appeared to be a lover's spat in another rowboat. And since neither of the amorous combatants were paying any attention whatsoever to their vessel, it eventually floated next to mine, at which point I said pointedly, "Excuse me, but I'm trying to enjoy the day here."

Needless to say, those two rather distracting individuals were too enraptured by their argument to pay any notice of me. So I took my oar and swatted the water with it, dousing the two of them and shutting them up momentarily.

"Hey, what the hell are you doing," the man said irately. "Can't you see that my wife and I are having an argument?"

"I see that quite well, sir," I responded, "but can't you see that I'm trying to enjoy this beautiful day."

The two of them then looked around, and after agreeing that it was a beautiful day, the woman said coquettishly, "Yes, you are right, this is too lovely a day to spend in this unseemly manner. May I introduce myself? My name is Madame Bovary, Emma please, and this is my husband Charles."

"The name's Sam and I'm a private investigator from San Francisco. But if I might intrude, what is it that occupies the two of you so fervently today?" I asked in marriage counselor mode.

"Well, it's a long and complicated story, as is any marital tale," began Charles. "I met my wife when I was already married, but fell in love with her nonetheless. Fortunately, my first wife died, and after a proper mourning period I married Emma.

"I know, you adored me beyond distraction," Emma added condescendingly. "But the problem was within me, for I was bored to tears. 'Before marriage I thought myself in love, but the happiness that should have followed this love not having come, I must, I thought, have been mistaken. And I tried to find out what one meant exactly in life by the words felicity, passion, rapture, that had seemed to me so beautiful in books.' I read everything I could of Paris and the gay life, and compared that world with the emptiness of my surroundings."

"Yes, my dear Emma," Charles interjected while looking at his wife, "but further troubles arose after you became ill, forcing me to move our home and my practice to a better climate. So we set up a new home in Yonville-l'Abbaye, though at least my practice finally took off once again."

Just then another rowboat approached us with a great deal of speed, and it was strenuously rowed by a man dressed in a leisure suit. "Emma," the man yelled, "'I need to have an affair. I may not look the part, but I'm a man who needs romance. I need softness, I need flirtation. I'm not getting younger, so before it's too late I want to make love...'" And with that, the man suddenly disappeared from his rowboat, which floated off towards the shore.

"Damn it, will Kugelmass never stop stalking me?" Emma said before she continued with her side of the story. "It was in Yonville that I became pregnant. But after I gave birth to a baby girl, it was clear to me that our love was over and that we 'had nothing else to say to one another?' I soon met Leon, a young clerk in town. But Leon eventually left for Paris without any admissions of our love for one another, so I began an affair with Rodolphe Boulanger, a wealthy neighbor whose love lasted only six months. Out of weakness, I eventually returned to my lover.

"After agreeing to leave for Paris with Rodolphe, I was fooled again when he abruptly left me. So I took to my bed, finding solace only in the false allure of Christianity. But after a few months I felt better, so Charles took me to the theater in Rouen, where I ran into Leon, with whom I consummated our love the next day in a carriage. Not surprisingly, he too began to fail at keeping a weekly rendezvous. 'I was not happy - I never had been. Whence came this insufficiency in life - this instantaneous turning to decay of everything on which I leant?'"

With Emma and Charles now clearly too distraught to continue and too overcome with grief for even life, I let their rowboat drift from mine. I wouldn't have thought about them again, except for a story on the TV that caught my attention a week later, one described by the reporter Gustave Flaubert. It was reported that a woman, Emma Bovary, the original desperate housewife, had committed suicide by taking a handful of arsenic. Her husband, Charles Bovary, was by her side at the time of her death. And it also came out in the story that after the burial, the poor man became so despondent that he died suddenly from a broken heart.

The School for Wives

Having drifted some distance from those two quite depressing people, I once again returned to the blue sky, the warm sun, and the white wine. However, just as I was about to doze off, a boat slid up next to mine, with the oarsmen laughing with pleasure, apparently at my expense. One of the oarsmen then said, "I'm sorry that we are laughing at you, but we always enjoy watching anyone trapped into listening to the never-ending domestic affairs of the Battling Bovaries. My name is Chrysalde and my friend is Arnolphe, and we come out here often to watch and laugh at the shenanigans of those two."

"Yes," added Arnolphe, "if only Charles had listened to our godfather Moliere, he might have avoided all his marital problems." Arnolphe next pulled out a little pamphlet and began reading from 'Marriage Maxims; or, The Duties of the Married Woman; with daily exercises.' With Arnolphes' ten maxims presented, Chrysalde then offered some conclusions from his friend's lessons: 'A gentleman should properly regard cuckoldry in a reasonable way? Since no one can ward off the blows of chance, this accident should not be taken to heart. For after all, the trouble comes entirely from the way in which you choose to treat the matter.'"

The Physiology of Marriage

The two young men then said their goodbyes and rowed over to another boat that had had the misfortune to drift alongside that of the Battling Bovaries. And after pouring another glass of wine, I thought back to a conversation I'd enjoyed with Honoré at his home. "Needless to say, the ups and downs of marriage, or any other amorous relationship for that matter, are common knowledge, though for husbands, the problem of playing the cuckold is always something to avoid at all costs. Of course, a man cannot avoid the inevitable walk down the aisle that sometimes accompanies a mad and passionate love. However, what a husband can and must avoid in a wife is her making him play the part of the cuckold. Firstly, a man must always remember that '... marriage in no way owes its origin to Nature.... Man is the minister of Nature, and society engrafts itself upon her. Laws are made in the interests of morality, and morality is subject to variation. Therefore marriage can be subjected to that gradual process of improvement which everything belonging to mankind seems to undergo.

"During my life I mostly played the part of the *raconteur*, which afforded me access to the homes of many husbands, as well as to the wives residing in those many homes. And throughout that time '... I found a far greater number of unhappy than of happy marriages, and I considered myself to be the first to observe that, of all human relations, that of marriage was the least advanced.'"

Honoré next explained how his thoughts on marriage were divided into three main categories, which were further divided into several related subjects. First were his "general reflections," or his views on the honeymoon and the first symptoms. Second were his "internal and external means of defense," or his ideas on finances, organizing the house, theory of the bed, love letters, spies, lovers, and catastrophes. And third were his thoughts on the "civil war," or his strategies for dealing with lovers, mother-in-laws, weapons such as headaches, compensation in advancement, and matrimonial peace once over. At the end of his lesson, Honoré concluded that a husband being made into a cuckold is almost inevitable.

Sentimental Education

After returning my boat to the docks, I made my way through the grounds of Versailles, past the palace, through the town and finally to the train station. After boarding the Gustave Flaubert car for the trip back to Paris, I went to the club-car for another glass of white wine, where I spied a breathtakingly beautiful woman in the seat next to me.

Hesitantly, I introduced myself to her, to which she offered her name, "Madame Arnoux." My first lesson in love soon had to leave, apparently in order to get back to her husband in another car of the train. So now heartbroken, I remained in the club car drinking another wine. And though I knew that my life would go on as usual, I could not say so as regards my heart, which had come under the spell of that most intoxicating woman. But I had no sooner thought this, than she returned to her seat next to mine. Then, suddenly crying, she told me about her adulterous husband.

Once back in Paris, Madame Arnoux invited me to walk her to her home. Upon entering, she instructed me to look about the place while she put herself back together. As luck would have it, while exploring "... I pushed open a door. Madame Arnoux was alone in front of a wardrobe mirror. Her dressing-gown was half-open, with the cord hanging down her hips.... Her figure, her eyes, the rustle of her dress, everything delighted me. I could scarcely restrain myself from covering her with kisses.... She was the point of light on which all things converged."

I immediately apologized for intruding upon her privacy, and then said that I must be going, especially as her husband might arrive at any moment. After a night of troubled sleep, and while wandering the streets of Paris throughout the next morning and most of the afternoon looking for my love, I ran into her on a crowed thoroughfare. Fortunately, there was a secluded café near where we met, so I asked her to join me for a glass of wine. It was then that I noticed that "... she was approaching the August of a woman's life, a period which combines reflection and tenderness, when the maturity which is beginning kindles a warmer flame in the eyes, when strength of heart mingles with experience of life, and when, in the fullness of its development, the whole being overflows with a wealth of harmony and beauty."

Sadly, our brief interlude of love ended that afternoon, and the next day I finally got back to my business as a philosophical investigator. But I'll not soon forget this episode, for "... the effect she had on me was that of a moonlit night in the summer, when all is perfume, soft shadows, pale light, and infinite horizons.... That picture blotted all the others. Why, I didn't so much as give them a thought, since in the depths of myself I always had the music of her voice and the splendor of her eyes."

Parisian Excursions

When I last saw Honoré at his home in the Chaillot Quarter, he gave me a list of places to investigate in areas outside Paris proper. The first was Versailles, which proved to be a pleasurable day in the pursuit of love. The next excursion on the list was to the financial district of La Défense, where I was to marvel at La Grande Arch. The third excursion was to the science and technology site of Parc de la Villette, where I was to explore the Cité de Sciences. And the last excursion was to a little slice of America, Disneyland Paris, where I was to investigate all the Disney lands.

La Défense

With the first generation of limited-height skyscrapers erected in the late Fifties, La Défense, sitting west of the city proper, is a major business district in Paris. The purpose-built site was selected to create a new home for leading French, as well as multi-national, companies. Today, its open-air layout of squares offers an investigator the feeling that he's walking through an outdoor museum.

As Jean Baudrillard notes in his travel book *America* (1986), La Défense differs remarkably from the financial districts in the United States: "By contrast with the American 'downtown areas' and their blocks of skyscrapers, la Défense has forfeited the architectural benefits of verticality and excess by squeezing its high-rise blocks into an Italian style setting, into a closed theater bounded by a ring-road. It is very much a garden *à la française*: a bunch of buildings with a ribbon around it."

In the early Seventies a second generation of buildings began to rise, followed in the early Eighties by a third generation. The most impressive of all the architectural wonders in La Défense is the 360-foot high La Grande Arche with its surrounding esplanade, which opened in 1989. The massive hollowed-out cube-shaped building is home to exhibition galleries and conference centers, and the top of the structure offers superb views of Paris.

After meandering about La Défense for most of the morning, and leaving La Grande Arche for the afternoon investigation, I joined the lunch crowd at one of the cafés to take in a bite to eat and to marvel at the architectural ambiance of the financial district. However, the café was so crowded that I ended up sharing a table with a most interesting older gentleman, a fellow American as it turned out.

"Excuse me," I asked politely, "do you mind if I share your table with you."

"No, not at all," he responded in an inviting tone.

After sitting, I continued, "The name's Sam and I'm a private investigator from San Francisco."

"Glad to meet you. My name is Daniel Bell and I'm from Boston," he replied. "I'm retired now, but I once conducted research and taught at Harvard University, where I wrote what many consider to be one of the most influential books of the second half of the twentieth century, that being *The Coming of Post-Industrial Society: A Venture in Social Forecasting* (1973). But let me offer you a few ideas from the book, as well as my thoughts concerning the world we now find ourselves living in.

"Man has lived through three industrial stages, the first referred to as "pre-industrial," which occurred from the dawn of agricultural societies to the beginnings of the Industrial Revolution around the middle of the eighteenth century. The "industrial" stage was evidenced by the application of new manufacturing and production processes, with this dramatic change occurring first in Britain and then later moving on to Western Europe and the United States.

"The third stage, the one that created today's "post-industrial" society, is characterized by the dominance of the service sector over the manufacturing sector in the economy. However, it should be noted that all three of these stages exist and interact with each other in modern developed societies, as well as in developing societies, though in different proportions within their economies.

"With the dominant mode of production now being post-industrial in developed economies, the majority of workers in those societies are engaged in service-related occupations at some level. 'The concept of the post-industrial society is a large generalization. Its meaning can be more easily understood if one specifies five dimensions or components, of the term: the change from a goods-producing to a service economy; the pre-eminence of the professional and technical class; the centrality of theoretical knowledge as the source of innovation and of policy formulation for the society; the control of technology and technological assessment; [and] the creation of a new intellectual technology.... The post-industrial society... does not displace the industrial society, just as an industrial society has not done away with the agrarian sectors of the economy. Like palimpsests, the new developments overlie the previous layers, erasing some features and thickening the texture of society as a whole.'"

Just then another gentleman walked over to our table and said, "Daniel, is that you? I haven't seen you in ages. May I sit down?"

"Why, if it isn't Michael Spence," Daniel responded. "This is my friend Sam from San Francisco. Are you still at New York University and the Hoover Institution? By the way, congratulations on receiving that Noble Prize in Economic Sciences."

"Thanks very much, Daniel," Michael said. "By the way, have you had a chance to read my latest book, *The Next Convergence: The Future of Economic Growth in a Multispeed World* (2011)." Daniel nodded no, so Michael continued, "If you've got some time, why don't I tell you and Sam about my thoughts in that book: '[My] book is about the third century of the Industrial Revolution, the one we are now living in.... This new growth was driven by the application of science and technology to production, logistics and communication, management and institutional innovation, and changes in governance and the way in which politics and government interacted with the economy - in short, to every aspect of the modern economy.... Starting after World War II... the countries in the developing world started to grow.... That was the start of a century-long journey in the global economy.... One could call the second revolution the Inclusiveness Revolution.'"

At that point, another gentleman arrived at the table and handed copies of a new book to both of my lunch companions. He then said in French, "Daniel and Michael, the two of you must come to my afternoon lecture in La Grande Arch. And please read the beginning of the introduction to my new book, *Capital in the Twenty-First Century* (2014), beforehand." And with that, he hurriedly walked off towards the conference rooms.

"That, Sam, was the acclaimed Thomas Piketty, Professor at the Paris School of Economics," Daniel informed me. "Shall we take his advice and read the first part of his universally well-received work: 'The distribution of wealth is one of today's most widely discussed and controversial issues. But what do we really know about its evolution over the long term?... What do we really know about how wealth and income have evolved since the eighteenth century, and what lessons can we derive from that knowledge for the century now under way?'"

La Grande Arch

With lunch over, Daniel and Michael left to attend Thomas' lecture, while I was left to now investigate La Grande Arch. And after meandering about this most impressive architectural wonder, taking in the exhibition galleries and peeking into the conference centers, I found myself atop the arch enjoying the superb views of Paris. From there, the panorama is of the Arc de Triomphe overlooking the Right Bank, the Eiffel Tower overlooking the Left Bank, and Sacré-Coeur overlooking all of Paris.

Now in dire need of a cool libation, I was just about ready to call it a day when I came upon a group of American investigators having an interesting discussion. Of course, being a nosy private investigator, I listened in to their conversation. And over the course of their talk, I managed to find out the names of the persons in the group: Alvin Toffler, the author of *Future Shock* (1970), and Paul and Anne Ehrlich, who co-wrote *One with Nineveh: Politics, Consumption, and the Human Future* (2004).

Alvin began first, "I agree with the two of you that the changes occurring in the modern world are inevitable, as I pointed out in my book. 'I coined the term *future shock* to describe the shattering stress and disorientation that we induce in individuals by subjecting them to too much change in too short a time.... This psycho-biological condition can be described in medical and psychiatric terms. It is the disease of change.... I gradually came to be appalled by how little is actually known about adaptivity, either by those who call for and create vast changes in our society, or by those who supposedly prepare us to cope with those changes.... But we know virtually nothing about how to do it.'"

"I could not agree with you more, Alvin," Paul replied. "The rate of change within modern societies is forcing nothing short of a revolution on how humans adapt themselves to the world. And as you know from our book, the rate of change is not only going to continue increasing in the future, but the directions of those changes are also going to have an ever-increasing effect on the future of the human race. 'In the world in general and the United States in particular, very few political leaders or members of the general public have been discussing the implications of continued growth of the global population, which is expected to be almost 40 percent larger by 2050, or expansion of current consumption patterns which threaten to outstrip Earth's resources in coming decades. There is also little recognition that increases in population and consumption underlie a plethora of today's most serious problems, from air and water pollution and land degradation to declining fishery yields, increasing risks of epidemics and famines, and climate change.'"

"If I might add, gentlemen," Anne interjected, "the *World Scientists' Warning to Humanity* (1992) is quite explicit about what will be required to steer and brake wisely in order to avoid the collision and achieve the happier result. 'Five inextricably linked areas must be addressed simultaneously: we must bring environmentally damaging activities under control; we must manage resources crucial to human welfare more effectively; we must stabilize population; we must reduce and eventually eliminate poverty; [and] we must ensure sexual equality.'"

Parc de la Villette

The next morning I took the Metro out to Parc de la Villette, a massive urban greenbelt measuring 136 acres. Building began on it in 1984 with the intention of making it a site for meetings and activities that might foster interests in the arts and sciences, though today it also hosts concerts, films and exhibitions. To accommodate all these urban activities, it is home to the La Cité de la Musique, the Zénith Theatre and La Géode, and the Grande Halle. In addition, the park offers the Children's Playground and The Follies, which are red cubes sitting throughout the grounds that provide day-care centers, cafés and children's workshops.

After exploring the grounds of the park, leaving the science museum to the afternoon, and while enjoying lunch in a café, I spent some time reading the English language *International Herald Tribune*. While doing so, I came upon an interesting article about a recent attempt in Louisiana to teach the Biblical story of creation in public school science classrooms. And according to the article, this wasn't the first time that an American state government has promoted the teaching of Creationism in the schools, the first incident being in 1925 with the passing of the Tennessee Evolution Statute, known as the Butler Act.

After the passing of this statute, a Dayton high school science teacher, John Scopes, who'd been recruited by the American Civil Liberties Union and some community citizens, was arrested and charged with teaching the Science of Evolution to his students. And with that, the "Scopes Monkey Trial" became the most famous American trial of the first half of the twentieth century, as well as a battle between religious tradition and scientific progress.

After the arrest, *The Baltimore Evening Sun* sent its most famous journalist, Henry Louis Mencken, to report on the proceedings of the trial. The paper also paid for Clarence Darrow, the most prominent defense lawyer in America, to lead Scopes' defense. He would do legal battle against the head of the prosecution, William Jennings Bryan, a three-time presidential Democratic nominee and a renowned Biblical scholar.

Unfortunately for the defense, once the trial began the court would not allow Darrow to call upon any of his authorities in the Science of Evolution, and so for some time the case appeared to be an easy win for Bryan and the prosecution. However, at some point the defense came upon the clever idea of putting Bryan on the stand to be questioned by Darrow about the stories in the Bible.

Darrow then cross-examined Bryan about Jonah being swallowed by the big fish and living inside it for three days, about Joshua commanding the sun to stand still in order to lengthen the day, and about the earth being only around six thousand years old. He also cross-examined Bryan on whether or not it took only six days to create the world, on whether or not Eve was made from Adam's rib, and on whether or not Cain's wife was really his sister.

While Darrow fought Bryan in the court room, Mencken fought pre-scientific ignorance in a series of newspaper articles, one of which was titled "Homo Neanderthalensis," contained in the book *A Religious Orgy in Tennessee: A Reporter's Account of the Scopes Monkey Trial* (1925): "Such obscenities as the trial of the Tennessee evolutionist, if they serve no other purpose, at least call attention dramatically to the fact that enlightenment, among mankind, is very narrowly dispersed.... the great masses of men... are precisely where the mob was at the dawn of history. They are ignorant, they are dishonest, they are cowardly, they are ignoble. They know little if anything that is worth knowing, and there is not the slightest sign of a natural desire among them to increase their knowledge."

After eight days of trial, the jury deliberated only nine minutes, finding Scopes guilty and ordering him to pay a $100 fine. The defense team appealed the decision to the Supreme Court of Tennessee, where, after many arguments, the Attorney General decided not to retry Scopes. And as to Darrow, he offered his philosophical and religious opinions in the essay "Why I Am an Agnostic" (1929): "The reasons for agnosticism and skepticism are abundant and compelling.... Skepticism and doubt lead to study and investigation, and investigation is the beginning of wisdom."

While on my way to Cité de Sciences, I asked myself why it was that the extremists of the American Religious Right are so hell-bent on introducing myths into the teaching of the sciences. For needless to say, those citizens have been, along with everyone else, the beneficiaries of modern scientific applications. And why is it that of the Western nations, only in America is it acceptable to allow the species *Homo Neanderthalensis* to have any influence whatsoever concerning the make-up of the science curriculum? But as it turned out, by the late afternoon I came to realize that it wasn't only the Right, but also certain entities on the American Left that attempt to influence what's taught as science to the public school children and university students of America.

Cité de Sciences

During the afternoon I visited the Cité de Sciences, the immense science and technology museum located in Parc de la Villette. The building rises to 133 feet and it stretches over seven acres, with water surrounding the structure and light flowing in from the huge cupolas above. The Explora exhibits occupy the first two levels, which present displays of scientific and technological applications. The other three levels offer cinemas, a planetarium, conference centers, the children's science center, libraries and shops.

After my day of scientific investigation, I boarded the Metro heading back to Paris and immediately made my way to the club car for a glass of white wine. Once situated at a quiet table, a gentleman walked in and asked if he might join me. Soon seated with a drink, he introduced himself to me, "The name is Alan Sokal, and I assume you've been exploring the science museum today."

I nodded yes and then said, "My name's Sam and I'm a private investigator from San Francisco."

"Excellent, Sam," Alan replied, "and as it turns out we are in somewhat the same business, the search for truth, though in my case, scientific truth. My fields of study are mathematics and physics, with my research conducted at University College London and New York University. Of course, an academic such as me generally lives a somewhat undisturbed life, going about my studies in the peace and quiet of the university.

"However, in 1994 I read a book, *Higher Superstition: The Academic Left and Its Quarrels with Science*, written by the biologist Paul R. Gross and the mathematician Norman Jay Levitt. That book brought to my attention what was occurring in the social sciences and humanities departments at some of our major American universities as regards the view that science is not the search for objective truth, but is instead the cultural construction of subjective truth. After finishing the book, and in response to it, I planned a little hoax, one, if I may, tell you about now. '[I] decided to try an unorthodox... experiment: submit to a fashionable American cultural-studies journal, *Social Text*, a parody of the type of work that has proliferated in recent years, to see whether they would publish it. The article... is chock-full of absurdities and blatant non-sequiturs.'

"Once the media attention died down, I approached my friend Jean Bricmont, the theoretical physicist and philosopher of science at the Université catholique de Louvain in Belgium, about writing a book titled *Fashionable Nonsense: Postmodern Intellectuals' Abuse of Science* (1998). 'The goal of this book is to make a limited but original contribution toward the critique of the admittedly nebulous Zeitgeist that we have called *postmodernism*.... our aim is to draw attention to a relatively little-known aspect, namely the repeated abuse of concepts and terminology coming from mathematics and physics.'"

Just then, another gentleman approached Alan and said, "I hope you're not filling this man's head up with your misguided notions on postmodernist thought." Then looking at me, he continued, "But excuse me, sir, my name is François Cusset. I am a writer and historian at the University of Nanterre, one of the thirteen successor universities of the University of Paris. And a few years back I wrote a book, *French Theory: How Foucault, Derrida, Deleuze, & Co. Transformed the Intellectual Life of the United States* (2003), that tried to explain how much of what was critiqued by Alan, Jean and many others was due to a misinterpretation of French theory.

Allow me to explain what occurred in America, and I'll begin in the Seventies. 'During the last three decades of the twentieth century in the United States, the names of a few French thinkers took on an aura that up to then had been reserved only for the heroes of American mythology or the celebrities of show business.... Their names, while hardly those of any screen idols, became no less intensely over-coded as they were gradually Americanized and their French accents faded; and these names became inevitable reference points across the Atlantic, whereas in their country of origin the scope of this phenomenon was never truly appreciated.'"

With those words still lingering in the air, the Metro arrived in Paris and the three of us went our separate ways. And as I walked along the crowded streets of the city, I became aware of the difficulties in translating texts from one cultural context into a vastly different one, namely, from French into American English. However, I did take satisfaction in the fact that discussions between scientists and sociologists, and between modernists and postmodernists, enable both groups to better understand and critique the others' point of view.

Disneyland Paris

On the train heading east the twenty miles to the Euro Disney Resort, I garnered a few pertinent facts concerning this vast holiday destination. The resort, which opened in 1992, spreads out over 1,500 acres, and it offers not only the theme park, but also hotels, campgrounds and sports facilities. The park itself measures 138 acres and is similar to the ones in America, though with two all-important exceptions. Due to lack of attendance, the park almost closed shortly after its opening. Fortunately, management quickly realized that two necessary French ingredients were missing, those being beer and wine. Needless to say, once they were available the park enjoyed a steady stream of visitors, French and otherwise.

My first stop in Disneyland was Main Street, USA, a wonderful reminder of how really boring life once was and still is in small-town America. Of course, the spotlessly clean Victorian-style building fronts are slightly at odds with historical facts, for in reality, the burning of coal in turn of the century America would have left those spic and span fronts forever tarnished with thick black soot. And the horse-drawn carts that meander up and down *this* Main Street would, in the old days, have left mounds of manure on the road just waiting to be tracked home on one's shoes.

Along with other attractions, the street offers a traditional barber shop, replete with the annoying reverberations of a barber shop quartet. Just imagine an America that once took such great pleasure in this sort of hokum, when in the "darker" sections of town could be enjoyed the melodic strains of early jazz. And even if one doesn't drop by for a cut or a shave, those irritating barbers show up once again for the nightly Electrical Parade, which also offers the usual plethora of ghastly looking illuminated floats, hopelessly out-of-step performers and imbecilic Disney characters.

Having had enough of that over-whelming display, I made my way to the first Disney bar I could find for a couple dozen glasses of wine. Once seated at a table, as usual a gentleman walked up and asked, "Mind if I join you? The name's Roland Barthes and I can see that you're having difficulty juxtaposing the myth of Main Street, USA with the reality of the main streets of America. You're wondering where are all the forgotten homeless, the dilapidated gin joints, the houses of easy pleasure, the corrupt city officials, and the victimized workers. And where are the Bible-waving clergy denouncing evolution and women's rights, the gun-toting rednecks yelping about second amendment rights, and the conservative heralds forever pontificating over traditional values.

"Well, let me offer you a few thoughts from my book *Mythologies* (1957): 'What is a myth, today? I shall give at the outset a first, very simple answer, which is perfectly consistent with etymology: "myth is a type of speech."... Of course, it is not any type: language needs special conditions in order to become myth... But what must be firmly established at the start is that myth is a system of communication, that it is a message.... it is a mode of signification, a form.'

"For example, take the gin martini, where the signified is the combination of gin and a variable amount of vermouth. On the other hand, the signifier is the coupling of the martini glass with possibly an olive. The signified and the signifier then combine to create the sign, which is the actual martini. Returning to a description of 'myth, we find again the tri-dimensional pattern which I have just described: the signifier, the signified and the sign. But myth is a peculiar system, in that it is constructed from a semiological chain which existed before it: it is a second-order semiological system.'

"Using the previous example once again, in the second-order semiological system the first-order sign, namely, the actual martini, becomes the Signifier in the second. The Signified in the second-order system might be an elegantly-attired woman or perhaps a tuxedo-clad James Bond. Either way, in this case the Sign in the second-order semiological system is the myth of say, 'sophistication'. With these ideas concerning myth in mind, I'll leave you to further investigate the many myths associated with Disneyland. But as you do so, remember that although many Americans believe Walt Disney was an incurable optimist, the truth of the matter is that he was merely an incurable mythologist."

Disney Lands

Disneyland Paris is so huge that, even after allowing for travel time, it takes at least two days to properly investigate all the myths that the theme park has to offer a philosophical investigator. My exploration for the second day began in Frontierland, where visitors discover, among other things, that there never was such a thing as Indians living in America, that myth having been invented by liberal Hollywood filmmakers. My only complaint about this particular Disney land was that it could have also included an entertaining myth about the Southern slavery system, one in which contented colored folks sing Motown numbers, though with references to the musical *Porgy and Bess*: "I've got my Bess on a cloudy day."

The next land I investigated was Adventureland, though here too there was a disturbing lack of creativity as regards certain aspects of adventure. Now *Peter Pan* and *Treasure Island* are both acceptable themes, but how about something a little edgier. How about a hands-on approach to the learning of history, with kids experiencing the adventures of rural America by throwing science books into a huge fire and singing the song, "Cast Thee Evolutionists into Hell's Inferno."

On the other hand, Discoveryland needs some much-needed improvement. First, eliminate most of the future as a "bed of roses" exhibits that are currently on display. Instead, visitors could experience the real world of the future: communities destroyed by the horrifying effects of unchecked climate change, urban cities and public schools devastated by continued civic neglect, and family finances ransacked by unaffordable university and healthcare expenses.

Lastly, I investigated Fantasyland, where the impressionable minds of children are filled with such quaint notions as that it's better to be born a princess in life than to work hard and be elected a President. However, I did come away from this particular Disney land asking myself why all the other lands weren't also considered fantasy. So finally having had enough of all the Mythlands, I tracked down the nearest bar and settled into another couple dozen glasses of wine.

Once seated at a table, Jean Baudrillard, who I met atop Printemps a few days before, walked up and said, "Welcome to 'the desert of the real itself'. We meet again, so mind if I join you? I can see that you're having difficulty understanding the overwhelming *Simulacra and Simulation* (1981) that permeates this cultural extension of America."

"But what do you mean by 'simulacra' and 'simulation'?" I asked out of ignorance.

Jean responded to my question, "'Simulacra' - 'simulacrum' in the singular - are copies of things that either never had a reality or that no longer have an original reality. For example, Peter Pan, a boy that can fly, never existed in reality. On the other hand, although pirates existed in the past, the one called Captain Hook is a pirate that exists only as a copy. And as regards 'simulation', that is the imitation of a real-world process or system over time. Thus, the story of *Peter Pan* is a simulation of real pirate events that took place centuries in the past, such as the ransacking of ships.

"Furthermore, the image evolves through stages: 'it is the reflection of a profound reality; it masks and denatures a profound reality; it masks the absence of a profound reality; [and] it has no relation to any reality whatsoever: it is its own pure simulacrum.... Disneyland is a perfect model of all the entangled orders of simulacra.... Thus, everywhere in Disneyland the objective profile of America, down to the morphology of individuals and of the crowd, is drawn. All its values are exalted by the miniature and the comic strip. Embalmed and pacified. Whence the possibility of an ideological analysis of Disneyland:... digest of the American way of life, panegyric of American values, idealized transposition of a contradictory reality... a hyperreal civilization.

"Excuse me," I asked again out of ignorance, "but what is it that you mean by 'hyperreal'?"

"'Hyperreality' is a description of a person's inability to distinguish the real from a simulation of the real," Jean said in answer to my question. "This inability is especially prevalent in postmodern societies due to the advanced state of information technology used in the media, which can radically alter, shape and filter a real experience.

Hyperreality blends the real and the simulation together until there no longer exists a clear distinction between the two. Needless to say, the United States is the epicenter of the hyperreal world, and it's a subject that I reflected upon in my travel book *America*: 'America is neither dream nor reality. It is hyperreality. It is a hyperreality because it is a utopia which has behaved from the very beginning as though it were already achieved. Everything here is real and pragmatic, and yet it is all the stuff of dreams too.... America is the original version of postmodernity.

With that, Jean bid me adieu. And after finishing my wine, I left the bar to catch the train back to Paris. Once back in the city, I stepped off the train and into the nineteenth century. It felt strange to once again be in the Modern world, as opposed to some postmodern simulation of it. And it also felt strange to once again be in the real world, as opposed to some hyperreal version of it. But there you are, welcome to "the desert of the real itself."

Parisian Solitude

When the hustle and bustle of modern or postmodern investigation finally comes home to roost, Paris offers a multitude of places that tender a little solitude for the pleasure and relaxation of the philosophical investigator. And while enjoying a few of those places, it dawned on me that I might one day want to explain to my fellow Americans about the concepts called "Modernism" and "Postmodernism," as well as the differences between the two.

Bois de Boulogne

Sitting to the west of the city between two stretches of the Seine, the 2,100 acres of the Bois de Boulogne is arrived at by taking the Metro to Porte Maillot, Porte Dauphine or Port d'Auteuil station. The park offers villas and gardens, nature trails and sports paths, and areas for picnicking and enjoying a glass of white wine on a warm Parisian day. And once ensconced in an ideal location for that glass of wine, I came upon the idea of first telling Americans about what Lawrence Cahoone wrote in *From Modernism to Postmodernism: An Anthology* (1996): "At a minimum, postmodernism regards certain important principles, methods, or ideas characteristic of modern Western culture as obsolete or illegitimate. In this sense, postmodernism is the latest wave in the critique of the Enlightenment, the critique of the cultural principles of characteristic of modern society that trace their legacy to the eighteenth century, a critique that has been going on since that time. Modernity has been criticizing itself all its life."

With Cahoone's ideas in mind, I thought that perhaps I might also tell Americans about what Robert Wicks wrote in *Modern French Philosophy: From Existentialism to Postmodernism* (2003): "Much of twentieth century French philosophy can be understood as a quest for freedom, stimulated by the problem of understanding one's place in the world as both an individual and as a social being. This quest was peculiar, though, because it was formulated against a confusing background, namely, an array of scientific and technological developments that appeared inconsistently to be both supportive and threatening to human well-being."

Although I realized that in America I'd have to keep my ideas on a fairly basic level, there was still much that might get in the way of any philosophical discussion with Americans. For in that self-absorbed nation of today, it's rather frowned upon to take an interest in any matter that doesn't have to do with either securing one's own financial future or satisfying one's own narcissistic passions. For after completing university, where most students spend four years studying from uninspired and uninspiring textbooks, graduates quickly realize that they have absolutely no intellectual interests whatsoever, despite the fact that such a vast amount of time and money was spent on their education.

Now as regards philosophy, when the eternal questions arise in everyday life, almost every American, even the supposedly well-educated, usually turn to the Holy Bible. Of course that seldom-opened book generally remains politely tucked away in a lower drawer of a bedroom dresser, except during times of crisis. Why, a relatively recent President - after being caught with his pants down - was even seen carrying that book around as a hypocritical act of self-serving contrition. Fortunately for the postmodern economy, that religious book seldom gets in the way of the average man's pursuit of all the material riches that are forever on offer in the postmodern world.

To further obstruct my plan to explain philosophical concepts to Americans, I'd have to take into account the great changes that have taken place in American education. Until the mid-Sixties, the modern university set as its goal the education of well-rounded citizens fit to maintain a democratic society. Unfortunately, the postmodern university has now replaced that former laudable institution, with the newer school an anemic entity that by and large merely seeks to indoctrinate students with the pecuniary canons of the business class.

Of course there are many reasons for this enormous shift in educational purpose, not the least of which is the debilitating lack of tax funds available to public universities. As a consequence, there is now far less financial assistance available to help students pay for dramatically increased levels of tuition. And since students know that they will leave school with huge educational debts, they tend to steer clear of majors that don't appear to them to contribute to their future financial viability in the marketplace.

It should be noted that the many problems within the postmodern university begin even before students enter its now not-so-hallowed halls. Using as its justification the catchphrase "diversity," the dons of the postmodern educational system demand that persons belonging to certain underrepresented groups be admitted whether or not those individuals are prepared to undertake higher studies. Sadly, pushing students into college work for which they are ill-prepared sets them up for failure, while also "dumbing down" what should be university-level courses. A far better course of action would be to have promising but poorly educated students attend a community college for two years, at taxpayer expense, and to then admit them to the university once they are academically prepared for higher education.

This postmodern or "multicultural" approach to admitting students is completely opposed to the traditional method, which was to select students according to their intellectual interests and educational abilities. It appears to be lost on the overlords of the postmodern system that one of the primary purposes of higher education is to show students the path to take in leaving their cultural heritage behind so as to become contributing *individuals* in a democratic society. Plato, the First Educator, well understood the importance of leaving the cave so as to see the world as it is, not as one's chance upbringing might have at first made it appear.

Needless to say, the many problems within the postmodern university continue even after students enter its now not-so-hallowed halls. For some time changes have been occurring in the social sciences and the humanities, where traditionally the doctrines of good citizenship and the need to read great books were impressed upon students, though admittedly often with very limited success. Beginning in the Seventies, the academics in those disciplines attempted to make their subjects more "relevant" to the lives of students. The resulting courses go under various rubrics: African American Studies, Latino Studies, Latina Studies, Women's Studies, Gay Studies, Lesbian Studies, Bisexual Studies, Transgender Studies, Intersexual Studies, and Autosexual Studies, to name but a few. This is an ill thought out educational agenda, for it leaves most students without the necessary knowledge to understand their duties and their responsibilities as thoughtful citizens in a democratic community.

As to whether or not the study of philosophy is alive and well within the postmodern university, sadly, it is not. For due to the educational changes mentioned, as well as for many other reasons of a political and social nature, most university students are never shown the road to travel down in the search for creating their own philosophical purpose within a democratic society. As a consequence, the most important reason for offering an education within the once hallowed halls of the modern university has been all but lost in the not-so-hallowed halls of the postmodern university.

Even more alarming, many academics in the social sciences and the humanities have now lost their own way on that all-important road. As of late, it has become fashionable for many academics, ones whose valuable time is paid for by both society and students, to spend that valuable time watching, analyzing and commenting upon American television shows and Hollywood movies. Admittedly, the shows and movies that garner their misplaced intellectual interest are, more often than not, the better ones on offer within those two very limited mediums, but that hardly justifies their so-called academic endeavors.

For example, collections such as *The Simpsons and Philosophy*, *Seinfeld and Philosophy* and *The Matrix and Philosophy* are more about the search for amusement than about the search for truth. The serious questions that modern academics once attempted to answer, often without success, are no longer even asked, for many postmodern academics are more concerned with entertainment than with enlightenment.

This is not to say that a veil of intellectuality isn't cast over the many entertaining articles to be found in those three books, as well as in another collection, *Buffy the Vampire Slayer and Philosophy.* In many of this particular book's articles the authors desperately attempt to concern themselves with real philosophical issues, such as the complex problems of science and knowledge. However, there must be more important issues facing our democratic society for academics to be concerned with than whether or not Buffy violently murders another disgruntled demon or indulges her libido within the arms of another vampire.

But in fact, the lack of any really serious issues to be dealt with in *BtVS* is at last posited in the final essay of that book. For in *Feeling for Buffy*, the writers Michael P. Levine and Steven Jay Schneider note firstly that "primarily, *BtVS* scholars are the ones who attempt to make the show out to be something else or something more." They then go on to say that "*BtVS* scholars are, in psychoanalytic parlance, repressing, projecting, and acting out their own fantasies in relation to the program." And finally, the two writers assert that "in attempting to bring scholarship or serious discussion to bear on *BtVS*, the scholars in question evince their own lack of understanding of, and insight into, the show, and perhaps more importantly, into the kinds of tasks, purposes, and methods that cultural theorists and others who engage with popular culture set for themselves and employ."

This is not to say that *BtVS* wasn't a thoroughly entertaining television show or that academics shouldn't write up their thoughts, though preferably not on the taxpayer's dime. Then again, why stop there? For admittedly, there's no end to the number of books possible in the "Whatever and Philosophy" genre:

Star Trek and Philosophy: From Modernism to Postmodernism
Starship Captains: From Two-fisted Womanizer to Limp-wristed Girly-man
The Enterprise: Engineering Aspects of the Postmodern Starship
The Prime Directive: From Oft-neglected Suggestion to Oft-neglected Paradigm

Mr. Spock versus Data: Opposing Modes of Cognitive Quasi-human Existence

Starship Women: From Agreeable Interstellar Sexpots to Moralizing New Age Feminists

Ozzie and Harriet and Philosophy: The Search for Existential Meaning in Suburban Life

Ozzie Nelson: Rebelling against the Protestant Ethic and the Spirit of Capitalism

Harriet Nelson: Homemaking and the Class Struggle from a Marxist Perspective

David Nelson: Dealing with Total Obscurity as an Organization Man

Ricky Nelson: Living and Dying as a Travelin' Man

Thorny Thornberry: The Cardigan Sweater and the End of Fashion

Leave it to Beaver and Philosophy: Growing Up Awkwardly in Suburban America

Beaver Cleaver: Acceptance and Rejection in the Worldview of the Child

Wally Cleaver: Adolescent Sexual Behavior from a Freudian Perspective

Ward Cleaver: Embracing the Protestant Ethic and the Spirit of Capitalism

June Cleaver: Fashion Consciousness from a Deconstructionist Viewpoint

Eddie Haskell: Just a Wise Ass, or, a Metaphor for the Moral Decline in Postindustrial Society

Once again, why stop there? For one could go on all day compiling a list of other possible publications for the "Whatever and Philosophy" series:

Mister Ed and Philosophy: An Exploration of Paranoia and Schizophrenia in Contemporary Suburban America

Gomer Pyle and Philosophy: The Pros and Cons of an All-Volunteer Army made up of Simple-minded Yahoos

Gilligan's Island and Philosophy: A Show about Nothing, no, Really, Absolutely Nothing

Friends and Philosophy: Excessive Self-indulgence and Dim-wittedness in Latte America

Sex and the City and Philosophy: Feminist Speculations about What Went Wrong in the Lives of Four Completely Boring and Sexually Promiscuous Women with Filthy Mouths and Minds

Lawrence Welk and Philosophy: Questions on Why the Only Brother on a Popular Musical Show was a Tap-dancer

Sesame Street and Philosophy: Speculations on How the PBS Routinely turns Rugged Little Boys into Lilly-livered Pansies

American Idol and Philosophy: The Transformation of Obscure Talentless Performers into Famous Talentless Performers

Sponge Bob Square Pants and Philosophy: Exactly What the Hell's Going on Here?

Television and Philosophy: Conjectures on Why the Boob-Tube is, in Theory, a Good Invention, and Why it is, in Practice, the Worst Technological Abomination ever Created in the History of the Human Race

Yes, there would be many obstacles in my goal to enlighten Americans about Modernism and Postmodernism, not the least of which was the question of who would want to listen to a private investigator in the first place. However, and before leaving the park, I did make one mental note, to remember to contact Alan Sokal and Jean Bricmont about writing a book titled *More Fashionable Nonsense: Postmodern Intellectuals' Abuse of Philosophy.*

Parc André Citroën

Named after the famed carmaker, Parc André Citroën sits along the Seine to the south of the Eiffel Tower and is arrived at by taking the Metro to Javel or Balard station. The park offers the urban investigator meadows, gardens, water sculptures, and glasshouses. And it also presents another lovely place to ponder over philosophical matters, in this case, the loss of the grand narrative in postmodern thought, in particular, the loss of the modern American western:

Though it is perhaps unknown to the general public, for many years now a fierce debate has occupied the valuable time of the most insightful academics within the School of Postmodern Studies at almost every major university in the world. And the question that these most learned men and women have been attempting to answer concerns Clint Eastwood's Spaghetti Westerns, which is a cinematic trilogy that consists of *A Fistful of Dollars*, *For a Few Dollars More* and *The Good, the Bad and the Ugly*. At issue is whether these legendary pieces in the history of film mark the end of the Modern Western or the beginning of the Postmodern Western, as many philosophers now propose.

After a careful review of the relevant literature on the subject, namely, after watching a lot of westerns, it appears that that trilogy is most definitely not modern, but postmodern in its scope and meaning. Of course to fully understand the differences between the modern and the postmodern cinematic genre as regards the western, it is necessary to first negotiate the intellectual chasm that divides those two historical, psychological and problematic film periods.

Without a doubt the most idiosyncratic hero in the period of the Modern Western was John Wayne, who showed the world the meaning of American virility in such films as *Stagecoach*, *Red River* and *Rio Bravo*, as well as in many more motion pictures in his *oeuvre*. Of course all of his manly and virile movies exhibit the major characteristics of this noble tradition: identifiable good guys, identifiable bad guys, and a beautiful and bountiful, though superfluous, female interest. However, the most important aspect concerning all of the Duke's manful characters are their unrelenting knowledge of good and evil, in other words, the guy in the white hat kills righteously while the guys in the black hats murder wrongly.

Before going on, it should be noted that many gay, lesbian, bisexual, transgender and transsexual writers in the field of Postmodern Sociology have often made mention of the fact that the Duke's birth name was Marion, which is quite an effeminate appellation. In addition, they have pointed out that in many of his films the Duke walks with a limp wrist while swaying his hips, thus introducing an element of gender confusion into the *élan* of the Modern Western. And though these disturbing insights are worthy of further research and possible discussion in postmodern journals, they should be treated as not being salient to the discussion at hand.

Though academics may disagree, the end of the Modern Western is clearly evidenced by three films, *The Big Country* (1958), *The Magnificent Seven* (1960) and *How the West was Won* (1963). Along with the three major elements that define this category of film, this trio of cinematic classics also introduced the concept of Manly Music into the subconscious of the modern male. Unfortunately, the use of a manful and virile film score has been all but lost in the Postmodern Western.

Turning now to the first of those three films, in *The Big Country*, Captain Jame McKay (Gregory Peck) is a wealthy and knowledgeable man of the sea who travels west to marry the well-chiseled, but self-centered, Pat Terrill (Carroll Baker). Unfortunately, Pat's no nonsense father, Major Henry Terrill (Charles Bickford), thinks McKay's manhood is questionable, and so he enjoys life once again when his foreman, Steve Leech (Charlton Heston), tries to pick a fight with the eastern dandy. And though he avoids manful combat at first, McKay ends up kicking the excrement out of Leech one night when the *femme fatale* is gusseying herself up to tease the men-folk. The final confrontation in the film has the Major and the rough-hewn Rufus Hannassey (Burl Ives) killing each other, with Hannassey's slack-jawed yokel sons left wondering if they should kill someone too. Lastly, the movie ends with McKay owning a sizeable chunk of the local real estate as a result of his capturing the heart of Julie Maragon (Jean Simmons), who's a prairie woman confronted by some nagging gender issues.

Most observers of the classic Modern Western agree that *The Magnificent Seven* collected together the manliest assemblage of manly men ever seen in a film, bar none, as well as the manliest film score ever brought to the screen, bar none. The movie begins in a poor Mexican village that's being raped, pillaged and plundered by the bandit leader, Calvera (Eli Wallach), after which some of the peasants head north of the border to find some manly men to help them with their pecuniary problems. They soon find Chris Adams (Yul Brynner) and Vin (Steve McQueen) manfully delivering a

hearse and a body to boothill, which is a not so popular
pastime given that the stiff is an Indian (Native-American?).
Later in the bar the peasants try to persuade Chris and
Vin to travel south and help them kill the forty miscreants
terrorizing their village, though they offer only room and
board in payment. But given the recent downturn in the local
bloodshed industry, the two hombres reluctantly agree to the
proposition, though only after bargaining for access to some
of the village's lithesome peasant-girls in which to deposit
their magnificent seed.

Although Chris and Vin are fairly certain that they could
handle the problem themselves, the title of the film indicates
to them that they need five more magnificent hombres to
manage the job. The first magnificent manly man they elicit
for their manful adventure is Britt (James Coburn), who can
outdraw any gunman with his knife and shoot a bandito from
seventeen miles away. They then find Bernardo O'Reilly
(Charles Bronson) chopping wood outside some cabin, and
persuade him that the profession of killing bandits is a lot
more manful than his present occupation. Lastly, Chris and
Vin take on Harry Luck (Brad Dexter), who's a likeable but
somewhat moronic character, and Lee (Robert Vaughn),
who's the only magnificent manly man in the film exhibiting
gay tendencies, not that there's anything wrong with that.

The next day the magnificent six travel south to Mexico, and
along the way they add to the title of the movie a seventh
gun, Chico (Horst Buchholz), whose only manful quality
is that he can catch a lot of trout for dinner, not that there's
anything wrong with that. Once at the village, the magnificent
seven quickly realize that, as should have been expected,
the peasants are all too timid, meek and useless to help kill
anyone, and that there are no lithesome peasant-girls in which
to deposit their magnificent seed. Nevertheless, they beat

Calvera in the first confrontation, though unfortunately he comes back to best them in the second encounter, after which he tells them to hightail it north. Of course the magnificent seven are all too manly to be told where to go and what to do, so in the third and final battle the bandit leader and most of his gang are killed, along with four of the magnificent manly men. This manliest of all westerns ends with Chico deciding to stay with the only lithesome peasant-girl in the village, and with Chris and Vin riding manfully off into the sunset to the strains of *The Magnificent Seven* theme.

The film that marks the cinematic finale in the genre of the Modern Western is *How the West was Won*, which starred just about every manly man in Hollywood, including Lee J. Cobb, Henry Fonda, Gregory Peck, Jimmy Stewart, John Wayne and Richard Widmark, to name only a few. But though all of those manful men do their manful best to raft raging rivers, to clear pristine forests, to kill their fellow citizens, and to torment dumb brutes such as buffaloes and Indians, there are far too many meddlesome women in the film. Needless to say, this monumental error on the part of the film's scriptwriters is undoubtedly what caused the entrance of the Postmodern Western into the milieu of twentieth-century film.

By the mid-Sixties the Modern Western had lost much of its appeal for audiences, this due to the deleterious influence of li-ly-li-vered li-ber-als. As disturbing as it may seem, European filmmakers were the ones forced to fill the daily manliness demands of the postmodern male. Financed mainly by Italian companies, the movies in this new genre were dubbed Spaghetti Westerns, and it's clear today that they were the precursors of the Postmodern Western. And though most of the early attempts were meager fare for men in search of a genuine manly movie, *Savage Guns*, *The Treasure of Silver Lake* and *Gunfight at Red Sands* were the few rare exceptions.

However, those first films did evidence to audiences that the potential was there for a really manful western, if only the right manly man would show the way.

Needless to say, Clint Eastwood's stint as pretty boy Rowdy Yates on *Rawhide* gave American audiences little indication that a genuine manly man was emerging into manhood. And shockingly, it took an Italian, Sergio Leone, with a Japanese script, *Yojimbo*, to inform the world of his arrival to film. So with only two hundred thousand dollars, some leftover film stock, and a film score by Ennio Morricone, Leone produced the first truly Postmodern Western - *A Fistful of Dollars* (1964).

Nowadays, most philosophers agree that *A Fistful of Dollars* contains all the elements that differentiate the Postmodern Western from the Modern Western. Firstly, and most importantly, there are no good guys, only The Man with No Name, who's only slightly less evil than the rest. So unlike the traditional hero in the Modern Western, who only uses his gun to protect the good townsfolk, the postmodern gunslinger is more than willing to kill anyone who gets between him and his sole motivation in life, which is a fistful of dollars. And that slaughter is never accomplished in a sanitized - "I really don't want to kill you" - sort of way, but with a manful and sadistic self-indulgence that takes pleasure in causing men to lose vast quantities of life-sustaining blood, as well as any number of body parts.

At the beginning of *A Fistful of Dollars*, Clint rides manfully into town wearing a manly serape and chewing on a half-smoked cheroot. He then goes about the normal business of a bounty hunter, which is to collect as many "wanted dead or alive" bodies as possible. And when not killing four hapless guys at a time, just because they poke a little fun at his mule, the Man with No Name exhibits an incredibly manful demeanor. And he does this by showing absolutely no human emotions whatsoever, by saying few if any unnecessary words, and by looking completely detached from everyone and everything, in other words, by being existentially cool.

The Man with No Name's incredibly virile disposition to the world brings out a second element that differentiates the Postmodern Western from the Modern Western. Unlike his modern counterpart, the postmodern gunslinger doesn't put up with any guff from dames. For whereas the traditional western hero moons over a beautiful, bountiful and superfluous *femme* throughout a movie, and then ends up marrying her, the postmodern hero has no real interest in women at all. Of course every now and then he'll save one from lowlifes, though only to have his way with her. In addition, the postmodern heroine is no longer a good church-going woman or a saloon girl with a heart of gold. No, she's now a sexually rapacious whore whose only goal in life is to fill her brassiere with a fistful of dollars.

Lastly, the third element that distinguishes the postmodern genre from the modern is firmly established in the film score for *A Fistful of Dollars*. The manful and heroic symphony that once accompanied the modern gunslinger is no longer present, and instead, the music, if one can even call it that, now consists merely of a long series of discordant though manly noises. Of course the symphonic qualities of the film score improved as the Postmodern Western evolved, and it reached its apex in the third of Clint's Spaghetti Westerns.

In *For a Few Dollars More* (1965), a new anti-hero was introduced into the emerging tradition of the Postmodern Western. Colonel Douglas Mortimer (Lee Van Cleef) travels through life for the same manful reasons that Monco (Clint) does, except that he carries a lot more manly and exotic guns around with him. That artillery soon comes in pretty handy, for both Monco and the Colonel are after El Indio, who's a hopelessly psychotic bandit with a huge price on his head. By the end of the movie, El Indio is no longer a problem for law-abiding folks and Monco has a few dollars more.

The Good, the Bad and the Ugly (1966) once again teamed Clint as Blondie up with Lee as Angel Eyes, though this time Leone added Eli Wallach as Tuco, who's a rather dim-witted and pleasantly sadistic man. This last of Clint's Spaghetti Westerns is set in the Civil War, though fortunately for the viewer, the complexities of that brutal conflict are only a minor annoyance to Blondie, Angel Eyes and Tuco as they search for hidden money, all the while attempting to torture, maim or kill one another.

Unfortunately, with the emergence of postmodern man throughout North America and Europe during the Eighties, even the Postmodern Western went out of fashion, this due to a general lack of manliness in a new generation that chooses to spend its time in limp-wristed coffee houses rather than in two-fisted bars. And though attempts are sometimes made to resurrect the Western, the scarcity of any real manly men in Hollywood, unfortunately results in productions that rarely please men of a manful nature.

Parc Monceau

Located on the western Right Bank, the twenty-two acre Parc Monceau is arrived at by taking the Metro to Monceau station. The park offers an elegant assortment of aesthetically-pleasing marvels: the colonnade of the *naumachia* basin, the Renaissance arcade, the Pavillon de Chartres, and any number of pyramids. And while investigating one of those pyramids, I came upon another method of explaining to Americans the concepts of Modernism and Postmodernism - a talk that would go under the title "Architectural Aspects of the Postmodern Beeramid":

> Having a number of empty beer cans at my disposal, I proposed to pursue a neoteric approach in the construction of what most architects consider to be the highest form of architectural design, the building of a beeramid. I knew from the outset that if my approach was to be a visionary one, and one that might encompass the complex and contradictory nature of the postmodern world, I would have to strive to avoid the parochial path which most architects, including myself, have followed in the past. Hence, my purpose that afternoon was to transcend the present architectural milieu by creating a postmodern beeramid.
>
> Traditionally, most approaches to building a beeramid do so by incorporating a Euclidean construct centered on a three-dimensional space-time manifold. In other words, the conventional approach is for the architect to first place one beer can in front of him. Of course, ever since the time of the ancient Greeks there has been the stipulation that the can must be empty. Most modern and postmodern architects still defer to the wisdom of the Ancients in this matter, for admittedly there would hardly be any point in wasting good beer while building anything, including a beeramid.
>
> The next step in the established construction rubric is to place another beer can next to the first one on the ground level, and to then center a third can over the first two, thus forming a two-story beeramid. At first, one might imagine that this hierarchical triumvirate is the most elementary beeramid possible. But if one ponders on the matter after quite a few beers, then it is immediately clear that the first beer can actually encompasses all of the teleological characteristics

of a beeramid. However, since those properties involve some rather advanced mathematical concepts from the physics of quantum singularities, I will not expound upon those features here, but will instead direct the interested architect to the graduate text, *Cosmology and Beerosophy: An Elementary Introduction.*

Now arises an important question, for if one beer can constitutes a beeramid, then every time an empty can of beer is set down, a construction of a beeramid has been actualized, at least within the local observational viewpoint of the architect. Of course, another question immediately arises as to whether the unitary-beeramid can be so designated without the architect's immediate cognitive acknowledgement that he is indeed building a beeramid. I will leave an analysis of this controversial proposition for another time, except to say that many writers in the burgeoning field of Beeramidology view the solution of this problem to be fundamental to any comprehensive understanding of the postmodern beeramid.

The established process of building a beeramid proceeds by placing another beer can on the ground level, and by then recursively adding a can to each higher level, the result being a beeramid that is one story higher than the previous beeramid. However, there are two important points that should be mentioned at this juncture. Firstly, the recursive building of a beeramid in this fashion is independent of the direction in the flow of time. In fact, an architect can recursively remove beer cans to form smaller beeramids, though many modern architects view this approach as reactionary and antithetical. For an insightful rebuttal to this somewhat antiquated view, it is recommended that the interested architect review the article, "Deconstructing the Modern Beeramid," which was originally published in the January 2010 edition of *Beerosophy Today.*

The second point to be mentioned regarding the traditional building process concerns a well-known proposition, *The Beeramid Theorem*, which states: "The number of beer cans needed to create a beeramid of height n is equal to n(n+1)/2." Given that a thorough understanding of the proof of this assertion is required of even the least experienced of postmodern architects, I will offer that exercise in mathematical induction here.

Applying the formula, a beeramid of height $n = 1$ should require

$$1(1 + 1)/2 = 1(2)/2 = 2/2 = 1$$

beer can, which is clearly the case, despite the rather troubling beerosophical notions alluded to earlier in this discussion. So if we assume that the proposition is true for a beeramid of height n, then a beeramid of height $n+1$ will require

$$
\begin{aligned}
&(1 + 2 + 3 + \ldots + n) + (n + 1) \\
=\ & n(n + 1)/2 + (n + 1) \\
=\ & n(n + 1)/2 + 2(n + 1)/2 \\
=\ & (n^2 + n)/2 + (2n + 2)/2 \\
=\ & ((n^2 + n) + (2n + 2))/2 \\
=\ & (n^2 + n + 2n + 2)/2 \\
=\ & (n^2 + 3n + 2)/2 \\
=\ & (n + 1)(n + 2)/2
\end{aligned}
$$

beer cans, and the proof is complete. And for the information of the so-inclined postmodern architect, many more interesting results in beeramatics can be found in the undergraduate text, *Elements of Mathematical Beerosophy*.

After dispensing with the conventional notion of a beeramid on that afternoon, I next considered building a four-dimensional hyper-beeramid. Most approaches encompassing this architectural model begin by placing three beer cans next to each other in a triangular formation on the ground level, after which a single beer can is then placed symmetrically on top of the other three. Of course the same teleological problem concerning the unitary-beeramid also arises in this case, but as before it is best to leave that discussion out of the context of the present polemic. And though I eventually chose not to build a beeramid of this genus, it should be noted that the number of beer cans necessary to create a hyper-beeramid of height n is still an unsolved problem in Mathematical Beerosophy. However, most beeramaticians believe that its solution may be closely related to Godel's Incomplete Beeramid Theorem.

At this point in my architectural quest I realized that I had emptied all the beer out of all the cans in my refrigerator, and that there appeared to be far too few empties for a revisionist approach in postmodern architecture. So I made my way down to the local shop to pick up a couple more six packs, though unfortunately, on the way there I inadvertently began pondering on the ramifications of the "Brewer's Paradox." This famed conundrum states: "If in a town a brewer brews the brew for anyone who does not brew his own brew, then who brews the brewer's brew?" This paradox should of course not be confused with "Brewer's Droop," which is a physiological abnormality that afflicts most, if not all builders of beeramids, at least at one time or another.

Once at the grog shop my mind was in such a confused state concerning that enigmatic circle of logic that I accidentally picked up a couple six packs of bottles, thus necessitating a return to the store a few hours later for six packs of cans. Of course by the time I left the store for the second time it was quite close to Happy Hour, so for all intensive purposes my efforts at a bold architectural beeramid design ended that day. But on a positive note, the next day I found myself with plenty of building supplies for continuing my construction of a postmodern beeramid.

Consequently, the following afternoon I once again turned my attention to the enterprise at hand by decisively placing one beer can in front of me. But my mind was still filled with doubts, at least until I pondered on the important thoughts of Charles Jencks in his groundbreaking book, *The Language of Post-Modern Architecture* (1984). In that work he states: "The main motive for postmodern architecture is obviously the social failure of modern architecture." Needless to say, this statement had such a profound impact on me that I actually halted work on my present beeramid to replenish building supplies in anticipation of a much more audacious effort in construction.

Before beginning once again, I also gave thought to the words of Robert Venturi in his work, *Complexity and Contradiction in Architecture* (1966): "Architects can no longer be intimidated by the puritanically moral language of orthodox modern architecture. An architecture of complexity and contradiction has a special obligation toward the whole. Its truth must be in its totality or its implications of totality. It must embody the difficult unity of inclusion rather than the easy unity of exclusion. More is less."

"More is less." What could that possibly mean? Was it a Zen koan imbedded within a Western narrative? And what ramifications did that bold linguistic statement have for my architectural efforts in the building of a postmodern beeramid? Fortunately, though only after cracking open more building supplies, its meaning came to me in a moment of sudden enlightenment. More "empty" beer cans must mean that there are less "full" beer cans. Of course, there was no other explanation. So with trust in the future and confidence in my abilities as a postmodern architect, I resolutely deconstructed the beeramid that I had previously begun and then placed one beer can in front of me.

My intention was to now begin my paradigm shift in architectural design within the context of a modern theme, and to then contrast that with a postmodern theme superimposed above it, thus expressing the on-going battle between the old and the new, and between the antiquated and the progressive. Needless to say, I can only justify these efforts by reference once again to Venturi: "Meaning can be enhanced by breaking the order; the exception points up the rule." A beeramid "with no imperfect part can have no perfect part, because contrast supports meaning. An artful discord gives vitality to architecture."

So after placing another beer can on the ground level next to the first, I placed a third can on the second level, though this time in the prone position rather than in the conventional upright. This effort had two extremely important results, and both were postmodern and progressive in nature. The first result was that I had abrogated the concept of symmetry from my creation, with disorder and chaos now entering into my architectural design. Although my beeramid was still controlled by the transcendental efforts of myself as the architect, the design also alluded to the essential complex and contradictory nature of the postmodern world.

However, the second result may have been the more profound of the two consequences. For some time now, postmodern feminist writers have viewed the creation of the traditional beeramid as evidence of the hierarchical patriarchy that governs the postmodern world. This is probably so, especially given that the beer can is seen by those insightful commentators as merely an extension of the male's enslavement organ. I will not go into a lengthy justification of this important feminist theme here, except to say that since most males seem to always have a beer in their hand, the observation is undoubtedly a most accurate one.

Although I am somewhat hesitant about mentioning it, at least within the context of the current discussion, there is one other possible interpretation of the second result. Looking at the beeramid holistically, the beer can in the prone position is alluding to an aspect of the universe that stands in opposition to the whole. In more concrete and understandable terms, the third can identifies a local topological anomaly. Of course, and as should be readily apparent from this discussion, I am referring here to the plight of the world's indigenous peoples, whose eventual extinction at the hands of evil global corporations is only a matter of time.

Unfortunately, my effort that day had to end with the placing of the third beer can, after which I sat back to enjoy another beer before heading off to Happy Hour. And while taking great pleasure in the "gestalt" of my daring architectural effort, I took to heart Venturi one last time: "And it is perhaps from the everyday landscape, vulgar and disdained, that we can draw the complex and contradictory order that is valid and vital for our architecture."

Canal St-Martin and Parc des Buttes-Chaumont

A most rewarding Parisian walk for any philosophical investigator is the three-mile Canal St-Martin, with the northern starting point arrived at by taking the Metro to Jaurès station. The canal begins at Place de Stalingrad, widens at Bassin de la Villette, the largest artificial lake in Paris, and finally ends at Port de l'Arsenal along the Seine. And while enjoying that stroll, I once again asked myself whether Americans would ever want to listen to a private investigator rant on about Modernism and Postmodernism, especially given my apparent lack of expertise in philosophical matters. However, and as it turns out, *this* investigator is well-versed in the subject of philosophy, at least as regards one particular item of clothing:

> Most experienced barflies will agree that it's quite common to exaggerate incidental details when meeting new folks, especially if in a new bar. Of course a good bar prevarication is seldom a problem, since half the time no one's listening, while the other half the message is completely garbled to the ear. So more often than not, the barfly can get away with stretching the truth while in a bar, at least that's what I thought until finding myself in a certain San Francisco watering hole. I'll tell the reader of this incident, but the bar and the individuals concerned must remain nameless so as to protect the innocent, of which I am definitely not one.

> I arrived late at No Name Bar, immediately garnering a cold one and mixing with the local clientele. A group of the bar's fine and respectable barflies, all members of a local literary club, soon invited me to join their crowd. Although I'm usually quite reserved about prevaricating, the beer must have gone to my head, for the biggest load of *equus crapuus* imaginable was soon spreading itself thick and heavy. And though I remembered little of that conversation the next morning, the fine and respectable barflies of the No Name Bar Literary Club possessed impeccable memories.

> My head was a bit sluggish the next morning, and sadly, a cold shower did nothing to alleviate the situation. But while drying off, I noticed sticking out of my pants pocket a note, one from the president of the No Name Bar Literary Club: "Dr. Sydney Goldstein, we are so pleased that you have agreed to speak at today's gathering of our bar's literary club. This is a great

honor for us, and we all look forward to hearing about your research into tropical dementia. And so that I might properly introduce you to other club members, please write down some of your many accomplishments."

Well, the proverbial was hitting the fan now. I first gave a momentary thought to slipping out of town for a day or two, but then decided my only option was to continue the big lie that I'd already begun, expanding upon it in new and creative directions. But what could I possibly talk about with any authority whatsoever? Reaching for an Aloha shirt, the words "tropical dementia" brought an answer to my dire situation. A plan had already begun to form, one that I believe is most impressive.

After lunch I made my way to the bar and was enthusiastically greeted by an assembly of the fine and respectable barflies of the No Name Bar Literary Club. One could see in their eyes the awe with which they held a visiting dignitary such as myself, and I soon felt a growing sense of purpose to my being there. Once everyone was seated, the president introduced me using the proper introduction that I'd written down over lunch:

"We are pleased to have with us today the world renowned authority on Pacific Island mental aberrations, Professor Sidney Goldstein, Director Emeritus of the Institute of Island Psycho-Biology in Hawaii. Dr. Goldstein is known for his seminal book on island beachwear, *The Aloha Shirt: Reality and Myth*, and for his highly controversial paper of last year, 'Don Ho: Animal, Vegetable or Mineral'. And now I'd like to welcome our guest for the day, Dr. Goldstein."

I greatly enjoyed the supportive round of applause from the club, and even found myself quite impressed by my own credentials. So after thanking the group for their invitation,

I began my lecture to the fine and respectable barflies of the No Name Bar Literary Club. And it must be admitted at the outset, that over the next hour I did indeed become Dr. Sidney Goldstein. But then again, and ain't it the truth, the most successful lie is always the one you half believe yourself.

"I'd like to speak today about a rapidly growing menace, 'Tropical Angst', or TA, which in some parts of Waikiki has reached epidemic proportions. Unfortunately, I see amongst you many with the early symptoms of TA. However, you are the fortunate ones, for this dreaded disease is easily dealt with early on. Only later, when sufferers take up reading books by the likes of Jacques Derrida and so end up deconstructing themselves, is there no known cure. The central tenet of my theory is that TA is best dealt with by selecting the most appropriate Aloha shirt to wear on a holiday. And with that in mind, my discussion today will deal with the importance of that apparel selection.

"The Aloha shirts of the 'Classic' period evolved from early attempts by native islanders to employ protective coloration in the hope of alluding Christian missionaries, a task quite difficult for even those of us living in the postmodern world. But as Europeans began populating the islands, there occurred a reverse cultural flow, with the now dominant group taking on the attire of the native peoples. Needless to say, that complex psycho-biological process culminated in floral images being emblazoned on almost any article of clothing.

"The next evolution in beachwear styles occurred in the early 1900's, this time within a group of Germano-Austrian settlers. Shirts created during this second era, or 'Transitional' period, are referred to in the literature as the 'Gestaltenshirten'. Unfortunately, the shirt's thesis, its more colorful side, could be turned inwards to evidence the shirt's antithetical side, one representing 'sturm und drang'. Since the 'Gestaltenshirten' couldn't be worn both ways at the same time, a synthesis of the two competing milieus was never possible. That rupture in the psychological triad caused the wearer, at least in layperson's terms, to go quietly mad.

"The wearing of those shirts brought about what are now considered to be the earliest documented cases of TA, first positively identified by the imminent psychiatrist Sigmund Freud during one of his many holidays to the islands. But due to the degenerative effects of the disease, he observed that all original members of the Germano-Austrian sect eventually went insane and jumped into volcanoes. This, he rightly hypothesized, was their natural desire to return to the womb.

"American influence in the islands increased dramatically during all of the twentieth century, and the popularity of the Aloha shirt ballooned during the Second World War, when the U.S. War Department determined it to be an effective aid in the relief of battle-induced dementia. Why, even Emperor Hirohito suggested in his memoirs that the Aloha shirt might have been the deciding factor in America winning the War in the Pacific.

"However, after the war the Aloha shirt remained in evolutionary stasis throughout the Fifties, Sixties and Seventies, with most shirts of the 'Neo Classic' period characterized by images of traditional island activities, such as ridiculing tourists and selling timeshares. Moving on, most authorities in the field of Psycho-Biology date the start of the 'Postmodern' period as being the early Eighties. That era saw not only the revival of the 'Classic' look, but also the creation of new styles to accommodate every conceivable consumer market.

"The 'New Age' look is characterized by images of crystals, star signs and Psychic Hotline numbers. The main drawback in wearing that style of beachwear is its expense, for individuals must purchase numerous shirts to accommodate the apparel needs of any of their past lives. I've predicted a renaissance in the 'New Age' shirt, especially as consumers enter the twenty-first century and continue their return to the Dark Ages.

"Interestingly, the 'Shroud of Hawaii' shirt was created by a group of born-again Christians living on one of the outer islands. Their leader, Boorish, claimed to have seen the image of Jesus on an Aloha shirt, an experience that convinced him to buy up an arsenal of weapons and have relations with ten-year olds of either sex. He eventually fled from FBI investigators, and now runs Personal Fulfillment Workshops in Beverly Hills.

"Not too surprisingly, Hawaii's high tech industry has generated a number of apparel styles. The 'Aloha 95' shirt arrived in Waikiki shops in 1996, but it was immediately a quick seller. Unfortunately, many suffers of TA were upset when they realized that the shirt didn't fit any better than 'Aloha 3.1', and that it required a new closet to hang it up in. And just last year, the 'DotCom' shirt arrived in Waikiki. But as it turned out, purchasers of that over-priced apparel found that after only a few months, the shirt came apart at the seams, making it no longer of any value to anyone.

"The highly competitive beachwear market has lately been embroiled in controversy, as evidenced by the recent publication of 'The G-Factor: An Analysis of Cognitive Intelligence and Island Beachwear'. The author of that paper makes the controversial claim that 'members of lower cognitive ability groups wear more Aloha shirts'. The audience will undoubtedly be pleased to hear that an international consortium of researchers will soon be analyzing the implications of his claims, with public moneys forever available in support of a much-needed discussion.

"That finishes what I have to say today, so are there any questions?... No, then I'd like to thank you all for being here, and I hope that my talk assures that your next stay in the tropics is a pleasant one. And I might add, soon to be available in a bookstore near you will be copies of my new book, *Jack Lord: Saint or Sinner*. Once again, thank you for inviting me here today."

I received a thunderous round of applause from the fine and respectable barflies of the No Name Bar Literary Club, and was assured by everyone there that my talk had been the best in recent memory. The club members and I then adjourned to the bar, where a pleasant time was had by all. To be on the safe side though, I made my way out of town for a few days early the next morning and decided that it might be best not to visit the No Name Bar ever again.

But about a week later, I noticed in the paper a most disturbing article concerning a strange occurrence in a San Francisco bar: "Government medical teams have been brought in to deal with an outbreak of dementia in the No Name Bar of San Francisco. Apparently, all the fine and respectable barflies, ones belonging to the same literary club, have taken up the wearing of brightly colored tropical shirts. Unfortunately, the cause of this malady is as yet unknown." Needless to say, after reading that I quickly packed away all my Aloha shirts, leaving them safely hidden in the confines of my closet until my next holiday to Waikiki.

After enjoying my morning stroll along the canal, I made my way to Parc des Buttes-Chaumont, which is arrived at by taking the

Metro to Botzaris or Buttes-Chaumont station. Sitting just east of the canal, this park perched on a hill offers a lake with footbridges to a rocky island and a Roman-style temple with a waterfall, streams and beaches. And while catching a few rays on the beach under a warm Parisian sun, I thought more about how to justify to myself why Americans might want to listen to a private investigator rant on about Modernism and Postmodernism.

As it turned out, the rather odd aftermath of that talk at the No Name Bar was that over time I became intensely interested in the concept of the Aloha shirt, in particular, the article "The G-Factor: An Analysis of Cognitive Intelligence and Island Beachwear." In fact, it fascinated me so much that I conducted a little research of my own at another local San Francisco bar, with my scientific investigation published in the article "The M-Factor: An Analysis of Manful Intelligence and Island Beachwear":

In the paper "The G-Factor: An Analysis of Cognitive Intelligence and Island Beachwear," the researcher made the controversial claim that "members of lower cognitive ability groups wear more Aloha shirts." And though that is indeed the case, the more important question is whether or not a causal relationship exists between those two variables, i.e., does wearing an Aloha shirt actually cause the wearer to experience a measurable loss in IQ level? To answer that penetrating question, I conducted a follow-up study on Aloha shirts, this time using thirty randomly selected subjects that I met one evening in a San Francisco bar.

To begin the study, I first measured each subject's IQ level using the psychometric testing tool known as the Stanford-Binet Intelligence Scale, after which, I measured each subject's MQ level using a self-devised Manlyness Quotient Test. Then, over the next month I had all the test-subjects record the number of days on which they donned an Aloha shirt. At the end of the month, I re-tested each subject as to his IQ level and MQ level, compiling for each one the number of Aloha shirt days, as well as any changes in the two levels.

Subject ID	Aloha Shirt Days	IQ Level Change	MQ Level Change
1	12	-15	44
2	21	-19	62
3	9	-13	39
4	17	-18	59
5	7	-9	29
6	9	-11	32
7	11	-14	43
8	12	-15	43
9	16	-17	51
10	17	-18	52
11	13	-15	45
12	15	-16	47
13	11	-14	42
14	21	-20	63
15	18	-19	61
16	9	-12	33
17	24	-21	63
18	9	-13	40
19	14	-16	46
20	5	-6	28
21	14	-16	46
22	16	-17	49
23	13	-16	46
24	15	-17	48
25	24	-21	67
26	15	-16	47
27	31	-25	74
28	9	-12	37
29	27	-22	70
30	15	-17	48

To begin the analysis, I calculated the "correlation coefficient" between each set of variables, though perhaps a short review of Sadistics 1 is in order here. Statisticians have arranged life so that a correlation coefficient always takes a value between -1 and +1, inclusive. As a consequence, a value close to +1 indicates a high "direct correlation" between the set of variables, meaning that a rise in one variable will see a rise in the other. On the other hand, a value close to -1 indicates a high "inverse correlation" between the set of variables, meaning that a rise in one variable will see a drop in the other. And to end this sadistic lesson, a value near 0 indicates that there is little correlation between the two sets of variables.

With all that horrendous nonsense in mind, the next step in my research was to create a correlation table for the three sets of data:

	Aloha Shirt Days	IQ Level Change	MQ Level Change
Aloha Shirt Days	1		
IQ Level Change	-0.966	1	
MQ Level Change	+0.972	-0.973	1

As expected, there was a strong negative correlation (-0.973) between IQ level change and MQ level change, thus confirming the popular opinion that thinking about things and being manly never quite works out. And also as expected, there was an equally strong negative correlation (-0.966) between the number of Aloha shirt days and IQ level change, thus confirming the results from the first paper on cognitive intelligence and island beachwear.

But what turned out to be of even greater interest to me was the strong positive correlation (+0.972) between the number of Aloha shirt days and the MQ level change, a fact that prompted me to study that particular relationship in much greater detail. To begin this part of the research, I conducted a statistical method commonly known as simple-minded linear regression, a process that determines a "best fit line," i.e., a prediction equation that relates the two variables in question. And after pushing just the right keys in Excel, I arrived at a prediction equation for Aloha Shirt Days (ASD) and MQ Level Change (MQLC):

$$MQLC = 19.38 + 1.95*ASD$$

Using the prediction equation, if the number of days that an individual wore an Aloha shirt during the previous month is known, then the expected MQ level change in that individual can be calculated with relative ease. For example, if a person wears an Aloha shirt every day in June, his expected MQ Level Change in that thirty-day month is the following increase in manliness:

$$MQLC = 19.38 + 1.95*30 = 77.87$$

Needless to say, my research offers anyone who's suffering from the symptoms of "Tropical Angst" a sure fire method of calculating just how many days he must spend on a tropical holiday so as to alleviate those symptoms and return to manful exuberance.

Bois de Vincennes

Located east of central Paris, Bois de Vincennes is arrived at by taking the Metro to Château de Vincennes, Porte de Charenton or Porte Dorée station. Once a royal hunting ground, the park offers a boating lake, a city zoo, the largest funfair in France, as well as gardens and a Buddhist center. And while enjoying a glass of white wine along the lake, I once again gave thought as to how best to explain Postmodernism. In particular, how to make the many inter-related philosophical concepts understandable to the American mind. I knew that I would have to keep things basic and to the point, as well as within a context that Americans might identify with in their own lives:

To understand Postmodernism one must first understand its roots in Structuralism, beginning with the linguist Ferdinand de Saussure and his most influential book *Course in General Aloha Linguistics*. In that seminal work he defined the nature of the "linguistic sign," which in the case of the Aloha shirt is composed of the "signifier," the material shirt itself, and the "signified," the concept the shirt is attempting to deliver to the world.

The monumentally-important anthropologist Claude Lévi-Strauss continued the discussion begun by Saussure in his two books, *Structural Anthropology and the Aloha Shirt* and *The Savage Aloha Mind*. His central aim was to discover whether there is a basic "human nature" across various cultures that wear Aloha shirts. For example, Aloha shirts in Hawaii portray basic island activities such as a tourist drinking a Mai Tai under a palm tree. On the other hand, in Australia the Aloha shirt may evidence a kangaroo drinking a beer under a eucalyptus tree. So the question arises, does an analysis of Aloha shirts across various cultures evidence that the patterns of thought in so-called "primitive" cultures show simpler patterns than those shown in the Aloha shirts of "civilized" cultures?

A common complaint concerning Lévi-Strauss is that he spent very little time amongst various cultural groups, instead relying mainly on the investigations of other researchers. In fact, there is no evidence - photographs, memoirs, holiday-letters, even postcards - that the man ever wore an Aloha shirt. So another question arises, can one really experience what it is like to be "inside" an Aloha shirt without having ever been "inside" an Aloha shirt?

The psychoanalyst Jacques Lacan approached the subject of tropical shirts from a quite different direction in his book *The Aloha Shirt: The Symbolic, The Real and the Imaginary.* In that work, Lacan attempted to understand the relationship between the "Subjective Self" and the "Objective Other," namely, the Aloha shirt itself. It's clear that in a holiday-makers' effort to become one with his shirt, he attempts to merge himself with the apparel, which is of course physically and psychologically impossible.

Although recent research indicates that the appropriate Aloha shirt is necessary when on a tropical holiday, Lacan would state that it is unimportant which shirt a tourist wears, for he will always be met with disappointment when on a vacation in the tropics. Also, as regards one's relationships with Others wearing Aloha shirts, clearly different Aloha shirts represent different world-views of the two wearers. And even if two tourists wear the same Aloha shirt, one cannot be certain that the "Other" wearing the same Aloha shirt has the same world-view as the "Self," thus making for a fundamental "decentering" of the individual from the rest of society.

To illustrate his point, imagine an island psychoanalyst attempting to counsel two men wearing the same Aloha shirt because they had gotten into a fight about the shirt's interpretation in a tropical bar. The psychoanalyst must deal with Subject One's subjective view of himself, as well as with his objective views of his Aloha shirt, Subject Two, Subject Two's Aloha shirt, and the psychoanalyst. Of course, the same concerns apply to Subject Two. Not surprisingly, it's been shown that psychoanalysts in Waikiki are not terribly successful at mediating conflict resolution involving tourists wearing similar Aloha shirts. Needless to say, bartenders and bouncers do a much better job, along with the help of Five-O.

As an aside, it should be noted that the sociologist Marcel Mauss offered an insightful view in his book *The Gift of the Aloha Shirt* of what it means to give a present of an Aloha shirt. According to his theories of "reciprocity" and "gift exchange," the presenting of an Aloha shirt builds fundamental relationships between groups, not individuals. In opposition to this view, the anthropologist Bronisław Malinowski argued that gift-giving does occur between individuals, but that presenting someone with an Aloha shirt is always a "non-altruistic" exchange. In other words, there is no such thing as a free Aloha shirt.

As another aside, the Marxist critical theorist Guy Debord in *The Society of the Spectacle of the Aloha Shirt* made the disturbing claim that the ability of the wearer of an Aloha shirt to live an authentic social life in modern society is threatened by the very shirt itself. So when an individual puts on an Aloha shirt, he not only suffers the loss of his "being" by wearing the shirt, but he also now projects himself as merely an appearance in the world. Consequently, in Capitalist society the individual becomes the commodity, he becomes merely the representation of a life.

Lastly on the subject of Structuralism, the literary critic Roland Barthes in his book *Mythologies of the Aloha Shirt* extended Saussure's linguistic theory concerning the science of forms known as Semiology. His theory stated that there was indeed a "linguistic sign," consisting of the "signifier," the material shirt itself, and the "signified," the concept the shirt is attempting to deliver to the world. These two unite to form the "sign," namely, the Aloha shirt.

In the second-order semiological system - the mythological language - the first-order sign "Aloha shirt" becomes the Signifier, and the second-order Signified concept is, say, "rebellion." Thus, the second-order Sign, wearing an Aloha Shirt, is a mythical expression and an ideological tool that aids in circumventing the cultural standards of contemporary bourgeois Capitalist society. Unfortunately, in creating the myth, the subjective "individualness" of the wearer of the Aloha shirt is lost to the objective meaning of the myth. Consequently, contemporary myths generally work in favor of and help support the bourgeois class that currently holds political and economic power. This helps to explain, in part, why job-hunters are constantly warned not to wear an Aloha shirt to an interview.

Roland Barthes broke with the Structuralist movement during the volatile year of 1968, and his new Poststructuralist views were mainly concerned with the interpretation of Aloha shirts. Backtracking slightly, and as mentioned earlier, my alter-ego, Dr. Sidney Goldstein, presented himself as an authority on the subject of tropical beachwear. Needless to say, it is a decidedly Modern conception that there are certain individuals designated by society, generally by the university or other professional organizations, who, because of their greater education and expertise, are better qualified to consider and discuss concepts of a philosophical nature. And as regards the Modern conception of the Aloha shirt, the authority on any particular shirt is the "Designer," and only he has the final say as to the meaning or interpretation of the shirt.

But from the postmodernist perspective, Barthes contends that as regards the Aloha shirt, multiple interpretations of any particular shirt are possible, and in fact desirable. In consequence, although the "designer" of an Aloha shirt does indeed have his own interpretation of the shirt, so does the "wearer" of that shirt, as well as any "observer" of that shirt, with all interpretations equally valid. Barthes outlines this approach in his book *Death of the Designer of the Aloha Shirt*, with the title not implying that the "designer" of any particular Aloha shirt doesn't have a valid interpretation of that shirt, but that it isn't the only valid interpretation. Clearly, the Modern concept that there is a hierarchy of Aloha shirt interpretations, with the "designer" as the highest authority, has now been replaced in the postmodern world by the concept that there exists an egalitarian multiplicity of interpretations.

The linguist and literary theorist Jacques Derrida extended the discussion of interpretations of the Aloha shirt by first introducing the concept of "differance," as opposed to the word "difference." Most Aloha shirts have a background and a foreground, with the background generally a solid color and the foreground commonly depicting phenomena regularly observed in tropical settings, such as flowers, palm trees and timeshares.

Needless to say, traditional interpretations of any particular Aloha shirt give preference to the foreground of the shirt, leaving the background of the shirt neglected in the interpretation. Derrida regards this as a most serious mistake, because if the background of the Aloha shirt is altered, say by a change in color, then the interpretation of the foreground of the shirt might also change. In consequence, a valid interpretation of any particular Aloha shirt must take into account both the foreground and the background of the shirt.

Of course, this brings up another serious dilemma concerning interpretations of the Aloha shirt. What if the background and the foreground of an Aloha shirt are identical? In other words, what if the shirt is one solid color? Then any shirt is essentially an Aloha shirt, thus calling into question the very nature of "Alohaness." Unfortunately, Derrida failed to address this grave issue in his book *Of Alohatology*.

It should also be noted that a few years back some Waikiki shirt designers attempted to market a Derridaesque shirt to tourists at the Ala Moana Shopping Center. Unfortunately, the design turned out to be quite unpopular with shopkeepers, and for one very good reason. According to Derrida in his seminal book, there really is no Aloha shirt to speak of, only interpretations of the shirt. As a consequence, there's really no actual shirt to purchase, much to the sorrow of the shopkeepers at the mall.

The historian and social theorist Michel Foucault was firstly concerned with the social dynamic involved in wearing an Aloha shirt, in other words, what does the wearing of a particular shirt tell the world about the wearer of that shirt? Generally, his view was that wearing an Aloha shirt is a form of liberation from the constraints of Modern society, thus allowing the wearer to self-construct his own freedom in postmodern terms. And rather than any particular shirt being interpreted independently of time and place, interpretations of a shirt must vary with respect to those two necessary constraints.

In his book *The Archeology of Alohaness*, Foucault defined three stages of Aloha Shirt interpretation. During the "pre-modern" stage designers offered no interpretation of any particular shirt, asserting instead that a valid interpretation of a shirt could only come from the word of God. On the other hand, the "modern" stage removed God from the discussion and appointed the "Designer" of an Aloha shirt as the only individual responsible for the interpretation. Finally, the "postmodern" stage allowed for far more complex interpretations of an Aloha shirt, as well as no interpretation whatsoever.

The social theoretician Jean-François Lyotard, in his book *The Postmodern Condition: A Report on Knowledge of Aloha Shirts*, asserts that any particular Aloha shirt cannot be interpreted through a scientific language game. In consequence, that shirt can only be interpreted through a narrative Aloha-language game, which in its turn can only be interpreted by a narrative Aloha-Aloha-language game, and so on *ad infinitum*. So ultimately, the Aloha Shirt cannot be interpreted definitively at all, it can only be worn by the wearer. Needless to say, this is a very serious postmodern challenge to any philosopher hoping to reflect successfully upon interpretations of Aloha shirts.

The feminist and psycholinguist Luce Irigaray views the interpretation of Aloha shirts as merely another example of the domination of male values in Western society, the very language of which assigns a masculine privilege to any apparel of acknowledged social value. To alleviate this oppression of women, she encourages them to design and interpret their own Aloha shirts. However, they must first understand the inherent sexual differences between men and women before ever attempting to design a shirt, and certainly before interpreting one.

Given his background in Freudian psychology, the philosopher and social psychologist Gilles Deleuz was not merely interested in interpretations of any particular Aloha shirt, but also in how the wearing of that shirt offered a window into the subconscious mind of the wearer. In such papers as *Oedipus Complex in Aloha Shirts*, *Anti-Oedipus and Alohaphrenia*, and *Civilization and Its Alohaness*, he discusses how knowledge of the early relationships of an individual, in particular, the "mommy-daddy-me" relationship, must first be dealt with before an individual is even capable of buying an Aloha shirt, much less wearing it. Only in this way can an individual find social liberation in the wearing of an Aloha shirt, thus allowing the wearer to self-actualize himself within the postmodern world.

Lastly, the sociologist Jean Baudrillard focuses on the concept of "seduction" as characterized in the wearing of an Aloha shirt. In a social setting, when others observe an individual in an Aloha shirt they generally interpret that individual as one from whom there is nothing to fear and that that person has the best of intentions towards them. However, the Aloha shirt often only serves as a form of "camouflage," for it seduces the observer into a state of casual acceptance of an individual that actually should be avoided at all costs. In his celebrated work, *Simulacra and Simulation in Aloha Shirts*, Baudrillard identified several phases in the evolution of Aloha shirt selection:

Archaic: Prior to the Renaissance;

Counterfeit: From the Renaissance to the beginning of the Industrial Revolution;

Production: From the Industrial Revolution to the beginning of postmodernity; [and]

Simulation: Postmodernity.

Needless to say, all four phases are ever-present in an all-inclusive wardrobe, thus allowing for an individual to switch between phases as often as he puts on a different Aloha shirt.

Cimetière du Père Lachaise

Also located east of central Paris, Cimetière du Père Lachaise is arrived at by taking the Metro to Père Lachaise or Alexandre Dumas station. Père Lachaise is the largest cemetery in Paris and it's considered the "Louvre of the Dead," for there are more famous stiffs there than in any cemetery in the world. Fortunately, a map of the place is available to help the philosophical investigator locate the gravestones of people that did something in life worth remembering, with apologies to the dead buried there that had done nothing in life worth remembering.

Although I could list the hundred or so famous stiffs noted on the map, I'll merely mention my favorite gravesites, the first being the last resting place of Oscar Wilde. Now the interesting thing about Wilde's gravesite is that any gal who visits it is required to first apply a liberal amount of lipstick to her lips, and then she must leave a smeary one for the long dead writer. Clearly, most gals are unaware of the sexual proclivities of this very gay man, for they can be assured that if alive today, he would not return the favor with a kiss.

My next stop was the gravesite of Marcel Proust, which oddly enough, was a writer I met the next day. Then it was on to the site of Jean Anthelme Brillat-Savarin, the author of *The Physiology of Taste*. Surprisingly, on the headstone he's only mentioned as a magistrate and not as a famed gastronome. Then again, according to Roland Barthes in his essay *The Death of the Author* (1967), it's not the writer that is fundamentally important to a book, but the reader's interpretation of the writer's book that is of utmost importance: "Thus is revealed the total existence of writing: a text is made of multiple writings, drawn from many cultures and entering into mutual relations of dialogue, parody, contestation, but there is one place where this multiplicity is focused and that place is the reader, not, as was hitherto said, the author."

My next to last stop in the cemetery was to the most visited gravesite in Père Lachaise, that being the final home of James Douglas Morrison, otherwise known as Jim Morrison, the lead singer for The Doors. The short and tumultuous life of this Surrealist poet and rock star began in 1943, only to end in 1971 with a drug overdose in Paris. The Greek epitaph on his gravestone reads: "Kata Ton Daimona Eaytoy." This translates either as "To the Divine Spirit within Himself," or as "The Devil within Himself," or as "The Genius in His Mind," or as "He Caused His Own Demons." Needless to say, no one rightly knows what the hell it means, but then that was Jim, always an enigma.

After approaching the site, I was immediately handed a bottle reading "Absinthe" on the label, and then told to take a swig of the green-colored liquid. For the uninitiated, Absinthe is a highly alcoholic spirit which is anise-flavored and derived mainly from botanicals such as the flowers and leaves of *Artemisia absinthium*. Its popularity with Parisian artists and writers of the late nineteenth and early twentieth centuries caused it to be condemned and outlawed by social conservatives and prohibitionists. However, today it's marketed throughout Europe, as well as in America.

With the absinthe quickly engulfing my mind, I sat down to enjoy "le poètes cimetière," three graveyard poets of the Parisian breed. They had gathered not only to commemorate Jim and his journey through life, but to also pay homage to his journey in death. The first poet was Paul Verlaine, who recited *The burial* (1865):

I know nothing that's more fun than a burial.
The sexton sings away, his pick-axe gleams,
The distant bell trills thinly in the air,
The white-frocked priest skips through the prayers.

After another swig from the bottle of absinthe, the second poet of the trio, Arthur Rimbaud, recited *Wandering* (1870):

I ran away, hands stuck in pockets that seemed
All holes; my jacket was a holey ghost as well.
I followed you, Muse! Beneath your spell,
Oh, la, la, what glorious loves I dreamed!

Lastly, and after yet another swig from the bottle, the third poet
of the trio, Charles Baudelaire, recited "Posthumous Remorse" from
Flowers of Evil (1857):

Then the grave, that dark friend of my limitless dreams
(For the grave ever readeth the poet aright),
Amid those long nights, which no slumber redeems...
Then the worms will gnaw deep at thy body, like Dread.

After we drained what was left of the bottle, a hand suddenly
surfaced from the gravesite. And with the help of the three graveyard
poets, Jim himself was pulled from the grave, fortunately, with a
second bottle of absinthe in his other hand. We all passed the bottle
around a few times, with each Surrealist traveler taking a long swig in
turn. When the bottle was almost drained, Jim lay back on his grave
and began to tell us the story of *The End* (1967):

This is the end
Beautiful friend
This is the end
My only friend, the end

Overwhelmed by the heady drink and the splendid lines of the four
poets, I offered them my own poem, *While Overlooking Cimetière*:

While overlooking *cimetière*
I chance to sip the absinthe dear
With thoughts of spring and love in mind
I look for one amongst her kind
My endless search in time and place

Brings forth one morn a pretty face
Then come the words I long to hear
While overlooking *cimetière*

While overlooking *cimetière*
I sip the splendid absinthe clear
With memories of summers past
The happiness swore both to last
But day arrives, dreams torn asunder
So travel I to lands down under
To face life then without the fear
While overlooking *cimetière*

While overlooking *cimetière*
I chance to sip an absinthe queer
With autumn breeze about to blow
The strength to journey dwindles low
So pen in hand I write, the clown
Reflecting on the roads gone down
Of memories that bring a tear
While overlooking *cimetière*

While overlooking *cimetière*
I sip the absinthe now with fear
For days turn cold, the nights grow long
The end in sight, the mind not strong
I contemplate a life now past
A day to come which is the last
And so I turn to friends most dear
While overlooking *cimetière*

After ending my poem and draining the second bottle, I closed my eyes and experienced an enlightening vision. I saw that though Modernity had progressed almost without stop for the past 500 years, there was always the inevitable backlash to it in the form of

Anti-modernity. Although the major backlashes in history had taken various forms over the five centuries, the last such episode was the decade of the Sixties, when the direction of Western Civilization was questioned and altered by the Modern world. Such episodes allow democratic societies to explosively let off the steam caused by their own internal contradictions. Much like a volcano, Western Civilization requires the occasional eruption of values and purposes, with Modern progress then proceeding unhindered until the next serious challenge to it.

When my eyes opened, the four graveyard poets were gone. So I got up and made my way to the cemetery gates, stopping only once at Honoré de Balzac's gravesite. Lying on the base of the site was an envelope addressed to me, with a note and a poem inside. The note contained instructions for me to be on the uppermost level of the Eiffel Tower the next day around noon, and once there to meet a middle-aged gentleman who would ask me for the time.

The Existential
Investigator

Eiffel Tower and Invalides Quarter

My investigation of Paris was now to take on a much different form, one that not only engaged the mind and the body, but also the heart. Needless to say, a private investigator usually sees people in only the most sordid of ways, and that especially goes for dames. But once a philosophical investigator learns to actually see and perhaps understand the people around him, instead of judging them from only easily-misinterpreted outward motions, he comes to realize that human existence is far more complex than at first thought. Fortunately, I soon met a man who helped train me in how to begin to observe the world as an existential investigator.

Eiffel Tower

The next morning saw my head still reeling from the dire aftereffects of that most potent of libations, absinthe. But after a long shower and a cuppa joe, I made my way to the Metro and caught the train to the station nearest the Eiffel Tower. I arrived about an hour before I was to be atop the edifice, which was most opportune, for there was a long line of tourists waiting to enter the lift that takes one and all to the first level. Fortunately, that long wait gave me plenty of time to memorize all the facts concerning one of the world's most recognizable erections.

The Eiffel Tower was originally built for the International Exhibition of 1889, though interestingly, it was only meant to be a temporary erection. But it must have taken a monumental dose of Viagra, for it's stayed up ever since, much to the delight of visitors to Paris. Also interestingly, it was once the tallest erection in the world, at least until 1931 when New Yorkers decided that they could come up with a taller erection in the Empire State Building. Still, today it remains the most memorable erection in the world, despite what many private investigators imagine about themselves.

At fifty-seven meters, the first level of the Eiffel Tower offers only a hummingbird's-eye view of Paris, and so more euros must be parted with in order to take the lift to the second level, which offers a mockingbird's-eye view of the city. Of course there's hardly any point in not shelling out more dough to take the third lift to the top level, and at two hundred seventy-some meters that eagle's-eye view of the city makes up for the slight dent in the pocket euro-holder. For needless to say, there's no better platform to view Paris from than the uppermost observation deck of the Eiffel Tower.

Of course a philosophical investigator who takes pride in honing his virility can skip the lifts altogether and instead walk up more than sixteen hundred steps to the top level, which is a feat that deserves the utmost of admiration and the highest of applause. Unfortunately, once at the top the view of Paris is essentially the same whether earned by taking the lifts or by walking the stairs, so there seems little to be gained by such an exertion, especially given that admiration and applause are such fleeting commodities in the postmodern world.

As directed by Honoré in his note, I arrived a few minutes before noon at the top level of the tower. After walking about and enjoying the view in all directions, I'd stopped to look down upon the Left Bank of Paris when someone asked me for the time. I turned around to see a middle-aged gentleman who immediately introduced himself, "My name is Marcel Proust and I work with Honoré at the agency. He told me that you would be here at noon. May I call you Sam."

"Sam's fine," I responded, "but exactly why did Honoré want me to meet you?"

"Now that's a rather long story," Marcel answered, "and it will take us many days to fully answer your question. First off, let me tell you a bit about myself. I'm most famous for a collection of books I wrote many years ago called *À la recherche du temps perdue*, which was published in seven volumes from 1913 to 1927."

After Marcel noticed that my French wasn't up to the task, he continued, "Fortunately for English-only readers, that series was translated by C. K. Scott Moncrieff as *Remembrance of Things Past* between 1922 and 1931. It was then revised by Terence Kilmartin in

1981 under a new and more accurate title, *In Search of Lost Time*. Today the book is most readily available to the English-speaking audience as a six-volume edition, one revised once more by D. J. Enright in 1992.

"I was born in Auteuil, a suburb of Paris, in 1871, at a time that saw the decline of the aristocracy and the corresponding rise of the upper bourgeois class during the social changes that occurred in the historical transition from the Third Republic and the *fin de siècle*. My father was a pathologist and epidemiologist, over his life writing important articles and books on medicine and hygiene. And my mother was a highly literate and well-read woman, who early on gave her son a command of the English language.

"Unfortunately, I suffered from serious asthma attacks from an early age, which disrupted my education, although not enough to stop me from excelling in literature. By 1890, I was publishing articles in literary magazines and founding a literary review. And in 1896, I published a collection of early pieces which was not well-received by the public. An early attempt at a novel was soon begun, and though abandoned a few years later, many of the themes in it appeared in my later masterpiece.

"After reading a wide field of other writers and working on various literary projects, I began work on *In Search of Lost Time* in 1909, with the first volume, *Swann's Way*, appearing in 1913. It was not until 1919 that *Within a Budding Grove* was published, with *The Guermantes Way* and *Sodom and Gomorrah* following over the next few years. Unfortunately, I died of pneumonia and a pulmonary abscess in 1922, and so was unable to see the publication of *The Captive*, *The Fugitive* and *Time Regained* from 1923 to 1927. And as you may have noticed yesterday, I'm buried in Cimetière du Père Lachaise."

Needless to say, at this point I wondered how Marcel knew that I'd been at the cemetery the day before, though I found out later that all my actions in Paris were being reported to the agency on a daily basis. How they managed to accomplish this feat I had no idea, but I greatly appreciated their many efforts in training me in the methods of a philosophical investigator. Of course, I'd long since given up worrying about talking to dead people, for it now seemed to me to be quite natural when in Paris.

Marcel, pointing to the part of the city spreading out from below the Eiffel Tower, then continued, "Please look upon the Left Bank, where we will begin our investigations. And off in the distance, do you see that church atop Montmartre? That's Sacré Couer, where we will end our philosophical investigations." With that, Marcel ushered me towards the lifts, which took us back to the bottom of the tower and to the beginning of our existential investigation of the Left Bank of Paris.

Champ-de-Mars

Marcel and I began our investigation along the Champ-de-Mars, or Field of Mars, the city greenbelt named after the Roman god of war and which extends from the Eiffel Tower to the École Militaire. During the construction of the military school, which began in 1765, it was determined that grounds were needed for military drills. Over the years the park has been used for celebrations such as the first Bastille Day, as well as the Paris expositions of 1867, 1878, 1889, 1900 and 1937.

After strolling slowly along the walkway to the Avenue I Bouvard, Marcel motioned me over to a city bench. And once seated, he asked, "So what have you learned thus far as Paris' newest *flâneur philosophique*."

"Marcel," I responded, "I'm sorry but I'm unfamiliar with that term *flâneur*."

"I see," Marcel continued, "I would have thought that Honoré had mentioned the term, but as I remember, his preferred investigator description is *raconteur*, or story-teller. However, the two terms are very similar, for an investigator begins as a *flâneur* and ends as a *raconteur*. As to the term *flâneur*, prior to the nineteenth-century its basic meaning referred to a stroller or a loafer, and it was often used to describe an idle man that cared little for accomplishing anything with his life.

"However, the poet Charles Baudelaire, who you met yesterday at the cemetery, changed the meaning of the term from a socially negative label, that is if one associates strolling and loafing as bad ways to journey through life, to a positive one. During the 1860s he altered, at least in the popular consciousness, the term so that it soon referred to an urban investigator or a connoisseur of city life, a man forever analyzing the modern experience.

"Let me offer you Charles' wonderful description from *Le Figaro* (1863) of this 'gentleman stroller of city streets', this 'botanist of the sidewalk', this *flâneur*: 'The crowd is his element, as the air is that of birds and water of fishes. His passion and his profession are to become one flesh with the crowd. For the perfect *flâneur*, for the passionate spectator, it is an immense joy to set up house in the heart of the multitude, amid the ebb and flow of movement, in the midst of the fugitive and the infinite. To be away from home and yet to feel oneself everywhere at home; to see the world, to be at the center of the world, and yet to remain hidden from the world - impartial natures which the tongue can but clumsily define.'

"A *flâneur* investigates the modern city as an urban spectator, as an amateur detective. Indeed, he is the very essence of the metropolitan writer or artist. And given the anonymity of his calling, which can take place in any part of the city without anyone suspecting, the detached observer may only make himself known once he becomes the *raconteur*. For in that event, his mind's journey is exposed for all to see in his story, at least to those that read books. Sadly, this is a rather inconsequential number in the urban population these days, especially in America."

Rue Cler

Motioning that it was time to move on, Marcel had us continue along the Avenue I Bouvard until reaching Place du General Gouraud.

We then made our way across the Avenue de la Bourdonnais and walked along the Rue Saint Dominique until reaching one of the most affluent neighborhoods in Paris, Rue Cler. The street market there is the most stylish in the city, and it offers a never-ending parade of astonishingly beautiful women shoppers. And though a few of them are undoubtedly wives, many more of them are probably mistresses. Needless to say, it is forever entertaining to watch these captivating creatures as they lead and direct their well-dressed but fiscally-concerned gentleman companions on how to properly carry the multitude of new bags acquired during the day's outing... at his expense no doubt.

Marcel and I seated ourselves at an outdoor table at his favorite Rue Cler café, which offered a panoramic view of all the comings and goings in the prosperous neighborhood. It is the perfect place for a budding *flâneur* to hone his skills as an urban investigator, with the two of us soon enjoying the elegant ladies seated around us, all of them reminding me of Leslie Caron in *An American in Paris* or *Gigi*, or perhaps Audrey Hepburn in *Funny Face*. Needless to say, these women are hopelessly unattainable to a man on a private investigator's salary, but still, even a PI can dream sometimes.

My *flâneurean* eyes began by watching a pretty teenage girl strolling far behind her mother, thus allowing her to flirt with every young man that might catch her virgin mood. The return of his smile reminded her that yes: "The mirror in my bedroom is correct, I'm so pretty." Such a delightful age in a young woman's life, for that youthful feminine innocence is still intact. Unfortunately, a few relationships over the next year or two will completely destroy that charming purity, and sadly, it will never return to her in her lifetime.

Then I noticed a stunning woman in her early twenties, that wonderful age when beauty begins to blossom, like a rose in a country garden. Every young woman enjoys her own color of that poetic flower: for the innocent it is the white, for the vivacious it is the yellow, for the serious it is the pink, and for the temperamental it is the red. Indeed, the rose captures the very essence of the youthful longing heart. That yearning soul waits impatiently for love to bud, to then bloom for the world to see, and sadly, to finally wither away, though soon replaced by another lovely flower. And as Marcel told me while referring to his youth, "The life of these pretty girls... appeared to me, as to everyone in whom ease of fulfillment has not deadened the power of imagining, a thing as different from anything that I knew, and as desirable, as the most marvelous cities that travel holds in store for us."

Is there not a pleasure in observing two young initiates falling in love, dancing to an imagined song that only they can hear and immersed in a glow that only they can feel? And when the two kiss in the little universe that is theirs alone, does that not take one's memories back to one's own first love? For youth is the only time in life when one believes that love will never end, though of course, the world is only biding its moments before teaching each lover a different lesson. Still, young love is such a beautiful sight that it brings tears to the eyes. It's amazing how much beauty there is around us at every moment, if only time is given over to mere observation, to being a *flâneur*.

There were also remarkable looking women in their thirties, the decade during which a woman displays her greatest beauty, as well as her greatest vulnerability. Some were glowingly pregnant or suckling a newborn, while others were directing their young ones. All of these women were desirable, though each in a wonderfully different way. One woman was leaving a bridal shop and I would have loved to see her on that most important day: the radiant bride hoping to change him, the beaming groom hoping nothing ever changes. Inevitably, both will be somewhat disappointed with the realities of marital life.

Lastly, there were women in their forties, fifties and beyond: stylish and elegant, worldly-wise and all-knowing, and well-versed in the arts of love and romance. Truly, from the outdoor tables of the café, *le flâneur philosophique* observes life to be a moving art gallery of splendid masterpieces, ones yet to be captured by an artist for all of eternity, but at least captured by the metropolitan investigator, if only momentarily. It's sad to think how many people in our restless and impatient urban world miss out on the magnificent splendor

225

surrounding them at all times and in all places of the modern city. Only the writer, the poet and the artist embrace existence as a sublime aesthetic experience... forever breathing in life as a contemporary aesthete.

Just then the most astonishing woman I had ever seen sat down at a table near ours, and I immediately asked Marcel, "Have you ever seen such an irresistible creature in your life? If I was an artist I would paint her so that all men could fall in love for the first time. Do you have any idea who she is?"

"I do as a matter of fact," Marcel answered. "She's Mme. Odette Swann, formerly Odette de Crécy, and I too fell deeply in love with her many years ago, as did a close friend of mine. I even wrote about her in my book, for not being an artist, the only way for a writer to capture a masterpiece is to paint it in words. But do not be foolish and do not approach her, for she is an infamous *femme fatale* and she may easily ruin you as she did my friend.

"I see by your questioning expression that you have never run into a *femme fatale*, a term which in English means a "deadly woman." The art of avoiding a *femme fatale* in life is an art that no man completely possesses, and sooner or later every man is overcome by the charms of these most mysterious and seductive of women. Always remember, this intense feminine magnetism that binds a man to an irresistible desire, one that incapacitates him from making rational decisions, that leads him into unforeseen dangers, is inevitable in every man's life, especially in the life of a private investigator."

Needless to say, I didn't listen to one bit of the prudent advice that Marcel offered me, for all that my eyes and mind could see was the loveliness of Odette in front of me. But, how do I approach such a beauty? I then remembered the poem, "The Camellia" from *Lost Illusions*, that Honoré left me in the cemetery the day before. Spotting a nearby florist, I left Marcel to his musings on the *femme fatale* and was fortunate to locate the only camellia left in the shop. I purchased it, and with the poem, returned to her table and cautiously laid the flower and sonnet next to her.

Odette looked at me with what I could see was a longing face, and then motioned for me to sit at her table. And I could see Marcel shaking his head nearby, undoubtedly warning me to beware of this woman. Needless to say, I took no notice of his wise counsel, for I was too mesmerized by her dark honey blond hair, a shade that reminded me of ambrosia, the golden nectar beloved by the ancient gods. Her eyes were a shade of brown as dark as the truffles of Périgord, as Marcel later described them to me, and they pierced my heart to the core. I then pulled out Balzac's poemand read it to her, all the while seeking her approval for my rather bold approach into her life:

Yet, in a theater, or ballroom light,
With alabaster petals opening fair,
I gladly see Camellias shining bright
Above some stately women's [honey] hair,

When I finished with the sonnet I offered it to her as a gift, whereupon she smiled for the first time. Many women have a pretty face and many women have a goddess-like figure, Odette enjoying both face and figure. But she also had a quality that made her almost unique among women, a quality possessed by very few of her species - an iridescent smile. It was capable of lighting up the world around her and warming the coldest of hearts, even ones that have not felt love in many years.

Odette then asked me, "So what is your name, sir?"

I think I responded Sam, but don't really remember, for I'd fallen irresistibly in love with her and my tongue was almost incapable of speech. To say that Odette was beautiful would describe almost nothing, for the more I looked at her the more her loveliness blossomed before me. Her eyes made me long to remain forever in her gaze, and her unaffected hair fell charmingly along the contours of her pretty face. She wore only a little make-up - more to acquiesce to the demands of society than to assure her beauty - and her lips evidenced a pale pink tint, which caused their moistness to glisten in the sun.

This object of my affections was attired in a lovely silk chiffon turquoise blouse, one with little regard for the ephemeral trends of the moment, for her elegance would never admit of anything transitory. Odette's top was cut just low enough to offer a glimpse of her beautifully formed breasts, though the garment in no way made her appear coquettish. But despite the loveliness of her appearance, perhaps what drew me even more to her was her Parisian accent, which seduced me with its sensuous undertones. And her warming smile caused me to always search for just the right words, if only that I might glow within her approval one more time.

I judged Odette to be around fifty, an age that younger men have little interest in, for they appraise women only by the contemporary aesthetics of extreme youthfulness and unconcealed sexuality. On the other hand, an experienced man sees past the fashionable trends of the present-day and searches for beauty that is eternal. In this sense, the practiced man is much like the artist, who sees beyond the ephemeral aspects of life to envision those often hidden qualities that give meaning to a beauty lasting forever.

Odette and I spoke for some time about her debilitating relationship with her late husband, Charles Swann, a man whose life she ruined during her early years as a much longed for *courtesan*. She also spoke to me of her now constant state of *ennui*, that emotional boredom experienced when an individual is left without anything in particular to do in the world and is no longer interested in any surroundings. This saddened me, for I think she realized that without the many men that once followed her every move around Paris, she almost ceased to exist.

We sat there talking of life for some time more until she explained that she had to leave to meet her daughter, whose story was far too complicated to render in one afternoon. I then took her hand and kissed it, and in that instant nothing existed in the world but two lovers, with at least one of them longing for the moment to never end. But this was not to be, even in Paris, where almost all things concerning the human heart are possible.

Needless to say, Odette could see all of these familiar feelings in my love-struck eyes, and so she cautioned me, "Be on your guard, or fear losing your heart and yourself to me, just as my husband did many years ago. Sadly, in love, my dear boy, what you see is not necessarily what you get. For as my good friend Marcel once told me: 'Even in the most insignificant details of our daily life, none of us can be said to constitute a material whole, which is identical for everyone, and need only be turned up like a page in an account-book or the record of a will; our social personality is a creation of the thoughts of other people.' Now, return to your friend and guide Marcel."

I returned to the table and Marcel, who was still shaking his head in disapproval at my indiscrete behavior. I then noticed Odette take out paper and pen, and then begin writing something down, after which, she stood up and came over to our table.

"Hello, Marcel," she said. "It has been many years since we last ran into each other. I read that your search for lost time has gone well, which pleases me. And, Sam, please take with you this little note and poem. I will think of you often."

Odette quickly turned and walked away along the Rue Cler, with my eyes following her until they could follow her no longer. I then opened her note and read it to Marcel:

My dear Sam,

I hope that you always remember me as I was today, for "when from a long-distant past nothing subsists, after the people are dead, after the things are broken and scattered, taste and smell alone, more fragile but more enduring, more immaterial, more persistent, more faithful, remain poised a long time, like souls, remembering, waiting, hoping, amid the ruins of all the rest; and bear unflinchingly, in the tiny and almost impalpable drop of their essence, the vast structure of recollection."

Love always,
Odette

P.S. And please allow your infatuated heart to take comfort in the lines of Shakespeare's *Sonnet XXX*:

But if the while I think on thee, dear friend,
All losses are restored and sorrows end.

Marcel then said to me, "As you no doubt just experienced, when in the throes of love, remaining a *flâneur* is impossible. For instead of engaging the world as an outwardly-focused observer, love draws the mind's eye towards only the object of one's love. There is darkness all around except in the warm light created by the two lovers, which only they can see and bask in. Fortunately, and inevitably, being in love is limited to a short period of time in anyone's life. This is probably for the best, for if everyone fell in love forever, the modern world would soon cease to exist, with nothing accomplished, with civilization lying in ruins."

Invalides Quarter

While still feeling the pangs of irresistible but impossible love, Marcel pulled me down to the end of the street Rue Cler, where he led us along the side-streets of the Invalides Quarter. Though home to many interesting old buildings, the most famous edifice in the neighborhood is the Dôme Church, originally planned in 1676 to house the remains of Louis XIV and other royals. Those plans were abandoned in 1841 by Louis-Philippe, who decided that the church should be the final resting place of Napoleon, as well as of other prominent military personages in French history.

After crossing Boulevard des Invalides, Marcel ushered me into the Musée Rodin, home to the most famous sculptures carved by the most famous nineteenth-century French sculptor, August Rodin. It was clear that Marcel had visited the museum many times before, for I quickly found myself admiring the sculpture that reminds every man of the pangs of irresistible love, *The Kiss*. To describe this sublime statue in words is impossible, for all a man can really do is long to be the recipient of the loving kiss from that angelically-formed nude woman.

Marcel eventually interrupted my thoughts and said, "I saw by your love-struck eyes at the café that you have never experienced a conversation in the key of love before today, nor have you ever experienced an affair of the heart."

"What is a conversation in the key of love?" I asked. "What is an affair of the heart?"

"Well, Sam," he answered, "a 'conversation in the key of love' and an 'affair of the heart' are quite often omitted in the postmodern world, where 'having sex' and 'making love' are considered to be synonymous in nature. But there was a time when life ordered human relationships differently, when a man made love first to a woman's mind through conversation, then through her heart which had grown warm to him, and finally through her body. The world today has rather reversed this time-honored arrangement, losing much of importance in the exquisite progression of two individuals finding love in one another.

"In more detail, what does it really mean for two individuals to find love in one another? For a man and a woman to first make love through their minds, which is to say, form a friendship, there must be openness and honesty to foster communication, as well as shared interests, goals and values. While this wonderful process is moving along, hopefully the hearts are following suit in a growing attraction between the two. These changes in the heart begin with curiosity, warmth and acceptance, and then grow into deeper feelings that culminate in desire and passion. This is what I call 'Mind-Heart Love', a type of deep affection that is more often than not left out of postmodern interpersonal relationships due to the compulsion to involve the bodies too quickly. Interestingly though, this type of love often results in relationships that last a lifetime.

"The third element of the triad is the body, characterized by sexuality, which at first involves touching and embracing. However, at this point everything must be put on hold while a discussion of sexual needs is dealt with by the two budding lovers. Unfortunately, the impatience of many couples to neglect forming connections through their minds and to deal only with 'Heart-Body Love', leads to disastrous consequences in all relationships. On the other hand, there are equally devastating problems associated with 'Mind-Body Love' in which the heart is disconnected from the relationship. Only when all three elements of interpersonal relationships come into play can the two finally find bodily love during foreplay, intercourse and afterplay. And only in this way can the mind, the heart and the body unite in what I envision as 'Sublime Love'.

"True, there is that burning desire that a man feels when he first sees an attractive woman, a *femme attrayante*, as opposed to his lack of interest in one that is merely *femme ordinaire*. Needless to say, each man has his own perspective in these aesthetic matters, for an ordinary woman to one man may be an attractive one to another. Then there is the *femme extraordinaire*, that extraordinary woman that one is compelled to approach in the hope of arranging a rendezvous. However, the magnificent woman, the *femme magnifique*, is too beautiful to approach, for in every man there forever lingers nagging doubts about himself.

"Finally there is the strongest desire of all, when a man sees for the first time a *femme irrésistible*, an irresistible woman such as Odette, at least in your case. If she were merely magnificent, a man would not have the courage to approach her. But with an irresistible woman, an inner drive overrides the sensible course of action, as you discovered for yourself earlier. This is the sort of Siren that even Odysseus would desperately attempt to untie his ropes for, to gladly accept death to hear the sound of her alluring song."

"However, what is often forgotten today is that attraction, at any level of desire, is only the beginning of love. A man must first make love to a woman as an *amie*, for conversations in the key of love allow each friend to share in the ideas and dreams of life. Only later, when their shared thoughts have warmed their hearts, does he become the *confidante*, which allows for more intimate conversations, as well as for overtures of love. If all goes well, she eventually becomes his *amant*, and that is the moment when the triad of making love is made complete between the two lovers, when they are made one. But how often we hurry the stages of making love, when because of uncontrollable carnal desire, the virtue of patience is lost in a man":

After admiring *The Kiss* for another moment, Marcel and I wandered through the museum doors to the garden, which is home to some of Rodin's other masterpieces, such as his monument to *Balzac*. It is considered by many to be the first truly modern sculpture, for Rodin attempted in the statue to portray not the physical likeness of Honoré, but the inner mental life of the great *raconteur*.

"It is important to remember," Marcel commented, "that the love between two lovers is not the only pleasure or bliss in life. Honoré showed us that this sort of enjoyment is also possible between a writer and a reader, though it took Roland Barthes to bring it to the popular consciousness. We French call this *jouissance*, or the 'textual orgasm', though it should not be confused with something like the postmodern pulp fiction concerning 'Fifty Shades of Smut'. No, *jouissance* occurs when the writer's text so consumes the reader that he exists in nothing but the moment, as in the physical orgasm, and as such, he never wants the moment to end. He longs for that moment to continue giving him pleasure and bliss forever, though of course, end it must.

"As a writer, how does one attempt to offer the moment of *jouissance* to the reader? Well, he must first view life as a continuous stream of moments, most of them ordinary and a few extraordinary, with all of them flowing forward in time together. It is the writer that must, while reflecting upon the past and telling his story, eliminate the ordinary in order to isolate the remaining extraordinary moments in any life experience. The writer must then compress those extraordinary moments into a short timeframe, thus heightening that life experience. And as with your brief affair with Odette, the extraordinary moments when you were together with her became a compressed version of memory, resulting in an intensity of experience that you may have never known before.

"Before parting for the day, let us walk over here to admire one of Rodin's most famous bronze sculptures, *The Thinker*, which depicts a man, perhaps a philosophical investigator, struggling with one of life's eternal questions. Let us imagine it is love that preoccupies this man's every waking moment: 'The truth is that this woman has only raised to life by a sort of magic countless elements of tenderness existing in us already in a fragmentary state, which she has assembled, joined together, effacing every gap between them, and it is we ourselves who by giving her her features have supplied all the solid matter of the beloved object. Whence it arises that even if we are only one among a thousand to her and perhaps the last of them all, to us she is the only one, the woman towards whom our whole life gravitates.'"

With his lessons in love now at an end, Marcel bid me adieu after giving me a list of places that I should investigate on my own in St-Germain-des-Prés the next day, and where to meet him for a glass of wine in the Luxembourg Quarter in the late afternoon. But before leaving the museum, I silently asked *The Thinker* what other questions needed answering about this long and often bewildering journey through life. Sadly, he remained quite mute on the matter, I suppose knowing that the important questions in life can only be asked by each individual for himself, and also answered only by each individual for himself. However, and without saying a word, he did remind me that I could always seek help during the journey from other philosophical investigators.

St-Germain-des-Prés and Luxembourg Quarter

A most pleasant way to begin a philosophical investigation of St-Germain-des-Prés is to take the Metro to Assemblée Nationale station, and after making one's way to the Seine, to enjoy the sights and sounds of the river while wandering along Quai Anatole France past Musée d'Orsay. After that, continue along Quai Voltaire to Rue des Saints Peres, and then on to Boulevard St-Germain, home to cafés and brasseries that once offered solace to any existential philosopher pondering those many important questions in life. And if after a few glasses of wine those thinkers make themselves known to a budding *flâneur*, then all the better, for that's a day well-spent.

Les Deux Magots

Mid-morning found me meandering up the busy thoroughfare of Boulevard St-Germain, with my first stop being the café Les Deux Magots, home to exquisite coffees and fine hot chocolates. After settling into an outdoor table with my cuppa, I noticed a somewhat inebriated and rather belligerent man looking at me nearby. As he continued to stare, I told him, "Knock it off wise-guy and don't piss me off or I'll slap you around a bit for good measure." Then, after patting my left coat pocket, I continued, "If that doesn't convince you, I've got a gat under here that's ready to talk business with you."

"I thought you were an American," the man said, "but you don't really have a gun under there, do you buddy?"

"Nah, I was just playing the tough guy," I responded. "But I'm finally glad to meet someone in this town that knows what a gat is. You want to join me for a coffee?"

"I'll join you, but not for a coffee," he answered. "I need something a little stiffer by this time of the morning."

While the man went inside to get a shot of something, I continued enjoying my cuppa, though all the while feeling a bit of a wimp for doing so. After he returned to the table with two shots of brandy, I asked him, "What's your name, and where do you hail from in the States?"

"The name's Ernest," he responded, "and I originally haled from near Chicago."

"So what are you doing here?" I inquired.

"As to how I got here," Ernest began, "after high school I tried my hand at journalism for a Kansas City rag. In 1918 I volunteered for an ambulance division, which sent me to a Paris that was enduring heavy bombardment from German artillery. I was soon sent to the Italian front, but suffered a severe injury from mortar fire. After returning to the States, I tried my hand at some writing while continuing as a journalist at a number of papers.

"After getting married to my first wife Hadley in 1921, we settled for many years in Paris, where I finally devoted myself to becoming a serious novelist, a story that I recorded in my book *A Moveable Feast* (1964): 'I always worked until I had something done and I always stopped when I knew what was going to happen next. That way I could be sure of going on the next day.... Going down the stairs when I had worked well, and that needed luck as well as discipline, was a wonderful feeling and I was free then to walk anywhere in Paris.'

"As you probably already know, there's no better place to walk than in Paris. Sometimes I'd saunter over to Gertrude Stein's place, and I remember one visit in particular. Apparently, her car mechanic had told her that all the young American expatriates in Paris were part of *une generation perdue*. Then she told me: 'That's what you are. That's what you all are. All of you young people who served in the war. You are a lost generation.' After hearing this I thought to myself 'that all generations were lost by something and always had been and always would be.'

"Other days I'd walk over to La Closerie des Lilas, located in Montparnasse. It was there that I wrote *The Sun Also Rises*, which unfortunately, literature professors now refer to as the first 'Lost Generation' novel. In those days I was constantly attacked by writer's block: 'I knew I must write a novel. But it seemed an impossible thing to do when I had been trying with great difficulty to write paragraphs that would be the distillation of what made a novel. It was necessary to write longer stories now as you would train for a longer race.' Well, I must be on my way now, for while I'm walking there's always something interesting for a *flâneur* to see in this magnificent city."

Brasserie Lipp

With my hungry stomach now begging me to fill the void caused by the coffee and brandy, I crossed the boulevard to Brasserie Lipp for a plate of sausages and sauerkraut topped off with a glass of cold Alsatian beer. After finishing the meal and wiping up the savory juices with a piece of bread, the waiter took my plate and brought me another beer. With that one soon gone, I was almost ready to doze off from the brandy and beer when a man approached me and struck up a conversation.

"Excuse me," he said, "but would I be correct in assuming that you are an American? My name is Jean-Paul, and might I join you?"

Pointing to the seat, which he'd already sat in, I realized any chance of enjoying a few winks was now going to be all but impossible. So I said, "You're right, I'm from the States."

As a warning to other philosophical investigators, a visitor to Paris must get accustomed to the forwardness of the inhabitants of this conversation-obsessed city, especially when the subject of America comes up. And in this Jean-Paul was no exception to the norm, "Allow me to comment on *Americans and Their Myths*, a topic I addressed in an article for *The Nation* magazine in 1947: 'Everything has been said about the United States. But a person who has once crossed the Atlantic can no longer be satisfied with even the most penetrating books; not that he does not believe what they say, but that his agreement remains abstract.... Perhaps nowhere else will you find such a discrepancy between people and myth, between life and the representation of life.'"

Café de Flore

Just then Jean-Paul became exceedingly distraught because some guy was yelling at him from across the boulevard. And after grabbing me by the arm, he forced me to cross the street to confront this man at an outdoor table at the Café de Flore. Seated at the table was a man clearly not at all happy to run into Jean-Paul, and I was worried the two of them were going to get into a punch-up. So I told a nearby waiter to bring us some white wine, and then got Jean-Paul to sit down.

With the three of us finally seated with a glass of wine, I introduced myself to the other gentleman, who responded, "My name is Albert, but it is this gentleman that I want to confront on a little matter of existentialist thought. I read in the paper this morning your absurd article on *Marxism and Existentialism* (1960), Jean-Paul. Where is it? Yes here it is. Allow me to read a few lines of it to you to remind you of your gibberish: 'Existentialism and Marxism... aim at the same object.... Far from being exhausted, Marxism is still very young, almost in its infancy; it has scarcely begun to develop. It remains, therefore, the philosophy of our time.'

"It is interesting that your Marxist discourse relating history and freedom seems to overlook the pertinent fact that all societies that have ever foolishly brought into force such a disastrous economic and political system as Marxism have been the very ones that severely limited the freedom of their populations, and to the point of massive executions."

"Excuse me gentlemen," I interjected, "but given that I'm new to your argument, could you tell me where this disagreement stems from."

"Well, it began about sixty years ago," Albert answered. "The political differences between Jean-Paul and myself started after the war, when, as the two main voices of the Left in postwar intellectual France, we began a philosophical argument that over time resulted in personal attacks that ended ten years of friendship.

"However, let me backtrack to the war and the Occupation of Paris. Both of us were already well-known writers when we met for the first time in June of 1943 at the opening of *The Flies*, a play by Jean-Paul. I moved to Paris in November, and though friends with this more famous philosopher, I remained my own man, independent. Of course the two of us had known of each other for years, and we had also reviewed each other's work since before the war.

"Perhaps the problem lay not in the similarities between us, but in the differences. True, we shared much in common, especially an outlook that at the very root of the human condition, existence is absurd. And we also both wrote works of philosophy, as well as novels and plays. But the difference lay in the fact that Jean-Paul approached the question of existence from an intellectual point of view, while my approach was that of a novelist, so an individual's point of view.

"In August of 1944 the first edition of the underground newspaper *Combat* came out in Paris, with me as editor. The Occupation was finally over and all of France was moving to the Left, for which both of us were the leading proponents of change. The two of us continued publishing together until the end of the next year, with each of us achieving fame, first in France and then internationally, though the political differences between us were becoming noticeable. Needless to say, we were both opposed to capitalism while always remaining steadfast supporters of forming a democratic socialist society. The problem was Marxism, with Jean-Paul a firm devotee of the French Communist Party and the Soviet Union. On the other hand, I believed that Communism was humanity's foremost enemy in the world.

"From 1946 to 1948 Jean-Paul began to support Communism and violent revolution more and more. Instead, I offered what I now admit was an overly-idealistic program to the world based on unity and democracy, one that rejected both sides in the Cold War, and one that also called for a concern for moral values and the rejection of violence. So it boiled down to a matter of ethics, a choice between violence or nonviolence, that brought our disagreements to the fore, and that resulted in the dividing of the Left in France.

"In reaction to this, in 1951 I published *The Rebel: An Essay on Man in Revolt*, and in the next year Jean-Paul wrote a scathing review of my book. I was outraged by it and published a reply condemning the review and Communism, implying, though not mentioning, Jean-Paul by name. In reaction, he published a nasty retort in a twenty-page letter titled *My Dear Camus*. In 1953 and 1954 I wrote more articles condemning the abuses of Communism, with Jean-Paul continuing to find excuses for the horrors of the Soviet Union and East Germany. And in the following year I published *The Fall*, which was my final response to the argument between us."

After Albert finished the story about the beginning and ending of his friendship with Jean-Paul, it was only a few moments before the two of them were arguing once again, this time about the meaning of some play written by their friend Samuel. As near as I could figure, *Waiting for Bardot* was a dark comedy about contemporary sexual mores in which two dames, Estrogen and Testosterone, wait outside a Parisian animal rights center in the hopes of shagging some broad named Bridget, who eventually joins them in a *ménage à trollops*.

Following another glass of wine and a few more disagreements, the two philosophers were eventually forced to go inside to the toilet to continue their bickering. This was mainly due to Jean-Paul staring too long at a knot on a nearby tree, which for some reason caused him to feel an intense nausea at his own existence. Of course this may seem rather odd behavior to any urban investigator who's never been to Paris, but I assure you that these sorts of psychological disturbances are commonplace in this most philosophical of cities.

However, I too was eventually forced to go inside to the toilet, though in my case for normal biological reasons. Once in the head, and as is my usual habit, I read the scribblings of a previous tenant, Walter Kaufmann, who offered a thought from his book *Existentialism from Dostoevsky to Sartre* (1956): "Existentialism is not a philosophy but a label for several widely different revolts against traditional philosophy. Existentialism is not a school of thought nor reducible to any set of tenets. One essential feature shared by all existentialists is their perfervid individualism."

After finishing my business and while washing my hands, Jean-Paul and Albert pulled me into an argument once again. It ended up one that caused me to become so disoriented that I couldn't find the exit - there was no bloody exit! Fortunately, I finally did find a way out of the toilet. And while leaving the café I asked myself an all-important question: "If Hell isn't other people, then what the hell is?"

Luxembourg Quarter

Finally away from those two quibbling philosophers, I made my way up Boulevard St-Germain in a hurry, for it was almost time to meet Marcel for that glass of wine. Turning onto Rue de Tournon, I shortly arrived at the Palais du Luxembourg, now home to the French Senate. I then wandered through the grounds until finding myself in the Jardin du Luxembourg, a beautiful garden that's home to the exquisite Octagonal Lake and a multitude of *flâneurs* that forever pass the time observing life, playing chess or just sunbathing.

After wandering about, I spotted Marcel occupying a park bench and so went over to join him for a glass of white wine. Just as I sat down, the smell of watermelon caused my mind to bring to consciousness an image of myself at about the age of seven standing in the backyard of my childhood home eating cold watermelon with great pleasure. I felt the happiness of that young *me*, a boy content to pass a warm summer's day in the time-honored tradition of enjoying a piece of watermelon and spitting the seeds hither and yon. When the image vanished, I smelled the bouquet of the wine, which indeed, displayed a slight scent of watermelon.

I mentioned this to Marcel and he commented, "You have just enjoyed what many would call your first 'Proustian Moment'. It is an instant in life that is unplanned in our search of lost time, and it comes upon us by some unforeseen event, in your case, the bouquet of the wine: 'Perhaps the immobility of the things that surround us is forced upon them by our conviction that they are themselves and not anything else, and by the immobility of our conception of them.... And so it is with our own past. It is a labor in vain to attempt to recapture it: all the efforts of our intellect must prove futile. The past is hidden somewhere outside the realm, beyond the reach of intellect, in some material object (in the sensation which that material object will give us) of which we have no inkling. And it depends on chance whether or not we come upon this object before we ourselves must die.'

"Let me give you another example concerning memory, this one regarding your meetings with Ernest, Jean-Paul and Albert earlier today. As you know, those three distinguished writers are all well and truly dead, and have been for quite some time, at least in the physical sense. So you see, a familiar street, for example, Boulevard St-Germain, is never just a street. No, it is also a collection of memories. And it's not just the streets, but also entire cities that are a compilation of past experiences, or should I say histories. For though you've never investigated Paris directly before your arrival here a week or so ago, you already knew the city quite well beforehand. Most likely those images and impressions were imbedded within you through television and movies, through newspapers and books, and through conversations with others that told you of their journeys to Paris.

"Now, if a tourist knows little about the historical significance of that famed boulevard, he merely enjoys a fine meal, in say Brasserie Lipp, and then perhaps entertains himself with observations of and scenarios concerning the other patrons. But if a knowledgeable traveler enjoys that very same meal, he contemplates not just the other patrons dining out on that particular day, but also on the ones who've dined there in the past, such as Jean-Paul. Of course this begs an all-important question: Which type of patron is more real, the ones who pay today or the ones who paid sometime in the past?

"Of course the current owner of Brasserie Lipp hopes that the patrons who pay today are more real, for he has very good reasons for desiring an objective world of debits and credits, of places and things, of the here and now. But from the existential investigator's perspective, there seems to be many good reasons for desiring that the experience in the restaurant be much more subjective in nature.

For if one meets up with Jean-Paul at Brasserie Lipp, and in doing so takes pleasure in his good company, has he not enjoyed a more rewarding dining experience than it might otherwise have been in the objective world of the uninformed tourist?

"While investigating Paris, have you not experienced a long series of curious meetings with distinguished people and literary characters, and were they not encounters that most definitely should not have been taking place? Of course, those encounters varied as regards their style. You met up with contemporary people who are still alive and well, but clearly in the wrong place. At other times you ran into historical figures that were plainly in the wrong time, if not necessarily in the wrong place. Even more strangely, sometimes in Paris you bump into eccentric literary characters that never existed at any time or in any place except in the pages of a book or a play or a poem."

With his lessons in the search for lost time now at an end, Marcel bid me adieu after once again giving me a list of places that I should visit on my own the next day, this time in Montparnesse, and where to meet him in the Jardin des Plantes Quarter in the late afternoon. Fortunately, Marcel offered me what was left of the bottle of wine and I spent the remainder of the afternoon enjoying it while watching other *flâneurs* contemplating life while storing all their images into memory. And would those memories ever be retrieved and contemplated once again? As with most things in life, and as Marcel well knew, only time would tell.

Montparnesse and Jardin des Plantes Quarter

Montparnesse offers the existential investigator the opportunity to continue his inquiries into the most influential, at least in the nonacademic sense, philosophical movement of the twentieth century, Existentialism. Jean-Paul Sartre and Albert Camus were the two leading existentialists, mainly because each advanced his philosophical ideas within novels easily understandable to any interested reader. However, a less-acclaimed philosopher, at least in the popular sense, was Simone de Beauvoir, the influential feminist writer. She advanced the cause of women in their modern battle to be viewed by men as autonomous individuals, ones that freely construct their own journeys through life.

Cimetière du Montparnesse

The next morning after making my way to the Edgar Quinet Metro station, I crossed Boulevard Edgar Quinet to the Principale entrance of Cimetière du Montparnesse, home to the final resting places of many an illustrious Parisian, including several that once called the Left Bank home. A thorough investigation of this cemetery offers the graves of the poet Charles Baudelaire, the novelist Guy de Maupassant, the photographer Man Ray, and the unjustly accused Jewish army officer, Alfred Dreyfus.

After turning right onto the cemetery walkway Avenue du Boulevard and strolling a short distance, I came upon the final abode of Jean-Paul and Simone, who, as life-long companions, were buried together. And as it turns out, Marcel sent me there to make conversation with this fascinating feminist, and to hear her story of the young woman Colette and her courageous efforts to construct meaning in her life.

One of the more interesting rituals of visiting Jean-Paul and Simone's adjoining gravesites is that it is customary to offer

Jean-Paul a cigarette, and the brand does not seem to matter much. The reason for this is that, as is evidenced in many a photograph, the acclaimed existentialist never had a picture taken without one dangling from what must have been his extremely tobacco-stained fingers. Apparently, existential choice-making also allows for one to occasionally make the wrong choices in life.

Just as I was moving on to explore other parts of the cemetery, I heard a woman's voice call from behind me, "Sam, mind if I have a word with you."

I turned around to find an attractive woman of perhaps sixty, who approached me and said, "May I introduce myself, I am Simone de Beauvoir, but please just call me Simone."

"Very pleased to meet you," I responded, "and I take it you already know my name. I assume that Marcel or one of the other philosophical investigators at the agency contacted you about me."

"Yes they did," she continued, "philosophers always keep in touch, though there's one thinker in particular that engages me in conversation far too much these days. Today I need a short break from the never-ending musings of my dear Jean-Paul. So let us walk about the cemetery, just the two of us, for I have what I think is a most interesting story."

With that, Simone took my arm in the French tradition and we slowly began our walk. After a few steps, she began, "This is the story of Colette, a young woman I met many years ago before the German Occupation of Paris. I remember her then as I always want to remember her, as young and very pretty, and as a woman with a captivating and disarming free-spirit. However, her story begins during the other war, the Great War, when her mother met a young soldier on leave from the front. Given the crisis in Paris, which was being incessantly attacked by German artillery, they fell in love quickly, and so made the most of what turned out to be a very short time together.

"After only a week, the young soldier was ordered back to the front, where he lasted but a few days before being killed in a mortar attack. Within a couple of months, Colette's mother found herself with a child on the way. Fortunately, her mother was a strong-willed woman. And though a single mother with few means at her disposal, she brought her daughter up with great care and parental love. But the times were difficult for everyone, especially when the economy failed at the beginning of the Depression.

"Not wanting her daughter to go without, Colette's mother pursued what she had always hoped to become, a celebrated dancer. Although there were very few jobs for dancers in those difficult times, she eventually joined the dancers at the Follies Bergère. This celebrated cabaret music hall was established in 1869, and by the 1890s achieved its greatest fame during the period of the Belle Époque. And though its popularity diminished after the Great War, it still remained emblematic of Parisian life.

"The young mother was eventually spotted at the Follies Bergère by the owners of the Moulin Rouge, or the Red Mill, who offered her a position in the acclaimed chorus line. Paris' most famous dance establishment was founded in 1889 near Place Pigalle, the red-light district of Montmartre, and it became known as the birthplace of the 'can-can' dance. And though it seems rather bland compared to today's over-sexualized entertainment industry, at the time Colette's mother joined the dance line, showing one's knickers in public was still considered quite provocative.

"As regards Colette at this time, the mother sheltered her as best she could from the world in which she worked, forever hoping to make a better life for her daughter. But like her mother, Colette enjoyed a love of dance, and by the late 1930s she was training in local academies for a possible career in the ballet. She also began sitting in on free lectures at the Sorbonne, where Jean-Paul and I offered a weekly talk on various issues in Existentialism and feminism. This is when I first met Colette, and when I began to encourage her interest in feminist ideas by giving her books to read.

"Our philosophical friendship lasted several years, with the two of us often going out to enjoy a glass of wine and each others' company after a lecture. Then two tragedies occurred in Colette's life, ones that greatly changed her outlook on the world. The first was on June 14, 1940, when German occupation forces entered an undefended Paris, remaining there until Paris was liberated in August of 1944. Of course, this was a tragedy for all Parisians. The second heartbreak occurred five weeks later, when Colette's mother died, mostly from illness, though partly from a feeling of hopelessness in life. And so Colette was left to engage the world on her own, and that's when I lost track of her for three years, mainly because my weekly lectures had been stopped by the newly installed government.

"It was in early October of 1943 that, quite by accident, I learned of Collette's whereabouts. I noticed a poster for a show at 'Un Club pour Hommes', in the Place Pigalle. The image on the poster was the exact likeness of her, and she was apparently performing as 'La Siren dans le mer'. As I had absolutely no idea what this could possibly be, I made my way over to the club one night in the hope of meeting up with her.

"I discovered that the Germans occupied not only Paris, but also the club, and so was denied entrance. Not to be dissuaded, I made my way to the back of the building to find the worker's entrance. And when no one was looking, I snuck in and eventually saw 'La Siren dans le mer'. The show took place in the private party room located in the basement of the club, also the site of a huge aquarium. Colette lay behind it, with her image magnified by a lens into the aquarium.

"To please the German crowd that always occupied the room, Colette, now a woman with a goddess-like body, wore nothing over her breasts and only a mermaid's outfit below. For the crowd's entertainment she danced the exotic dance of a mermaid, continually waving her arms as if swimming with the fish. It would have been a most beautiful and mesmerizing optical illusion if not for the crowd, who'd make crude and drunken comments about Colette. She told me later that she always put wax in ears, just like Odysseus, to avoid the sound, not of the Sirens, but of the occupiers.

"After the show ended, I managed to catch Colette's eye and motioned for her to meet me outside on the street. As soon as we met she was in my arms, with both of us so very pleased to have found each other again. It is so very true, the moment when we once again meet a long-departed friend is one of the most gratifying moments in any life. We immediately made our way to a nearby café, where she told me what had happened since we'd last seen each other.

"Colette said that after her mother died she was forced to withdraw from her dance classes and take a job, any job. But with work difficult to come by in occupied Paris, the only way she found to survive as a dancer was in the clubs of Place Pigalle. Tears came to my eyes when she told me of the humiliation and loneliness of taking her top off to please the occupiers, but it was either that or starve. Fortunately, she was eventually offered the job as 'La Siren dans le mer'.

"We then returned to our previous discussions of philosophical issues, with Colette now offering me a most unique view of her act. Each night while in the aquarium, and to avoid thinking about the situation, she would enter into her own private world and think back to our talks on feminism. Interestingly, she'd come to what I believe is a most accurate description of the relationship between men and women. Men always view women through a lens, seeing what they want to see and only what they want to see. In this sense, all women live in an aquarium with respect to men.

"It was quite late when we left each other that night, and before we parted I gave Colette a ticket to Jean-Paul's play *The Flies* at the Théâtre de la Cité. She promised to attend, and to also join me for drinks after the performance. I remember to this day that on the night of the show she arrived in a loose-fitting black and white polka dot blouse, with a lovely red tie at the neck lying just off to the side. She literally caught the eye of every man in the theater, and being Paris, quite likely some of the women. To say that Colette was beautiful that night would describe almost nothing, but I would have to say that at that moment she was quite possibly the most captivating woman in Paris, a city where beauty is hardly a rare commodity.

"Colette sat next to me during the play, and she remained entranced for the entire performance. *The Flies* was Jean-Paul's adaptation of the Orestes and Electra myth, which tells the story of the killing of King Agamemnon of Argos, by his wife Queen Clytemnestra and her lover Ægisthus, upon the leader's return from the Trojan Wars. The play itself recounts Orestes' homecoming to Argos and his decision to join with his sister Electra in avenging the death of his father.

"However, *The Flies* only uses the story as a cover to send the message that the people of France must now make a decision, whether to continue under the yoke of the Occupation or to choose to be free and accept the responsibility of that choice. The flies in the play represent the occupiers, with Clytemnestra and Ægisthus being the traitorous French who choose to live under tyranny rather than fight for freedom. They kill Agamemnon, who represents what was formerly free France. And of course, Orestes and Electra are the youth of the country that must make the ultimate existential choice, whether or not to act to be free.

"I can remember to this day how in Act II, after Orestes kills Ægistheus and his mother Clytemnestra, and then goes to meet with his sister Electra, how Colette moved forward to the edge of her seat when she heard the lines: 'I am free... Freedom has crashed down on me like a thunderbolt.... The heavier it is to carry, the better pleased I shall be; for that burden is my freedom.'

"Colette moved forward in her seat once again in Act III, when Zeus confronts Orestes and Electra over the murder of their mother and her lover: 'Neither slave nor master. I am my freedom.' Further along in the act, I noticed Colette almost trembling when Zeus attempts but fails to turn Orestes back to his former condition as his slave: 'What they choose. They're free; and human life begins on the far side of despair.'

"With that said, Colette turned to me and laid her head on my shoulder, sobbing quietly and almost unable to speak. She then whispered in my ear that she was no different than Electra, denying her own freedom with the choice not to be free. When the curtain went down, we walked out to the street and to a café around the corner, one popular with philosophers, students and members of the French resistance movement. After she sipped a glass of wine in silence, she said to me that she needed to join the resistance, to help in the common cause to free Paris and the rest of France.

"Although I still regret my decision to this day, not in my mind, but in my heart, for I truly loved her dearly, I introduced Colette to a member of the movement in the club that night. This young Parisian was a philosophy major at the Sorbonne before the beginning of the Occupation, but he quickly became a member of the resistance after realizing that philosophy was a luxury that would have to wait until less turbulent times. Jean-Paul had known him for some time as a promising intellectual, and he had introduced him to me a year or so before. What I didn't know would happen was that as soon as Colette met him, the two would fall passionately in love.

"I still remember the two of them sitting at a far away table, both unable to take their eyes off one another. It was as though before their meeting, life had been a puzzle, with all the other pieces never fitting precisely into the piece that was them. But after this union, the two pieces fit where they were meant to, two souls clinging to each other in a war-torn world that had mixed up all the pieces of life's puzzle. And when they danced near the end of the evening to *Polka Dots and Moonbeams*, it was clear to me that each finally understood the meaning of love.

"When the song ended, Colette put her arms around the philosopher's neck and they kissed for the first time, thus sealing their two fates into one. They were now lovers and compatriots, with both of them firmly committed to the eradication of 'the flies' that held France hostage. And they also now understood that they'd made the ultimate choices in life... that of love and only love, that of freedom and only freedom.

"Throughout November the resistance organized a plot to plant explosives at 'Un Club pour Hommes' on Christmas Eve, but the key to optimizing the impact of the attack was dependent upon 'La Siren dans le mer'. Colette offered the movement the most feasible plan, though it was also the most dangerous for her. She'd advertise a holiday show that featured her not only with her breasts in view, but also without her usual mermaid outfit. Because of demand, tickets for such an event would be too expensive for all but the highest of

German military staff, so it was assured that a large number of them would be in the basement during the performance.

"But there remained one difficult problem, how to get the explosives into the basement without the Germans observing what was going on. Colette had a plan for this as well, for she knew of a brick wall behind the aquarium where a tunnel could extend into an adjoining building to the club. So with a large enough tunnel dug between the two buildings, and with proper guidance, she could wire the explosives during the intermission when the curtain in her act was drawn.

"By Christmas Eve everything was in place, and Colette performed her first act as usual. Even from behind the aquarium she could see that the basement was filled with high-ranking military personnel, as well as with influential German politicos. So during the intermission, which only lasted fifteen minutes, she removed the bricks hiding the tunnel and pulled on the rope that brought the explosives and wires from the adjoining building to her. She then nervously connected the wires to the explosives, turned on the timer, and left the aquarium as she normally did during intermission.

"Colette went immediately to the toilet, where a change of clothing was hidden. After changing, she eased herself through the window to the outside of the club. Walking slowly so as to remain inconspicuous, she turned a corner just as the explosion went off behind her. The concussion knocked her to the ground, but she quickly got up and fled to the rendezvous point to meet her lover and compatriot.

"The next day the word was out that the operation was a complete success, with seventeen high-ranking German officers killed and dozens more seriously injured in the explosion. The German high command in Paris ordered an all out search for Colette, who was deemed the one most likely to be responsible for the plot. Colette and her young philosopher remained in hiding for the next week, though they were moved to new locations every few days by members of the resistance movement.

"But it was clear from the start that it was only a matter of time before they were caught, and that moment occurred on the first day of 1944. Not knowing exactly what went on, I'd like to think that when the two lovers heard the approaching footsteps of the SS unit, they said their final goodbyes and enjoyed a last kiss. What I do know is that the young philosopher was killed almost immediately in a desperate attempt to gun down the enemy and protect his lover and compatriot. And I also know that Colette was taken into custody, given a mock trial, and then sent to Alsace-Lorraine, to Natzweiler-Struthof, the only Nazis concentration camp built on present-day French territory.

"Colette never returned to Paris from Natzweiler-Struthof, her life ending in the harsh and brutal conditions of the work camp. In fact she was never heard from again, though her legacy lives on in the annals of the French resistance movement, as well as in the memories of her friends. And though the story of Colette may sound a sad one, it is really one to be celebrated, for her choice to embrace freedom meant that all of France would one day be free."

I'd been so entranced by the story of Colette that I hadn't noticed that our walk was now where it started, the gravesite of Jean-Paul and Simone, and she soon continued with her conversation, "I want you to see a small plaque that I placed next to my site many years ago":

Colette
1918 - 1944
Dancer, Feminist, Resistance Fighter

"But let us sit down on that bench over there, for I'm not used to long walks anymore. I told you the story of Colette for a very good reason, and that is to evidence to you that a freely-chosen existence is not only just for every man, but also for every woman. I wrote down my thoughts on this matter in my book *The Second Sex* (1949): 'If her functioning as a female is not enough to define a woman, if we decline also to explain her through *the eternal feminine*, and if nevertheless we admit, provisionally, that women do exist, then we must face the question: what is a woman?... Humanity is male and man defines woman not in herself but as relative to him; she is not regarded as an autonomous being.... He is the Subject, he is the Absolute - she is the Other.'

"Allow me to touch upon one more illustration as regards Existentialism and feminism. Perhaps you have seen in a museum somewhere my good friend Pablo Picasso's 'The Bull', a series of sketches that begins with a drawing of a complete bull. Then over the next seven or eight drawings, Pablo removes one aspect of the bull in each new sketch. In the end, all that is left of the bull is a curved line representing its penis. And given his sexual proclivities in life, this is a most appropriate metaphor for Pablo's view of men.

"But if a woman was to design a series of sketches of herself as an individual in the world, what would she draw? I think the first drawing would be a curved line representing the vagina, the aspect that initially defines her in the world as the Other. In the next drawing she would add her womb, the cradle of both man and the Other. And in the next the curves of her body, all characteristics that differentiate man from the Other. Eventually she would complete a sketch showing the features of her entire body, her complete Other, the one adored and controlled by man.

"However, if a woman has engaged in freely chosen projects, then the metamorphosis of that woman away from her Otherness cannot end there. For the next drawing would have to show her as a writer, as an artist, as a doctor, as a scholar, or perhaps as a mother or a carer, any life freely entered into by her. And finally, the last sketch would be a blank drawing, which indicates that the unknown future would involve her in other freely chosen projects yet to be determined by her, but instrumental in her evolving womanhood.

"Well, I have to say that I am terribly tired now and probably should get back to Jean-Paul. I hope our conversation today has opened your mind to a new view of women." Simone then hugged me, kissed me on both cheeks, and returned to her place alongside her companion.

Catacombs

Though rather overwhelmed by my long conversation with Simone, I collected my thoughts on the way to the next destination on Marcel's investigation list. After returning to Boulevard Edgar Quinet, I turned right and proceeded to Boulevard Raspail. Turning right again, I walked to the next huge intersection, then crossed it to find myself at the entrance to an often overlooked spot in Paris called the Catacombs. In 1786 the cemetery of Les Halles was deemed unsanitary, so the bones of the less than famous were brought to Montparnesse and placed underground. It's a fascinating and chilling place, and as well, it was used by the French Resistance during the Occupation. And to hide this fact, the resistance fighters engraved at the entrance the phrase *Arrete - Cest ICI de la mort*, which translates as "Stop! This is the empire of death."

While following the path that traverses about the chambers of the Catacombs and investigating the millions of old bones, an older gentleman, Dr. Rieux, said to me, "Allow me to tell you about my intimate knowledge concerning the realities of death, what I prefer to call *The Plague* (1947). All these catacombs remind me of the 1940's when I lived in Oran, a port on the Algerian coast. It was there that I first experienced the first death in the plague. At first, I wasn't certain whether or not it was the dreaded disease. But as more and more people came down with the symptoms and died, I began to reluctantly imagine that it might be the plague.

"Needless to say, the town denied it was the pestilence, at least until the authorities shut us down and isolated us from loved ones caught outside the perimeter. The plague took its course as more and more sick were treated each day, though all were fated to the same inevitable outcome. The days drifted into weeks, which then drifted into months, with all citizens now working towards a common cause. The plague progressed into the hot months of summer, and as it continued, I reconsidered my role as a doctor: 'For many years I've been ashamed, morally ashamed, of having been, even with the best intentions, even at many removes, a murderer in my turn.... Yes, I've been ashamed ever since; I have realized that we all have plague, and I have lost my peace.'

"The plague finally ended, the gates of the city opened, and loved ones were reunited, with the city once again happy: '[I] knew what those jubilant crowds did not know but could have learned from books: that the plague bacillus never dies or disappears for good; that it can lie dormant for years and years in furniture and linen-chests; that it bides its time in bedrooms, cellars, trunks, and bookshelves; and that perhaps the day would come when, for the bane and the enlightening of men, it would rouse up its rats again and send them forth to die in a happy city.'"

Finally at the end of the path traversing the chambers of the Catacombs, the Doctor and I climbed the stairs to the outside world and parted company. Feeling a slight case of *Nausea* (1938) after being far underground for the better part of an hour, I made my way to a local café and ordered a glass of white wine to settle my nerves. After draining the first glass quickly and still not feeling much better, I ordered a second one and decided to "determine the exact extent and nature of this change."

In so doing, I took out a pen and a piece of paper that I might keep a record of my state of mind: "Things are bad! Things are very bad: I have it, the filth, the Nausea.... And since that time, the Nausea has not left me, it holds me.... And it was true, I had always realized it; I hadn't the right to exist.... Nothing. Existed.... I am free: there is absolutely no more reason for living... Today my life is ending."

La Closerie des Lilas

Fortunately, after another fifteen minutes all my symptoms of nausea completely cleared up and I proceeded on my merry Parisian way. Leaving the café, I staggered along Avenue Denfert Rochereau until reaching one of the great literary restaurants of Paris, La Closerie des Lilas, which opened its doors in 1847. The tables of the "Pleasure Garden of the Lilacs" have given comfort to the likes of Gertrude

Stein and Alice B. Toklas, Paul Verlaine and Charles Baudelaire, Jean-Paul Sartre and Simone de Beauvoir, Vladimir Lenin and Leon Trotsky, Pablo Picasso and James Whistler, Henry James and F. Scott Fitzgerald, and Ernest Hemingway, who wrote *The Sun Also Rises* there.

Since I hadn't made any reservations, and given that this is one of the most popular restaurants in Paris, I contented myself with a light snack and a glass of wine at the bar. After ordering, I noticed a strange looking man sitting next to me, one who clearly needed to talk to someone. He appeared to be in quite a state, so I indicated to him that my ears were open. Unfortunately, I never found out the name of this young man, so I'll merely refer to him as *The Stranger* (1942). After the meal and wine arrived, The Stranger said, "Allow me to tell you a rather odd tale.

"When Maman died, I traveled by bus to the rest home on Thursday and stood vigil around the coffin with the other old people, who gave me 'the ridiculous feeling that they were there to judge me.' I buried Maman on Friday and returned home, spending the night with Marie, then Sunday as usual. The next morning I returned to work and the boss asked if I'd like to work in the new office in Paris. The following Sunday I went with friends to a beach house and had a run-in with a group of Arabs, one of which I shot. I was taken to jail and met with a lawyer, who questioned me about the death of Maman.

"After a few days I was taken to talk to a magistrate, but the interview only provoked him to anger: 'Drawing himself up to his full height and asking me if I believed in God, I said no.... He said it was impossible; all men believed in God, even those who turn their backs on him. *Do you want my life to be meaningless?* he shouted: As far as I could see, it didn't have anything to do with me, and I told him so.'

"I spent almost a year in jail, but the case eventually came to trial. After a few more days came the judgment of guilty and the sentence of death on the guillotine, after which, I was sent back to my cell. I was not terribly bothered, for '... everybody knows life isn't worth living.... Since we're all going to die, it's obvious that when and how don't matter.' When the final day arrived, I understood that it is possible to begin life again at every moment. 'And I felt ready to live it all again too.... I opened myself to the gentle indifference of the world. Finding it so much like myself..."'

With his story over, The Stranger bid his adieu without telling me how he'd gotten out of the mess he was in, though I assumed that at the last minute the court had stayed his execution. With lunch over, I was just about to order a martini when an older man came up to me and said, "Good afternoon." I indicated to him that he should stay.

After retrieving his drink, he sat down next to me. The man then ordered another gin, and once our drinks arrived he resumed the conversation: "'If you want to know, I was a lawyer before coming here. Now, I am a judge-penitent. But allow me to introduce myself: Jean-Baptiste Clamence, at your service.... we cannot assert the innocence of anyone, whereas we can state with certainty the guilt of all. Every man testifies to the crime of all the others - that is my faith and hope.... I'll tell you a big secret, *mon cher*. Don't wait for the Last Judgment. It takes place every day."'

With that, Jean-Baptiste bid his adieu and left me to my gin martini. And I'm certain that as he once again walked the streets of Paris, he knew that *The Fall* (1956) that had occurred to him so many years before would undoubtedly occur again, when he would once more fail the test. For as Jean-Baptiste so rightly knew, one is what one is in life.

Jardin des Plantes Quarter

After leaving the restaurant, I walked down Boulevard de Port Royal to Boulevard Saint Marcel to find myself in the Jardin des Plantes Quarter. I proceeded along the boulevard in the direction of the river until reaching Boulevard de L'Hospital, and then continued towards the river until arriving at the entrance to Jardin des Plantes, with its beautiful gardens and the Muséum National d'Historie Naturelle. And after making my way to the Ménagerie, I wandered about the zoo until finding the monkey house, where Marcel was patiently waiting for me on a bench.

I first told Marcel all about the day: my conversation with Simone, the story of Colette, the doctor in the Catacombs, the bizarre fit of nausea, and the two strange persons in the café. He found it all very entertaining, and after thinking for a moment, said, "Let me see, I spoke about love the other day, and then about memories yesterday, so perhaps today I might turn the conversation to that most beguiling of our little luxuries, philosophy. Fortunately for our friends the monkeys over there, as well as for most of the human race, they exist in the world never feeling the need to methodically construct meaning in life, with that preoccupation left to the mind of the philosopher.

"However, even the philosophical investigator is prone to many errors in the eternal search for truth: 'A large part of what we believe to be true (and this applies even to our final conclusions) with a persistence equaled only by our good faith, springs from an original mistake in our premises.... We may have revolved every possible idea in our minds, and yet the truth has never occurred to us, and it is from without, when we are least expecting it, that it gives us its cruel stab and wounds us forever.'

"Well, enough of these meandering thoughts for one day, for philosophical notions are always at hand if one only takes time to consider them. And, *mon cher*, we can always return to them tomorrow." So with the conversation at an end, Marcel first stood up and then bid me and the other monkies adieu. And as before, he gave me a list of places that I should visit on my own the next day, this time in the Latin Quarter, and where to meet him in the afternoon, this time in Montmartre.

Latin Quarter and Montmartre

Just as in Montparnesse, the Latin Quarter offers existential investigators and other students of philosophy many opportunities to continue their inquiries into Existentialism. Fortunately for me, on the day of my investigations Jean-Paul Sartre was offering a lecture at La Sorbonne and Albert Camus doing the same at the Collège de France. And as requested by Marcel, in the afternoon I traveled to Montmartre, atop which stands Sacré Couer, where I said goodbye to my now beloved Paris.

La Sorbonne

After taking the Metro the next morning to Cluny la Sorbonne station, I walked away from the river along Boulevard Saint Michel to Rue des Ecoles and La Sorbonne, the seat of the University of Paris. Established in 1253, the school eventually became the center of scholastic theology and remained so for much of its existence. Its then traditional academic methods forced its closure during the Revolution, though it was re-established by Napoleon in 1806. Of course these days its academic approach is anything but traditional, and on the day of my visit I was fortunate to attend a lecture by my friend Jean-Paul entitled *Existentialism is a Humanism* (1946).

After finding a seat in the lecture room, the famed philosopher began his talk: "We can begin by saying that existentialism, in our sense of the word, is a doctrine that does render human life possible; a doctrine, also, which affirms that every truth and every action imply both an environment and a human subjectivity.... This is humanism, because we remind man that there is no legislator but himself; that he himself, thus abandoned, must decide for himself; also because we show that it is not by turning back upon himself, but always by seeking, beyond himself, an aim which is one of liberation or some particular realization, that man can realize himself as truly human."

Collège de France

Once the lecture ended, and realizing myself to now be an Existentialist and a Humanist, I projected and almost lost myself getting back onto Rue des Ecoles. After continuing along until hitting Rue Saint Jacques, I crossed the street to the Collège de France, which was founded in 1530 as an institute of research and learning. Even today there remains on display its long-standing motto, *docet omnia*, or, "all taught here." And nothing could be more accurate, for the college indeed took me in that morning and showed me a seat in the hall of learning.

My friend Albert offered the lecture, *The Myth of Sisyphus* (1942): "... Sisyphus teaches the higher fidelity that negates the gods and raises rocks. He too concludes that all is well. This universe henceforth without a master seems to him neither sterile nor futile. Each atom of that stone, each mineral flake of that night-filled mountain, in itself forms a world. The struggle itself toward the heights is enough to fill a man's heart. One must imagine Sisyphus happy."

Shakespeare & Co

One must also imagine me happy as I left the lecture hall, and as I proceeded down Rue Saint Jacques in the direction of the river. As well, one must imagine me happy as I turned right on Quai de Montebello and discovered the antiquarian bookshop Shakespeare & Co, the most chaotic house of books in the world. After browsing about the shop for some time in a mostly disoriented fashion, I finally found a book that might possibly suit my needs. So I purchased it, had them stamp the traditional logo "Shakespeare & Co Kilometre Zéro Paris" onto the front page, and ventured back outside to a bench overlooking Notre-Dame cathedral, where my investigation of Paris began two weeks back.

Over the last few days it had dawned on me that perhaps I might write up all the little excursions I'd gone on in Paris, and also tell any possible readers about all the philosophical investigators I'd run into on those excursions. But where to start, that was the question? And with that in mind, I opened up my new book of essays, *Literature and Existentialism* (1949), one penned by my friend Jean-Paul. Firstly, I had to ask myself three pertinent questions, ones that he asked of all writers in his essay "What Is Writing?": "What is your aim in writing?... What aspect of the world do you want to disclose?... Why do you want to change this rather than that?"

Then I discovered in his essay "Why Write?" that Jean-Paul also asked all writers to consider various aspects of this modern and widespread literary malady, this overwhelming compulsion to write something: "Why does it have to be 'writing,' why does one have to manage his escapes and conquests by 'writing'? Because, behind the various aims of authors, there is a deeper and more immediate choice which is common to all of us.... the writer, a free man addressing free men, has only one subject - freedom."

In the final essay of his book, Jean-Paul would have me consider one last question, "For Whom Does One Write?": "... since the freedoms of the author and the reader seek and affect each other through a world, it can just as well be said that the author's choice of a certain aspect of the world determines the reader and, vice-versa, that it is by choosing his reader that the author decides upon his subject."

Montmartre

Returning to Boulevard Saint Michel, I walked up to the Saint Michel Metro station and boarded a series of trains to eventually exit at the Blanche station in Montmartre, where as planned, Marcel was waiting for me. It was still only the early afternoon, so we decided to enjoy a slow but steady investigation of the area. Beginning first along Boulevard de Clichy, Marcel showed me the Moulin Rouge and Place Pigalle. Both places were very quiet, I suppose because it was the time of day when men are generally less-preoccupied with gawking at the bare bottoms of the opposite sex.

From Place Pigalle we walked up Rue des Martyrs, and then turned left onto Rue des Abbesses, which we strolled down, enjoying Place des Abbesses on our way to Cemetière de Montmartre. As with all other Parisian cemeteries, the one in Montmartre is home to many a celebrated Frenchman, one of the more famous being the film director François Truffaut. After wandering about the cemetery for some time, Marcel had us sit on a bench, where he spoke to me about the pleasurable, though these days rather old-fashioned, act of reading a book.

After offering me his thoughts on the act of reading, Marcel and I left the cemetery and walked up the hill along the winding Rue Caulaincourt to where it meets Rue Lamarck. And turning right onto Rue des Saules brought us to "Au Lapin Agile - Cabaret Artistique," a place originally called "Cabaret des Assassins" as a result of a band of assassins that broke in and killed the owner's son many years ago. Its current name came about in 1875 through the efforts of the artist Andre Gill, when he painted a restaurant sign depicting a rabbit jumping out of a saucepan. Today it is the meeting place for a mixture of ordinary and out of the ordinary types, who all enjoy the cabarets' renditions of traditional French songs.

While we sat at one of the tables in the front courtyard of the cabaret, Marcel spoke to me about the pleasurable, though these days far from old-fashioned, act of writing a book. Marcel then told me about how he envisioned the relationship between him, the writer, and the unknown readers of his book: "So, if I were given long enough to accomplish my work, I should not fail, even if the effect were to make them resemble monsters, to describe men as occupying so considerable a place, compared with the restricted place which is reserved for them in space, a place on the contrary prolonged past measure, for simultaneously, like giants plunged into the years, they touch the distant epochs through which they have lived, between which so many days have come to range themselves - in Time."

After offering me his thoughts on the act of writing, Marcel and I continued up Rue des Saules until finding ourselves at Place des Tertre, a square that's so Parisian you expect to see Gene Kelly in *An American in Paris* selling his paintings there. Once through with walking about the place, we followed the streets to the steps leading up to Sacré-Coeur, the basilica that commemorates the saving of the French nation during the Franco-Prussian War. The building of this unique and impressive church began in 1875, with construction continuing for the next forty years. And though it appears to offer the highest point in Paris, the Ovoid Dome that sits atop Sacré-Coeur actually comes in second to the eagle's-eye view from the crown of the Eiffel Tower.

Standing outside the front of the church, Marcel mentioned that he had to organize a meeting to take place in an hour or so with some of the philosophical investigators from the agency. He recommended that I take this time to investigate Sacré-Coeur, so I entered the church and explored every nook and cranny for the better part of that hour. Near the end of my investigation I walked to the back of the basilica, where candles cast shadows of various objects on a wall. And though those images appeared to be real, I realized that they were nothing but reflections of the actual world.

With my hour up, I made my way to the front of the church and began to walk outside, though the sun was so bright that I immediately turned back to the door of the basilica. As my eyes began to adjust to the brightness, I saw that the church door now appeared to be nothing but the entrance to a cave, and as such, it offered no refuge for a philosophical investigator. So I turned away from the entrance to find my good friend Honoré, who took me by the arm and led me away from the church.

As we walked along, Honoré told me, "I trust you will never forget all the philosophical investigators that I informed you about and that we met during our modern investigation of the Right Bank. Always keep in mind, though Modernity appears to be missing these days, it most definitely is not, for the scientists, the technologists, the engineers, the mathematicians, and of course, the philosophers are always extending knowledge to new frontiers. And if you ever have any doubts about this in the future, you should return to France and visit my good friend Voltaire, who always welcomes philosophical investigators to his home in Ferney."

Now at the top of some stairs, Honoré dropped my arm, said goodbye, and told me to walk down to the next level, where I was greeted by all the philosophical investigators that I'd met during my postmodern investigation of the city. There were the aficionados of all aspects of Parisian culture, the text writers that give the reader so many pleasures, the modernists and postmodernists that quarrel so that knowledge remains objective and devoted to truth, and lastly, the poets and writers that bring us important ideas that no others can possibly bring to our subjective journey in life.

Walking over to the top of another set of stairs, my friend Marcel took me by the arm and walked me down to the next level. There I was greeted by Jean-Paul, Simone and Albert, the three existential investigators that forever ask all of us to choose to be free and committed in life. Marcel then let go of my arms and said to me, "Please continue to the far end of the level for the wonderful view of Paris, and also to say goodbye to two loving friends."

Once at the observation wall I enjoyed one of the grandest sights in the world, the panoramic view of Paris spreading out as far as the eye can see. I then felt someone take my arm and turned to see my friend Odette, who lovingly brought her lips to mine. However, when my eyes opened from the kiss it was not Odette that I saw before me, but a younger woman, one that I immediately knew to be the famed Colette. In that instant, I realized that both women had only led different lives because their existences were so dependent upon the time and the place and the circumstances in which they found themselves living in.

I then looked at her and said, "I'm so glad to finally meet you, Colette." And after looking up towards the top of the stairs, I asked, "Where has everyone gone? Will I ever see them again?"

Colette looked at me, and with her hands she caressed my face and said, "Sam, they are still here and will always be here, just as

Odette and I will always be here for you." She then moved one hand down to my heart, warming it with her touch, before she whispered, "We will always be here, both in your mind and your heart, just as all of Paris will forever be in your thoughts and memories."

In the next instant she too disappeared, leaving a book on the stone wall of the viewpoint that forever overlooks Paris. And when I opened it, I found the pages blank, realizing immediately why she had left this special gift for me. Paris, like any relationship of love, is a book continually being written, but with blank pages always left for the future. She is a lover that constantly calls you back to her arms, forever hoping to embrace you once again.

At that moment I knew that when I returned to San Francisco it would be necessary to write down my thoughts and memories concerning my first philosophical investigation of Paris. I'd first begin with my experiences as a modern investigator, and follow that with my time spent as a postmodern investigator. Finally, I'd tell the story of Odette and Colette, of Jean-Paul and Simone and Albert, of love and memory and philosophy, of reading and writing, to remind myself of all my experiences as an existential investigator. Throughout life, the book would always remain close to me so that I might forever remind myself of those long ago moments spent in the loving arms of Paris. When I returned to her arms once again, which I knew I would, she'd remind me of how I'd changed since we'd last seen one another. And she'd encourage me to continue gathering my memories about her to help fill in the remaining pages of the book.

After picking up the gift and before leaving, I enjoyed one last glimpse of Paris spreading out before me. And in that final moment, I thought back to what another American traveler once said about this beloved city: "There is never any ending to Paris and the memory of each person who has lived in it differs from that of any other.... If you are lucky enough to have lived in Paris as a young man, then wherever you go for the rest of your life, it stays with you, for Paris is a moveable feast."

The Philosophical
Investigator

The Philosophical Investigator

After returning home and enjoying a day of rest, I called Will and asked him to meet me at the office in the late afternoon. Once there, Will asked me to tell him about my philosophical investigations in Paris, with the journey pleasing him greatly. I told him that I'd found his missing Modernity, which, of course, hadn't been missing in the first place. And that I'd learned an important lesson, that Modernity is always around us and that we can't, nor do we want to escape it. It binds our lives together with its ever-increasing knowledge-base, its scientific approach to solving problems, its abundance of useful technologies, and its secular and democratic institutions. Needless to say, Will knew all those facts before sending me on the case.

Will was also pleased that I'd fallen in love with the City of Light, with the sights and the sounds, and the foods and the wines, of the most culturally-preoccupied city in the world. And he was especially delighted that I'd fallen in love with the two women that had made the investigation so memorable, Odette and Colette. Will told me that I now clearly understood what he'd said when we first met: "Paris is there to be loved through the mind, the body and the heart."

He then said, "But if you don't mind, I'd now like to tell you my story, the story of William James Durant, born in Massachusetts in 1885. With my mother hoping that I would eventually enter the priesthood, I was enrolled in the Catholic schools there, as well as in New Jersey, where my teachers urged me to enter the Jesuit Order following graduation. But this was not to be, for at some point on my youthful journey I discovered the works of the great philosophers, as well as their search for truth.

"After graduating from college in 1907 I became a cub reporter for the *New York Evening Journal*, though the grisly nature of the paper's articles meant my career would be a short-lived one. So later in the fall I went to teach languages and mathematics at Seton Hall College in South Orange, New Jersey. The college housed an excellent library, and given my great interest in books, I was also made the librarian. I moved to New York in 1911, and once there I joined with other liberal thinkers in pondering on the great ideas of the time, with my personal interest being Socialist thought. And around the same time I joined the staff of the Ferrer Modern School, where we experimented in progressive education.

"Following a summer spent traveling in Europe, I returned to the school, where I met my future wife, Ada Kaufman, who was a Russian immigrant that I affectionately called Ariel. After marrying her in 1913 I resigned my teaching position and entered graduate school at Columbia University, where I studied philosophy under John Dewey. And the dissertation for my doctorate in philosophy ended up my first book, *Philosophy and the Social Problem* (1917).

"After graduation I became an instructor at Columbia University, though that position only lasted until the beginning of the First World War. So now having few academic openings in life, Ariel and I established our residence in an old New York Presbyterian church, which we renamed the Labor Temple. Once organized, I gave lectures there on philosophy, history, literature, science, music and art. And as well, we established the Labor Temple School for adult education.

"Then an event occurred that changed Ariel's and my life forever, and it sent us on the intellectual journey of a lifetime. By pure happenstance, E. Haldeman-Julius, who was the publisher of the popular 'Little Blue Books', passed by the Labor Temple and noticed that I was to give a talk on Plato that Sunday afternoon. The publisher attended it, and he so enjoyed my lecture that he asked me to turn the talk into a 'Little Blue Book' publication, with that first essay followed by a similar publication on Aristotle. But it did not stop there, for after I had produced eleven 'Little Blue Books' by 1926, they were all bound together into one of my most popular works, *The Story of Philosophy*, which sold two million copies over the next few years. And following that first success, three years later I published *The Mansions of Philosophy: A Survey of Human Life and Destiny* (1929), which was also known as *The Pleasures of Philosophy*.

"Strange for a philosopher, I now found myself financially secure enough to pursue my long-held dream of writing *The Story of Civilization*. My original plan was to divide the work into five volumes, which I hoped would appear at five-year intervals. However, over time those five volumes turned into eleven and those twenty-five years turned into forty-five. However, let me offer you some of my thoughts from the preface of the first volume, for they are ideas that explain my purpose and my method in writing *The Story of Civilization*: 'I have tried in this book to accomplish the first part of a pleasant assignment which I rashly laid upon myself some twenty years ago, to write a history of civilization.'

"So was born *The Story of Civilization*, with its eleven volumes appearing over a period of forty years, from 1935 to 1975. It began with *Our Oriental Heritage*, and was followed by the history of pre-modern Western Civilization in *The Life of Greece*, *Caesar and Christ*, *The Age of Faith*, and *The Renaissance*. The final six volumes, *The Reformation*, *The Age of Reason Begins*, *The Age of Louis XIV*, *The Age of Voltaire*, *Rousseau and Revolution*, and *The Age of Napoleon*, covered the history of modern Western Civilization until 1815.

"Of course such an arduous and time-consuming project could never have been accomplished by one person alone. So with the eighth volume I added Ariel's name to the cover, though needless to say, she had been instrumental throughout the writing of every volume. And our tenth volume, *Rousseau and Revolution*, received the highest of American literary tributes, the Pulitzer Prize."

After hearing all about *The Story of Civilization*, I asked Will, "Have you ever thought about how you might have continued your story of civilization after the year 1815, if only time had allowed you to do so?"

Will responded, "I have given that idea much thought over the years, during which time I have outlined one possible continuation of the story. Backtracking slightly in the next volume, *The Birth of America* would in the beginning be a brief history of native America up to the arrival of the European explorers. It would then follow the history of the founding of colonial America from 1607 to 1763, of the establishment of American independence from 1763 to 1789, and of the beginning of American civilization from 1789 to 1815.

"Following this, *The Age of Expansion* would be a history of European civilization and its expansion throughout the world from 1815 to 1870, and of the start of the Industrial Revolution in Great Britain. It would also be a history of American civilization from 1815 to 1865, with emphasis on its expansion across the continent of North America and the Civil War. And the next volume, *The Age of Industry*, would be a history of European civilization from 1870 to 1918, and of American civilization from 1865 to 1918, with special emphasis on the spread of the Industrial Revolution and the remarkable discoveries in the sciences and technology.

"The fifteenth volume, *The Fall and Rise of Civilizations*, would be a history of European and American civilization from 1918 to 1945, and it would cover the aftermath of the First World War, the Depression and the Second World War, with emphasis on the expansion of American influence throughout the world. And to complete my long story of civilization almost to the beginning of the new millennium, *The Triumph of America* would be a history of European and American civilization from 1945 to 1989. This volume would cover the rise of the Soviet Union, the Cold War, the dominance of America worldwide, the continued growth of science and technology, and the renewed conflict between philosophy and religion. It would also include a brief history of the Third World colonial nations, covering their movements for independence from European and American control, as well as their evolution from agrarian to industrial societies."

After saying this, Will turned his eyes downward, clearly deep in thought, for I think he already knew what my next question would be as regards *The Story of Civilization*. And needless to say, it's the question that historians, professional and amateur alike, always ponder on during moments of reflection. So I asked him, "Have you ever thought about what the future might bring to the world, and whether volume seventeen in your story would be one of hope and promise for all of Mankind, or instead be a tome chronicling the decline of civilization?"

Will next raised his head, smiled at me, and then told me about the two possibilities for the writing of that story, "Speaking as an optimist, I'd like to be able to title that volume, *The Beginning of World Civilization.* It would be a history of how America, given its worldwide influence, took the lead in showing the world how to house all the poor, how to heal all the sick, and how to educate all the ignorant on earth. It would also be a history of how America took the lead in showing that science and technology were gifts to be shared by all, and that the work of international business was not only to make a profit, but to change the lives of democratic people for the better. It would also be a history of how America took the lead in showing the world that the quantity of life's comforts should never outweigh the quality of life's comforts, and that Man is not merely the reaper, but also the guardian of everything on Earth. And lastly, it would be a history of how America took the lead in showing the world that freedom and justice are not safeguarded through bombs and bullets and bullying, but through reason and discussion and compromise."

Will stopped there for a moment, which gave me the opportunity to say to him, "That would be a wonderful book with which to continue *The Story of Civilization,* for it would be a history of hope and promise for all of Mankind."

Will agreed, but he then looked at me sadly while losing his ever-present smile for the first time. I then noticed a different mood come over him as he began to speak to me once again, this time on the other possibility for that story, "However, and speaking as a realist, I fear that that volume would more likely be titled *The End of Civilization.* It would be a history of how America never took the lead in improving the lives of the poor and the sick and the ignorant, and of how democratic institutions fell into disrepair, at home and abroad. It would also be a history of how unregulated profiteering brought about the end of opportunities for many people in the developed nations, as well as enslaving the lives of workers in developing nations. It would also be a history of how Man's creature comforts outweighed the comfort of Man's fellow creatures, and of how unfettered industrialization brought about the destruction of the Earth's resources. It would also be a history of how people and governments stopped talking to one another, and of how violence and terrorism became the only options in settling conflicts. And lastly, it would be a history of how the divisiveness of religion once again overwhelmed the wisdom of philosophy, resulting in a return to the pre-modern world that existed prior to the youth of our modern civilization."

Will immediately saw the disappointment with which I listened to his last words, especially his thoughts on philosophy, which was a way of viewing the world that I'd recently come to love, thanks to my conversations and experiences in Paris. He then said to me, "You must not feel too dejected about a future that may or may not come to pass, for philosophy always makes her return. She remained sleeping for over a thousand years after the fall of the Roman Empire, only to resurface five hundred years ago, bringing with her all of modern civilization. So even if she has to go into hiding once again, philosophy will remain strong in the hearts and minds of a few, and she'll always bide her time until the dawn of a new and more modern civilization. For even in the darkest of times, there is always lurking in the shadows other Voltaires, and it is their light that will lead the way."

I next asked him, "Could you tell me more about your book *The Story of Philosophy*?"

Will responded, "*The Story of Philosophy* began with the founders of philosophy: Socrates, Plato and Aristotle. I then continued my story with the philosophers that created the modern world: Francis Bacon, Baruch Spinoza, Voltaire, Immanuel Kant, Arthur Schopenhauer, Herbert Spencer, Friedrich Nietzsche, Henri Bergson, Benedetto Croce, Bertrand Russell, George Santayana, William James, and John Dewey. But let me offer you some of my thoughts from the preface of that book, for they are ideas that explain my purpose and my method in writing *The Story of Philosophy*: 'There is a pleasure in philosophy, and a lure even in the mirages of metaphysics... Most of us have known some golden days in the June of life when philosophy was in fact what Plato called it, *that dear delight...*'

"Let me finish my discussion, not on the role of philosophy itself, but of the teachers of philosophy: 'The function of the professional teacher is clear. It should be to mediate between the specialist and the nation; to learn the specialist's language, as the specialist has learned nature's, in order to break down the barriers between knowledge and need, and find for new truths old terms that all literate people might understand.'

"I would also like to offer you a few words from the philosopher Mortimer J. Adler, ones that he wrote in an essay 'The Great Conversation' in *A Reader's Guide to the Great Books of the Western World* (1952): 'The goods of the mind are information, knowledge, understanding, and wisdom. We seek these goods not just in order to live, but in order to live well. Possessing them lifts us above the plane of animal existence, for these goods enhance our existence as human beings, as well as providing enjoyment and pleasure.'

"Also contained in that reader's guide are the thoughts of Robert Hutchins, at one time the President of the University of Chicago and the Chairman of the Board of Editors for *Encyclopædia Britannica*: 'The tradition of the West is embodied in the Great Conversation that began in the dawn of history and that continues to the present day. Whatever the merits of other civilizations in other respects, no civilization is like that of the West in this respect. No other civilization can claim that its defining characteristic is a dialogue of this sort. No dialogue in any other civilization can compare with that of the West in the number of great works of the mind that have contributed to this dialogue.'

After Will finished with his thoughts, he offered me a gift, shook my hand, and then left the office. Turning to the gift, I discovered a copy of Will's *Story of Philosophy* with the following inscription:

Sam,

As Socrates advised us so many years ago: "The unexamined life is not worth living." I know that your philosophical journey has begun and that it will continue throughout all the years ahead.

Your friend and teacher, Will.

The next day I began reading the *Story of Philosophy*. And over the next year I read Will's *Story of Civilization*, always keeping in mind the lines of Alexander Pope in *An Essay on Criticism*:

A little Learning is a dang'rous Thing
Drink deep, or taste not the Pierian Spring
There shallow Draughts intoxicate the Brain
And drinking largely sobers us again

In the following year, I read many more books on philosophy and history. I also traveled to Europe and other parts of the world, becoming over time a philosophical investigator, if only as a student of the great philosophers. But while living this *flâneurean* way of life, it dawned on me that at some point I too must help in furthering the "Great Conversation" that Will had spoken of on that now distant day. Where and when that would take place I knew not, but my future would one day make itself known to me. For just like a philosophical idea, a man's mind takes time to grow and find direction.

The Philosophical Investigation

Which is the best book of philosophy to help an investigator make sense of the world? Which philosophical thinker best answers the countless questions concerning the world? Of course, these questions can only be answered by each philosophical investigator, and only then after a sampling of ideas by intellectuals that are all too often contradictory - rather like life itself. But since everyone has plenty of time to leisurely pursue the answers to these questions, here's a list of some of the philosophers that over the years have offered this philosophical investigator suggestions on how best to pursue philosophy, what Plato called "that dear delight." (Note: Contact the author for a free and more detailed copy of this list.)

Mortimer J. Adler
Great Books of the Western World (60 volumes)
The Great Conversation
Syntopicon (2 volumes)

Honoré de Balzac
The Human Comedy (90+ books)

Jacques Barzun
From Dawn to Decadence: 500 Years of Western Cultural Life, 1500 to the Present

David Bodanis
Passionate Minds: Emilie du Châtelet, Voltaire, and the Great Love Affair of the Enlightenment

Lawrence Cahoone
From Modernism to Postmodernism

Ian Davidson
Voltaire in Exile

Will Durant
The Story of Philosophy
The Story of Civilization (11 volumes)

Walter Kaufmann
Existentialism from Dostoevsky to Sartre

John Morley
The Works of Voltaire

Marcel Proust
In Search of Lost Time (6 books)

Bertrand Russell
A History of Western Philosophy

S. G. Tallentyre
The Life of Voltaire
Voltaire in His Letters

Voltaire (selection)
Candide
Essay on the Manners and Spirit of Nations
Letters on England
Memnon
Micromégas
Philosophical Dictionary
Questions on the Encyclopédie
The Lisbon Earthquake

Treatise on Tolerance
Socrates
Story of a Good Brahman
Zadig

<u>Robert Wicks</u>
Modern French Philosophy: From Existentialism to Postmodernism

The Proustian Investigation

During these less than literary times, it's probably asking too much for anyone to wander through all the winding corridors of the six volumes of Marcel Proust's masterpiece, *In Search of Lost Time*. However, for those who wish to at least experience some of the thoughts of this famous and influential French writer, please get in touch with the author and he'll send you a complementary list of the more intriguing quotations from the over 4,300 pages of the collection. The references listed in parentheses offer the interested reader the volume abbreviation and the page number of the quote from D. J. Enright's version of the classic.

The Philosophical Invesigator Purpose

The reasons for writing this book are threefold. The first reason is to offer the general reader a travel story based in and around Paris. The second is to present a user-friendly introduction to the history and philosophies of France. The third reason is to use the materials in the book with secondary students as one way of introducing learners to the philosophical concepts of Modernity, Postmodernity and Existentialism. The current secondary curriculum in the United States covers mainly the fundamentals of the American intellectual experience, but it fails to adequately cover the basics of the British experience, neglecting French intellectual history completely. Given that Mother England and Father France gave birth to the child America, perhaps this book will open the minds of learners to the experiences of another Western people.

All royalties from the sales of this book go to support the Data Analysis Project, an educational concern coordinated by Ken Ewell. The first goal of the project is to work with public school teachers to increase their quantitative and statistical literacy skills, and to develop curriculum to improve the classroom learning experiences of their students in mathematics. The second goal is to prepare educators and learners for the *Common Core State Standards for Mathematics* program and the online *Smarter Balanced* testing system. The third goal is to organize a parent and guardian support group to address concerns and questions brought on by the *CCSSM* program and the *SB* system. The fourth goal of the project is to establish a two-year team- and technology-based workplace in exploratory and confirmatory data analysis as an alternative to the traditional one-year *Advanced Placement Statistics* course.

Ken can be contacted at *kenewell.noworriesmate@yahoo.com* or at the The Investigator Trilogy page on Facebook.